CONSTITUTIONALISM AND LEGAL REASONING

Law and Philosophy Library

VOLUME 79

CONSTITUTIONALISM AND LEGAL REASONING

MASSIMO LA TORRE
"Magna Graecia" *University of Catanzaro*
Italy
University of Hull
England

Springer

A C.I.P. Catalogue record for this book is available from the Library of Congress.

ISBN-10: 1-4020-5594-3 (HB)
ISBN-13: 978-1-4020-5594-2 (HB)
ISBN-10: 1-4020-5595-1 (e-book)
ISBN-13: 978-1-4020-5595-9 (e-book)

Published by Springer,
P.O. Box 17, 3300 AA Dordrecht, The Netherlands.

www.springer.com

Printed on acid-free paper

TABLE OF CONTENTS

PREFACE

This book, which consist of three chapters and two appendices, is intended to connect subjects that have usually been considered as detached or not strongly connected: constitutionalism, legal argumentation and legal ethics. Its main contention is that contemporary constitutionalism pushes towards a new style of legal reasoning, which needs to take into account moral criteria and principles and that eventually the interpretative and moralist approach will lead to a somewhat unorthodox and *less authoritarian* concept of law.

A constitution to be taken seriously and as a distinct and superior source of law, will end up referring to some sort of constitutional justice or judicial review. And constitutional reasoning and justice need to make recourse to principles but principles to be given an operative content should be elaborated through some form of moral reasoning. This reasoning however, if it does not want to betray the spirit of constitutional democracy and the very idea of a constitution as a special moment of self-determination, could not be just Platonism, a cognitivism without roots in the practice of public discourse and deliberation. So that constitutionalism will not really do without a public sphere and some activism of the latter. But if this is so, the traditional concept of law based on hierarchy, commands, prescription, sanction, and in the last instance violence, becomes obsolete. A law which is a command cannot be congruent with a practice ruled by discourse, that is, I argue, with constitution.

Furthermore – as shown in the second chapter – legal reasoning and adjudication as such, if they want to avoid the danger of working merely as *ex post factum* rationalization of decisions taken on grounds not pertinent within the law, have to be shaped in terms of argumentation, of giving good reasons. And the claim of being supported by good reasons has of course to be justified in a way that could be acceptable to the audience and which also takes this seriously, ascribing to it a normative dignity. Good reasons and justification thus are the core of legal practice and cannot be really reduced to just commands or even rules or fragments of rules. One can easily spot the same development within advocacy, which though very much neglected in legal philosophy, is a relevant part of legal reasoning. Indeed, if we accept advocacy as part of adjudication, we are more or less obliged to see morality or moral principles once more as internal to legal practice.

Advocacy in fact – as shown in the third chapter of the book – cannot do without legal ethics. And this cannot just be again proposing a morality of legalism (which is what the legal positivist asks us to do), since a legalistic morality will in the end be uninformative and could not fill in gaps in the black letter of the law. Moral legalism is in a sense the thesis that black letter law should be reiterated as a deontological professional standard – which is finally an admission of the irrelevance of legal ethics. If black letter law as such is able to produce a professional deontological standard, why should we have explicit professional standards at all whenever we have a black letter law? The final assumption of the book is that rules do not apply themselves and therefore, principles have to be appealed to in order to make sense of rule application. Such a sense, in a contest driven by a fundamental claim to justice such as contemporary legal practice, is constitutionalism as the morality of a self-defining public sphere.

There is a stubborn prejudice about the law, which still imbues large parts of legal doctrine and legal practice. That law is eminently a coercive phenomenon; it mainly consist of coercion and violence, though centralized or monopolized. This idea is mirrored through the concept of law that is most permanent in the history of legal ideas: that law is command backed by a sanction, a menace, a threat of an evil, which would be inflicted in case that command is ignored or disobeyed. Even if this idea is explicitly formulated and elaborated by a particular jurisprudential approach, the same idea is reflected nearly everywhere, especially since a particular political form has arisen as the paradigm of law and order, the modern State. Though it is true that this historical institutional figure is nowadays exposed to some decline and seems to be overcome by the new range of globalized social affairs, it remains the point of reference of much legal thought. The legal and the coercive seem to be irremediably intertwined.

Now, the ambition of this small book is to put in doubt such connections and to disentangle – as it were – the legal practice and reasoning from the myth of authority and State. My contention is that such connection is already contested by the rise and progress of constitutionalism. A constitutional State, where so many limits are set to political supremacy and sovereignty, is no longer a State in the paradigmatic Hobbesian sense. This I try to show in the first chapter. legal positivism and the command theory are usually connected with a high dose of scepticism about the possibility of finding rational or reasonable criteria of rightness in the domain of values and social rules. Their assumption is that values and rules of human conduct are highly controversial and that there are no objective or intersubjective principles to which we could appeal in order to solve the controversy. Values are plural and they clash one against the other, and there is no rational way to build a hierarchy among them and render it effective. There is only one way out: someone could cut the Gordian knot of that plural mess and through sheer decision impose an order. Such an act of cutting the knot can only be the command of a sovereign. By producing order it therefore deserves the dignity of being recognized and acknowledged as the law of the country. Thus law that is command or prescription is needed because of the impossibility of solving the conflict of values.

For the legal positivist, morality is a perpetual source of controversy, while law claims to be the solution. The solution therefore is seen an amoral power, in that such a neutral power could not itself again refer to some value to be justified. Values in fact are judged as not accessible to justification. In such a view, justification works only in so far as theoretical propositions are concerned, that is, statements of fact. However, values, being not of this kind, are intractable by theoretical rationality. Nor is there any other available. The domain of ought is a battlefield, not an audience that might be persuaded through the better argument. There is no practical reason, a reason impinging upon values and the ought of human conduct. Values are a source a disagreement, since they base in the end to be effective on agreement. This is not the case of power; power does not need agreement to be operative. This is why it can compensate for the deep disagreement afflicting values.

Such an attitude, deeply embedded in the positivistic conception of law, contributed, together with the parallel rise of empiricism in philosophy, to neglect all those long-established doctrines and practices that centred around the possibility of finding solutions to cases of moral and legal controversies by arguments. Practical reasoning was – as it were – abandoned and despised to exalt the great success of theoretical, mathematical and empirical demonstration. Since – it was contended – there is no cogent or stringent demonstration in morality and law, what we can rely on is only the decision, the fiat of the sovereign and the fact of his superiority. Law in the best case can be transformed into a descriptive practice, where the judge has only to proceed syllogistically or mechanically. But if she cannot, her ruling will be fully discretionary and rightly so.

Such a view of course did not favour the pre-modern doctrines and practices of moral and legal argumentation. "Prudence" as a distinctive third way of human conduct beyond knowledge and will was discarded. There is no room for prudence in philosophy – says Hobbes (*Leviathan*, Part IV, Chap. 46).[1] Likewise, there will be no place for prudence as a special kind of reasoning in legal practice and education. Meaning or "sense" was to be either strictly theoretical or representational or volitive and irrational in the end. Argumentative approaches were declared obsolete and accordingly forgotten, until however a dissatisfaction about the irrationalistic consequences of legal positivism and the myth of force which lurked behind it made things stir again.

Lawyers, especially after the sad experience of Fascism, which both in Germany and in Italy had seized power in a more or less "legal" manner (at least according to positivistic standards), started looking for better guarantees and new paradigms in legal reasoning. The alternative "either controversy and conflict or decision" was considered too narrow and rigid. There was an acute perception of a nihilistic implication in such sharp disjunction. A decision is justified by reasons and values, but these, according to the premises of the legal positivist, remain a matter of unresolved controversy. Or the decision is not and cannot be justified by reasons and values at all. In the latter case however, it will be without a foundation, its "cause" will base on "nothing". Accordingly, the escape from controversy, will in the end only be possible through an appeal to the "nothing" of justification – which is actually a sort of "nihilism".

To avoid such nihilistic implications, a third way was sought. Some, like Gustav Radbruch after World War Two, appealed to natural law. But the more promising path was considered to be found in the rehabilitation of old "prudence" and ancient doctrines and techniques of practical argumentation. Classical "topic" and "rhetoric" were now studied again. Beyond such a revival it was the very notion of a practical reason – which had previously been despised ("Kritik der *sogennanten* praktische Vernunft" reads the title of a famous book by the Danish realist Alf Ross) – that was mobilized. It served now to redeem the concept of law from its imperativistic decay. This is the issue of my second chapter, where I briefly present a narrative of that revival and of the new attempts to reconstruct practical reasoning as a reliable tool for the legal domain. In this chapter I also try to look at some more general consequences of such a development, especially as far as the idea (and the ideal) of law is concerned.

The great success of positivism as the theory of modern law has not only overshadowed the doctrines of practical argumentation but has also nearly expelled moral considerations from the province of law. One popular assumption of positivism has been a sharp separation between law and morality. Such a view has had a strong impact on the way we have conceived *inter alia* professional obligations and responsibilities of judges and lawyers. Judges according to the positivistic paradigm were considered as neutral tools of the application of law, "law-machines", *Rechtsautomaten* – as said by German nineteenth-century legal theorists. Once this approach was applied to lawyers' deontology, that meant that legal ethics was a contradiction in terms and had to disappear from the map of law. Since the only relevant source in the legal domain is thought to be the command or the prescription by the legislator and whatever further materials can be drawn or descend from such *Urquelle*, any other rule or criterion is considered to be irrelevant. Accordingly there was not much room for deontolgical rules guiding lawyers' conduct beyond the standard of a strict application of the regal rule. In a sense, legal rules were considered to be self-executing, that is, as applying themselves to cases. What the lawyer had to provide was – as it were – flesh and blood to the law, but not its sense, meaning, scope or even acceptance.

In such a context there could not be any moral dilemma with direct legal implications for the lawyer. Now, this view has always been falsified by the sturdy resistance of lawyers' professional ethics. This has certainly been reduced to something which sometimes made it nearly unrecognizable to the practitioners themselves. Legal ethics has nevertheless survived and has proven stronger than any doctrine of separation of law and morality. It is true that deontological codes, especially in Europe, are quite a recent development; deontological dilemmas however and institutional domains of such dilemmas had survived the positivistic era and have now reemerged with more strength then ever. It is true, nevertheless, that the dilemma between a separationist legalistic approach and the one defending a connection between law and morality is then retranslated in different terms within the very domain of legal ethics and deontological codes. Here, we face the alternative between the "moral amorality" thesis, defending a legalistic view of the lawyer's role, and a moralistic approach, which unfortunately attempts to reshape the lawyer's figure according to the noble example of the judge. In this second approach, the lawyer should be fully oriented to the fulfilment of justice ideals, while for the legalistic perspective, lawyers' ethics should centre around the client's interests. In the third chapter thus, I try to progress in the overview of legal positivistic failure in dealing with the issue of lawyers' moral obligations and their corresponding dispositions. Law indeed cannot do without virtues.

I am in search of a better model for legal modernity. Mine is not intended as a Utopian enterprise; the humane law that I am looking for is not for the future, nor is it meant as a reform project or as a programme for new institutions to come. My contention is that *positive* law is better understood if it is not too easily equated with power, force, or command. Law – I believe and try to show – is more a matter of discourse and deliberation, than of sheer decision or of power relations. Constitutionalism, legal argumentation, legal ethics – three fundamental moments of our daily experience with the law – are there to witness that I may be right. Now a "constitutional" view of the law and its practice and the connected discoursive approach to legal reasoning can also offer interesting solutions to legal ethics.

For instance, if we take legal reasoning seriously and conceive it in a "liberal" way as comprising both lawyers and judges, so that adjudication is both a task for advocates and judges, the requirement of separation of powers on the one side is already full of implications for lawyers' deontology: the role of a lawyer will not be allowed to encroach with the one fulfilled by the statesman. On the other side, the claim of rightness intrinsic in legal discourse cannot avoided by lawyers. So that they could no longer be seen as defenders of clients' interests, but of their rights. And rights are *claims to be right*. Dworkin's "rights thesis" is just such a contention. Thus, the requirement of justice or better, a certain threshold imposed on the tolerable injustice of the legal claim raised, will be inescapable not only for the judge, but to the lawyer as well.

My final assumption is that rules do not apply themselves. Wittgensteinian philosophy, contrary to some more recent idiosincratic interpretation, clearly shows that rules are a practice and that a practice is a principled and interpretive enterprise – which is therefore to be assessed from the internal point of view. Any external or "exclusive" positivism should go well back to a pre-interpretive methodology and think of the "nature" of law more or less in terms of a "natural kind concept",[2] that is, an inanimate object, kind of stone – we might say –, or ballistic missiles, not "open" or sensitive to or modifiable by, the conceptions of those who manipulate and use it. My contention on the contrary is that ideals (which imbue the distinct forms of life) and principles (by which ideals are operationalized) have to be referred to in order to make sense of rule application. Such sense, in a contest driven by a fundamental claim to justice such as contemporary legal practice, is *constitutionalism* as the morality of a self-defining public sphere.

I am aware that the general idea of this book unfortunately runs counter to recent developments in the international arena and more generally in the less palpable *Zeitgeist*. It might well be that like Hegel's owl that takes flight at sunset, I am trying a conceptual pattern when the corresponding institutional practice is beginning to die out.

According to a new "climate" States and State agencies may not be bound to a superior law checking their strategic moves.[3] There is now much talk of international law as no longer being binding over States and of a revival of "force".[4] The latter would now be allowed to overcome law and its gentle civilizing function. *Pacta sunt servanda* is suddenly degraded and marked as an obsolete principle. Normative equality of legal subjects (be they States or simple persons) is declared as withered away by the factual disequality of power forces. After Carl Schmitt's "exploits" in the past century, war and an "exceptional situation" marked by an imminent terrible danger are once again seen as the paradigm for political and legal relations. In such an "exceptional" constellation, institutional guarantees and human rights are outplayed and legally void. Presidential perogatives and the executive power are said to be exempt from parliamentary control and judicial review. The cruelty ban is broken. Even the unspeakable is spoken: *torture* is brought back in the law's limelight. Nonetheless, a "constitution" of such brutality will not be what we still think to be our legal tradition. Constitutionalism is not a *régime* where violence may be unleashed and celebrated as the law.

ACKNOWLEDGMENTS

This book, its brevity not withstanding, is the outcome of many years of research and teaching in several academic institutions and of discussion with friends and colleagues. The first chapter is based on arguments that can be found in my contribution to *Developing a Constitution for Europe*, edited by E. O. Eriksen, J. E. Fossum and A. J. Menéndez, Routledge & Kegan, London 2004, while the second chapter is a development of an article on *Theories of Legal Argumentation and Concepts of Law. An Approximation*, published in "Ratio Juris", Vol. 15, 2002. Appendix A is an expansion of my contribution to the seminar on "Law, Discourse, and Moral Judgment" held at the University of Hull on the 14th of October, 2005, now published in *Ratio Juris*, Vol 19, 2006; Appendix B elaborates on a paper given at the ARENA of Oslo University in March 2003, now in print as a chapter of *Constitutional Rights Through Discourse*, ed. by E. O. Eriksena and A. J. Menéndez, Springer. I am grateful to Blackwell Publishers for the kind permission to use the two articles printed in *Ratio Juris*. Thanks also are due to Tony Ward for reading and giving advice on the manuscript.

This book I would like to dedicate to Giulia, my daughter, for the time taken to write it was actually hers.

NOTES

1. As is well known, for Hobbes "prudence" is a capacity to predict future events based on the memory and succession of past circumstances and is common to human beings and other animals (see e.g. *Leviathan*, ed. by C. B. Macpherson, Penguin, Harmondsworth 1982, pp. 13, 97, 117, 682). Cf. W. Hennis, *Politik und praktische Philosophie*, Luchterhand, Neuwied am Rhein 1963, in particular chap. 6, and Q. Skinner, *Reason and Rhetoric in the Philosophy of Hobbes*, Cambridge University Press, Cambridge 1996.
2. Cf. R. Dworkin, *Justice in Robes*, Belknap Press, Cambridge, Mass. 2006, pp. 10 ff.
3. For a report about this change of "climate", cf. E. Denninger, <<Recht, Gewalt und Moral – ihr Verhältnis in nachwestfälischer Zeit. Ein Bericht>>, in *Kritische Justiz*, Vol. 38, 2005, pp. 359 ff.
4. See, for instance, J. Yoo, <<Using Force>>, in *University of Chicago Law Review*, Vol. 71, 2004, pp. 729 ff.

CHAPTER 1

LAW AS CONSTITUTION

I. CONSTITUTIONALISM OF THE ANCIENTS AND OF THE MODERNS

I. 1. Ancient Constitutionalism

We all may remember Benjamin Constant's famous essay on the notion of the Ancients' freedom compared with the Moderns. Constant on the one side identified a sense of freedom based on participation and membership and laying besides on civic virtues, while on the other side he believed he saw a different view emerging. The latter rather referred to privacy, its rights and guarantees and was supported by a search for individual happiness and lack of social constraints. These two senses of freedom were then played one against the other in order to argue for the superiority of the Modern need for private autonomy and security.

Now, it might well be that such opposition was functional to a special understanding of the emerging constitutionalism after a decade of revolutionary turmoil and a longer period of populist authoritarianism. However, the irony of such distinction and opposition is that it reversed the truth of the matter, at least as far as modern constitutionalism is concerned. Constant's picture of Ancient freedom was one that centred around the figure of an active citizen involved in a time-consuming and morally demanding exercise of collective decisions. While the Moderns' most intense desire is to secure a peaceful enjoyment of their property, delegating most public affairs to a special body of professionals appointed to government and legislative office as their own "representatives" and deputies. This picture may capture some of the essence of *Zeitgeist* at the time when Constant wrote his celebrated essay: a restoration of institutional moderation and private security against public revolutionary excesses. That picture however, does not render justice to the important not only temporal distance between Ancient and Modern constitutionalism. By Ancient constitutionalism I do not mean any Ancient Greek or Roman political system. Both Greek and Roman "classical" societies and their political principles and doctrines were ever influential all through the history of Western political and legal thought.

The idea of *Res publica* is a permanent source of inspiration and legitimation for later Medieval institutional orders. However, the Christian conception of political power as corrective and repressive of human sins and depravity and its claimed derivation from God's will did not allow for a real continuity of the Ancient notion of polity as a public sphere of (tendentially) equals and citizenship as the capacity of a simultaneous work of ruling and being ruled. Rex, monarchy, in classical Roman times always an illegitimate political status equivalent to tyranny, was rehabilited through the convergency of the shepherd myth and the hellenistic concept of "*kyrios*", the Emperor-master. In the long centuries of Roman political life nonetheless the Emperor, to be appointed, needed the fiction of a special delegation coming from the people, the so-called *lex regia*, seen as the ground rule of his nearly absolute powers. The Roman Empire was ideologically conceived, until very late, as a *res publica* with a tripartite structure: senate, people, consuls, that is as a "mixed commonwealth" according to the ideal handed down by authors like Polybius, Cicero and Tacitus. It was Byzantine and medieval society that reintroduced the ideal centrality of monarchy in an exercise of simplification and reduction. Actually, such a sphere is reshaped through the notion of pastorship and thus privatized as fundamentally equivalent to a family. Whereas in Greek and Roman culture, family is excluded from the political sphere as such, because it is private and hierarchical, it is just the fact of being thus characterized that renders it paradigmatic for the new concept of a political society. Kingdoms are considered to be big families, and families are seen as flocks requiring a shepherd, a *rex*.

Here, however, I will not raise the question of whether it would be possible to think of a constitutionalism of the ancient Greeks and Romans. It is a subject far too remote from the problems I intend to deal with in this book. The question raised preliminarly should instead be whether there is, and if so, what is, a Medieval constitutionalism, given that contemporary constitutionalism sometimes projects itself as a development of such a historical figure. My contention is that "constitutionalism", in the sense of a special limitation of political power, which does not impinge upon the very formation of such power is indeed of Medieval origin and a specific Middle Ages cultural artifact. To understand this we may follow Professor McIlwain's suggestions[1] centred around two fundamental concepts, *iurisdictio* and *gubernaculum*. In his studies of the English constitution, the American scholar points out a permanent tension between these two main domains into which the law was distinguished according medieval jurisprudence. Due especially to the practice of "common law", we see English lawyers referring to two basic areas in the law of the country: one concerning mainly individual entitlements and contractual relationships between private subjects, which was covered by *iurisdictio*. This was a competence of "saying the law" which was taken away from the tendentially almighty monarchical powers. The Medieval king is certainly seen as the supreme judge. However, in the domain of *iurisdictio*, his judgment and ruling are subject to the common law and are actually delegated to specialized officers whose decisions build up a body of rules upon which the king has no right to infringe.

Opposed to *iurisdictio* we find another domain of competences, that of *gubernaculum*, which concerns all that has to do with political activities, government and administration. Within this domain the king is proclaimed fully free and subject only to a "reason of State". Here lawyers should keep silent and bow to the king's majesty and supremacy. Now, the constitutionalism of the Ancients, that is, its Medieval form, was – I would maintain – just an attempt at safeguarding that institutional separation between a domain of *iurisdictio* and one of *gubernaculum* and to strike the right balance in their relationship and operations.

In this constellation are the two features that we have to stress. First of all, a "constitution" in such a context is the given and customary order of political institutions: it is something conceived as "ancient", "old", and deriving its legitimacy from the fact of being rooted in past times. In this sense Medieval constitutionalism would not object to King James I of England when he proclaimed that <<all novelties are dangerous in politics as well in a natural Body>>.[2]

A second and most fundamental feature of Ancient constitutionalism is that the fundamental laws it is based on are not rules concerning the organization and operations of political power; they rather concern what we would nowadays label as private law relations. *Iurisdictio* deals with, and guarantees, individuals' private rights, their property, their entitlements, their purchases, their contracts. *Iurisdictio* does not cover the exercise of political power as such. It regulates private goods and transactions; and by doing so it excludes from such sphere the king's supreme prerogatives. We are therefore confronted, when conceptualizing monarchical supremacy, with two notions of *potestas*: one, *potestas ordinaria*, which operates in the domain of *iurisdictio*, and is equivalent to this, where the king is subject to the law of the land, to "common law"; and a second, *potestas regia*, intrinsic to monarchical dignity, which is operative within the domain of *gubernaculum* and coincides with this, within which the king should apply himself only to God's laws and where he is directed not by the law of the land, but by *ratio regum*, the kings' reason.

The problem however – as remarked by professor McIlwain – is that in Medieval constitutionalism there is no positive and effective legal remedy against king's trespassing across the line that divides (and somehow protects) *iurisdictio* from *gubernaculum*. The king, by violating common law, is not subject to any special legal sanction. This actually is the field of the many parliamentary battles fought in XVII century England and a powerful reason for vindicating specific parliamentay powers concerning law-making, which might impinge upon *iurisdictio* and its borders. Judicial review of legislation on the one side and government responsibility towards the people and their representatives (the Commons) for political acts on the other, slowly emerge as the possible tools for re-establishing a balance between *gubernaculum* and *iurisdictio*. In this process of re-adjustment, nevertheless, *gubernaculum* as an absolute and opaque prerogative is put into question. Edward Coke already in his long fight against James I stated that, although the king's prerogative is legal, "sovereign power" is not a parliamentary term. And he concluded by saying that Magna Carta is such that it cannot bear a sovereign.

The step from pre-modern to modern constitutionalism is made possible thanks to a deep change in the prevailing political paradigm. "Constitutional" or "fundamental" would now be a law only if it dealt with the public, not private, sphere; only if it was directed to shape and regulate expressions and acts of political power. In the constitutionalism of the Moderns, thus, we are confronted with a kind of overturn of those two features I have singled out as essentials of Ancient constitutionalism. The main objective of a "constitution" there is not political power exercise, but criteria governing private entitlements and agreements. The Moderns' constitution conversely has as its main objective to constitute and shape legislative power, *gubernaculum*. To be able to fulfil such a function, a constitution will have to establish some sort of government responsibility towards the people, thus introducing a dynamic element, which will no longer be able to refer to the past or to customs and tradition as its legitimation basis. A constitution, from now on, will be somewhat "new", a "novelty", a project for the future, not the registration of a past history.

I. 2. From Fundamental Law to Social Contract and Self-Institution

In Eighteenth century Germany[3] *Konstitution* still means – following Roman law – a law issued by the Emperor, while *Verfassung* refers to the concrete political and social setting of a State and can sometimes overlap with what we would to-day call a "form of State", that is, for instance, a monarchy, a republic, a presidentialist régime, etc. This second linguistic use is as well rooted in classical Roman political science: Cicero for example, when speaking of his beloved "mixed commonwealth", referred to it as <<haec constitutio>>(*De Republica*, I, 45, 59).

In the German, as well in general in the European, pre-modern legal culture constitutional laws were called *leges fundamentales* (*Grundgesetze* in German). It is however interesting to remark that in Eighteenth century natural law doctrine, which is contractualistic in essence, *Verfassung* takes a meaning much closer to the modern democratic notion of "constitution". As is well known, the prevailing German natural law doctrine favoured a triadic model of social contract. This was conceived as developing along three progressive stages: (i) *pactum unionis*, a basic agreement to gather together and constitute a society in order to exit from the "natural state"; (ii) *pactum ordinationis*, an agreement on the shape to give to government; (iii) *pactum subordinationis*, an agreement to obey the laws and commands issued by the form of government previously chosen. Of these three agreements the second, the collective decision about the form that government has to take is called "constitutional agreement": "constitution" here is a basic law on the internal structure of the State and the way and procedures by which its powers have to be employed.

Contractualist doctrines, however, conceive of the agreement that the State imposes as a conceptually necessary assumption. This means that *whatever State* is assumed as conceptually based on a contractual agreement independently of the existence of any form of factual collective will. A further implication of such an approach is that every State will have to be considered a *constitutional* order. Wherever a constitution (agreement) is missing, we will not be confronted with an authoritarian régime but rather with the "state of nature", with a pre-legal and pre-political condition, where individuals are not yet a "people" or a "society" but only a "multitude". For such an approach therefore, whatever form of government *is* and *can be*, the outcome of a constitutional compact. This as such does not determine any of the many possible forms of government.

Now, the evolution from this doctrine to modern constitutionalism is in need of a further step. Common and preparatory to modern constitutionalism is the idea that history, tradition, or nature (families, for instance) are not sufficient conditions for constituting the fact of society, a commonwealth. Paradigmatic in this respect is Locke's criticism of Robert Filmer's patriarchalism. Contractualistic natural law takes a strong individualistic stance – at least in principle and hypothetically.

We need to get a strong connection between the constitutional moment and the notion of democracy into the modernity of constitutionalism. Modern constitutionalism is distinct from the Ancient one precisely in so far as it is focused not only on how government should be exercised but also on *who should govern* or even in a sense on *whether there should be a government*. Or we could better say that Modern constitutionalism is an evolutionary step with regard to the Ancient one in so far as it poses and tries to solve the question of government's limits (of *iurisdictio* – one might still say) by pointing out that such limits are strictly connected with the question of who is given the power of government. In short, Modern constitutionalism solves the question of "*iurisdictio*" by dramatically raising the problem of the "*gubernaculum*" holder and finally by referring the latter to the former, by making "*gubernaculum*" internal to "*iurisdictio*". In the first move it is democracy which is seen as the answer to the problem of limits to political power; in the second move it is judicial review which is ascribed the task to legalize the notion and the practice of (democratic) popular sovereignty.

As has been remarked by an Italian constitutional lawyer, <<in Modern constitutionalism the concept of constitution is the outcome of a convergency of two notions: that of fundamental law seen no longer as immemorial custom but as a law given by a legislator and that of constitution as the structuring of State powers>>.[4] We should then add a further feature: the legislator in question, the constitutional lawgiver, the one who produces the constitution, is not a subject, but the "people", or the community of those individuals who are requested to abide by the constitution. *Quod omnes tangit, ab omnibus approbetur* – a Medieval legal principle with a limited application range is extended tendentially to the entire system of legal powers and to the whole body of persons residing within a given territory and asking to live under a common institutional asset. Constitution in this sense also means the self-understanding of community members and their practice of self-institution, that is of instituting themselves as citizens. This self-institution has two possible basic variables: one which sees the "people" as such as an outcome of a constitutional decision and therefore has a more individualistic view of what a common social life requires and implies.

A second variable presupposes at least a subject, the "people", which to be active does not need a radical moment of reflexivity and which, accordingly, can be considered the "constituting power" of the constitutional asset. Such is the French idea of a "nation", Sieyès' "pouvoir constituant". The former notion of constitution as a compact by which a people is produced together with the constitution we find, for instance, in Kant's political writings, where a constitution (*Konstitution*, not *Verfassung*) is said to be an act of general will by which a multitude is transformed into one people (<<den Akt des allgemeinen Willens, wodurch die Menge ein Volk wird>>(*Zum ewigen Frieden,* BA 25)). On the other side, there are two main variables as far as the extension of self-institution is concerned. For a first approach, self-institution is absolute, has no limits nor boundaries, since all matters are covered by that act of self-institution: in short, it is equivalent to full sovereignty. No justification is here required nor expected to determine those areas invested by the self-instituting act. For a second approach, in contrast, self-institution is anchored to certain principles and is subject to strict criteria of necessity, proportionality and fairness. Here self-institution is no longer omnipotent, but lays upon a substantive justification. Sovereignty is accordingly not absolute but restrained within that precinct of measures that are needed to make possible a peaceful and sociable common life and the enjoyment of individual fundamental rights.

In terms of moral philosophy, we could say that in the first approach the self-institution of political society is a matter of "ethics", by which a substantive notion of good life is implemented, whereas according to the second approach self-institution (constitution) is only a matter of "morality", of the "right" not of the "good", that is, of those basic normative conditions that are supported by overlapping consensus and by the functional basic need for social survival.

I. 3. Modern Constitutionalism

A Modern understanding of constitutionalism can be found in Thomas Paine's political writings. As is well known, Paine wrote his most celebrated essay, *The Rights of Man*, as a rejoinder to Edmund Burke's powerful attack against the French revolution and its political and legal reform ideals. Burke in particular put in question French revolutionary constitutional practice by referring to, and somehow coining, a notion of "constitution" strictly linked with the concept of tradition and history. Constitution in this sense, which was then immediately handed down and radicalized by reactionary political thought, re-established the priority of automatic over reflective, of hereditary over self-assumed commitment, of customary rules over agreement and deliberation. Constitutional practice should work <<after the pattern of nature>>.[5] It is also an attack against the Enlightment and its principle of the self-esteem of human reason. "Prejudice", "unreasoned habits" are vindicated against self-discovery, obedience against discussion. Human rights were the main target of such powerful attacks in an attempt to revive against them the old "franchises" and historical entitlements of the pre-Modern English political order.

In the second part of his *Rights of Man* for an entire chapter Paine discusses "of constitutions". Here, the first point raised is that a constitution is not the act of a government. It is not – he says – a self-regulation that State sovereignty imposes upon itself. It is rather the source of government. There would be no proper State without a previous constitution. A State not produced through a constitutional moment would be mere force deprived of legitimacy. <<A Constitution is not the act of a Government, but of a people constituting a Government; and Government without a Constitution is power without right>>.[6] It is not as if in the political realm the house – as it were – would be given through the State and a constitution could only offer decoration and furniture, but no more. Paine's view is just the opposite of the one evoked in a most celebrated parliamentary speech by Prince Otto von Bismarck. Ontological priority is to be given to constitution, not to States.

The second point stressed by the British political writer is that the constitution has not only the task of offering legitimacy to the State but also and especially of limiting and directing State powers. It serves <<not only as an authority, but as a law of control to the Government>>. It is <<the political bible of the State>>.[7] Legislation is considered a part of Government, not in the sense that executive and legislative power coincide, but in the sense that government as the whole of political institutions comprises legislation. Accordingly, a constitution cannot be changed or reformed by ordinary State agencies, including legislation. <<No article of this Constitution – says Paine referring to the American model – could be altered or infringed at the discretion of the Government that was to ensure>>.[8] This limitation is explicitly extended to the legislator, since – it is added – <<it is repugnant to the principles of representative Government that a body should give power to itself>>.[9] Ordinary laws are not sufficient to control State powers. Laws are addressed to individuals and are effective as far as their conduct is concerned. Different is the case of State powers activities. These need to be directed through a stronger rule.[10]

On the other side, the self-constituting act of constitution is not produced *ex nihilo*. The constitutional moment presupposes a mutual recognition of individuals who integrate in a common enterprise by reciprocity of fundamental rights. The "rights of man" therefore are the bedrock of the constitution. This foundation has to be acknowledged at any step of constitutional and State actions. This implies that human rights are assumed as a substantive, foundational part of the constitution and that they should be institututionalized. Such institutionalization is made possible only if the exercise of those rights is somehow reproduced within the precinct of State powers. Now, within this area a clear respect for human rights asks for a general separation of powers. "Rights of man" and separation of powers are in this perspective the essential elements of a constitution. A State infringing upon human rights and separation of powers could not be said to be constitutional – as is emphatically proclaimed in article 16 of the French Declaration of the Rights of Man and Citizen: <<Every community in which a separation of powers and a security of rights is not provided for, wants a constitution>>.

Paine is well aware that democratic constitutions are quite different from pre-Modern constitutional arrangements. A constitution is not another Magna Carta – he says. <<Magna Carta [...] was no more than compelling the Government to renounce a part of its assumptions. It did not create and give powers to Government in the manner a constitution does>>.[11] A constitution is not an act of self-restraint of an already instituted power nor is it a bargaining or a contract or alliance between such a power and its subjects. The model for a modern constitution is no longer the alliance agreed between God and His people. Though Paine is deeply influenced by Protestant theology, his constitutional model is – we might say – an atheistic one: there is no Sovereign prior to the people.

A modern constitution has – stresses Paine – a double function: it produces the State power and gives this its shape. And it fulfils such a double function, while reproducing through the shape given to State powers the originary normative position of human rights and citizenship. Thus, though a constitution can be changed by civil society, there is something in it that cannot be altered: the structure of fundamental rights and the necessity of reflecting such rights in the internal functioning of political and legal institutions. The latter are required because of the weakness of natural rights as applied to public affairs. So that <<the power produced from the aggregate of natural rights, imperfect in power in the individuals, cannot be applied to invade the natural rights which are retained in the individual, and in which the power to execute is as perfect as the right itself>>.[12] If we maintain the alliance paradigm, one should then say that the basic compact here is no longer between a pre-ordained and superior power and its own subjects, the people, but rather between a people and their fundamental rights.

Paine's thought indeed reflected ideas that were decisive during the French revolution crisis. In particular, his approach is quite close to Emmanuel Sieyès' influential constitutional views. Sieyès' first theoretical move was to assert the fundamental unity of the body politic. This he achieved through the appeal to *nation*. A commonwealth – he says – is not the sum of traditional corporative "orders", but a society of individuals that are equal because all are subject to the same law. One common law makes one nation. However, positive law is the outcome of a nation's will. There is no nation without the will of common laws. Such will is first manifested through association. At first we are confronted with a bundle of individual wills. Once this association projects itself as a long-term scheme concerning individual basic needs and associates plan to give "consistence"[13] to their union, a further step is needed. Here the question is to find permanent and functional establishments: an institutional framework. At such a stage we have no longer to do with individual wills but with a public decision, that is, a decision taken by the generality of associates.

However, in a large and populous country like France, associates will be too many and scattered in a too big a territory to be able to gather together and express an articulate common will such as required for legislation. A further institutional device is required: this is representation. The formation of a body politic therefore is a process in three steps: (i) a first gathering of individual wills whereby private subjects acknowledge each other as associates; (ii) a public sphere of action given by a common will; (iii) articulating and implementing common will through representation. But to have the exercise of a representative common will we should already presuppose a constitution in force. A representative body and a government are the product, not the producer, of a constitution – which expresses the content of a not yet representative public will. The latter, but not the former (legislative and executive power), is not bound by constitutional rules, which however, are not able to "authorize" the nation to its foundational act. This is what Hannah Arendt will later call "Sieyès' vicious circle".[14]

Associates – says the French abbot – have a great interest in submitting government and representation to follow their common will. This can only be achieved through constitutional law that establishes and structures those bodies. Nation's will is supreme: only natural law could prevail over it. <<La nation existe avant tout, elle est l'origine de tout. Sa volonté est toujours légale, elle est la loi elle-même! Avant elle et au-dessus d'elle il n'y a que le droit naturel>>.[15]

We have seen that according to Sieyès, a body politic takes its shape through an evolutionary movement along three epochs: a first of individual decisions, a second of unrepresented common will, a third of action taken through representation. It is in the first movement that we originally have a nation. This is not subject to any constitution: <<la

nation n'est pas soumise à une constitution>>.[16] Constitution is a product of the second epoch: <<Nous avons vu naître la constitution dans la seconde époque>>.[17] While the nation is subject only to natural law, the government depends on positive law and especially on constitutional norms. This amounts to saying that a nation is bound to a constitution and legality only in so far as it is the very source of any form of positive law. A nation as such never exits from the state of nature. Its "constituting power" remains unimpaired and independent from any form. On the contrary, governments take just that shape that a nation has decided to give them. Thus, even ordinary law cannot be but an expression of *governed* people.[18]

In such a view, a constitution would never be an act of self-limitation undertaken by government. Before the constitution there is no representation and therefore no genuine government. Moreover, now the separation of powers is not the mirror of a fracture embedded in society unlike the idea of "mixed commonwealth" widespread in pre-modern political régimes where different classes are at least ideally entitled with distinct powers.[19] It is rather a distinction of functions within government agencies.[20] Indeed, a constitution here is not meant as a picture of a given state of society; it is on the contrary the deliberate institutional project of a *new beginning.*[21] There are designed novel political forms, which society (the "nation") believes are the best ones to promote or render possible its own collective action. Institutional powers are not a simple, irreflexive emanation of society and its internal hierarchies; they are mediated and *invented* by the constitution and its "epoch".

It might be argued that Modern constitutionalism indeed is not an outcome of Modernity, since it is anticipated in many of its forms and expressions by pre-Modern republicanism. The theory and practice of late Medieval and early Renaissance city-republics offered a model that democratic constitutionalism only tries to re-establish and re-initiate. However, republicanism in its various versions remains an ambiguous and spurious concept. It especially lacks two distinctive features of Modern constitutionalism: (i) the egalitarian background of inalienable human rights (which ideally makes a community of "equals" of the nation) and their formal declaration; (ii) the foundational moment manifested and registered through the institutional emergency of a "constituting power" (the American "convention", the French "assemblée nationale") and written down in a constitutional charter. In republicanism, in short, we do not encounter the idea of a *novo ordo saeclorum*, of a "new beginning", which actually marks the sense of the most modern of all modern terms: *revolution.* Nor is there any hint of a "pouvoir constituant" in the "mixed commonwealth" so much cherished by pre-Modern republicans. These would have never dared to claim that <<une constitution suppose un pouvoir constituant>>.[22]

II. CONSTITUTIONALISM AND LEGAL POSITIVISM

II. 1. Law as Fact

In jurisprudential circles legal positivism is a perennial source of both reassurance and of controversy. There is a strong competitor and an alternative to deal with: natural law. And there is, especially in recent times, an effort to redefine legal positivism, so to eschew the bulk of conceptual and practical obstacles with which it has ever been confronted. Unfortunately, much of this very recent discussion is not relevant to our subject. In several refined and highly sophisticated scholarly essays the looked for definition of law, within a positivistic approach, is so wide that it would make of many historical fierce opponents to positivism indeed supporters of the latter. Moreover, such sophisticated redefinitions are sometimes so idiosincratic that they would not be acceptable or even understandable for the many positivists who are still crowding our courts and law schools. Just to give an example, what is now called "inclusive positivism"[23] – which acknowledges moral principles as a source of law – would be palatable for several principled legal moralists and it would accordingly happen to be repugnant to many traditional legal positivists. The "separability thesis", on the other side – which draws a sharp dividing line between law and morality – said to be the master tenet of legal positivism by many Anglo-American jurisprudents, would not be agreed upon by a few founding fathers of European continental positivism, according to whom law is rooted in the "spirit of the age", in ethnicity or in the morality of national community.

What would then be a better definiton of legal positivism? To find it, I think two main features should be taken into account. First of all, "positivism" means that law is "posited", man-made, artificial and that this is what makes natural law (which is not equally disposable by human beings) a somehow useless notion. In this sense, we could speak of legal positivism *lato sensu*, in a wider sense. However, in nearly every version of positivism the idea of "artificiality" is connected with that of a *specific* form of man-made law, the one produced by the *State*. The law of the legal positivist is the law of a special historical political formation, the modern State. This is mirrored through the obsession that legal positivists (John Austin, for instance) have with regard to commands, sanctions, and hierarchies. Here the law is inextricably linked with sovereignty and this is rooted in sheer force and so-called political superiority. The positivist's obsession with the State is so acute that he is tempted to say in the end that law is so much the same as State law that citizens or citizenship are an irrelevant category from the legal point of view. Accordingly, in a first phase law is said to be gapless (for instance, by the French *Ecole de l'Exégèse* or by German *Begriffsjurisprudenz*), considered to be in a second phase, in response to much criticism, as indeed exposed to gaps but nevertheless to be filled up through the discretion of its own officials, eminently judges.

Such positivist obsession is so strong and permanent that it marks a continuity of attitudes in the good two centuries of the positivistic era. Such continuity is featured by another strange idea, which is again functional to the view of the law as merely State law. The addressees of legal rules – say such diverse scholars as Hans Kelsen, Alf Ross, Karl Olivecrona, or H. L. A. Hart and most recently a number of post-Hartian jurisprudents – are only judges and State officials. Law is considered as an autonomous social sphere also because it is such with regard to the rest of society and to individuals. Law is only addressed to, and concerned with, law officers. Normal citizens with their needs and their inclination to break the law or to protest can conveniently remain out of the picture.

A second feature of positivist law is the obsession with facts. Law here is not only conceived as man-made but is also and primarily a *fact*. And a "fact" in such a view is something endowed with immediate evidence and overwhelming coercive force. "Facts" here are opposed to "ideas", "beliefs", and "values", but also to language and rules. A "fact" moreover is contrasted with "freedom" or "free will". In the end, from this point of view, it is the fact that it is a fact that gives the law its validity and legal force – as is shown, in a paradigmatic way, by the "normative force of the factual" pointed out by Georg Jellinek or by the centrality given to effectiveness by Hans Kelsen's "pure theory". For Kelsen – as is well known – only an order which may be considered "im grossen und ganzen" as effective can be ascribed a "fundamental norm" and thus legal validity. A similar strategic role plays the so-called "social fact thesis" within the Hartian jurisprudence and the notion of "convention" in some post-Hartian theoretical developments; all of them centring around the idea of "law as fact". Here, once again, *ex facto oritur jus*.

This tendency is related to the ever frustrated effort of offering legal studies a noble and "hard" epistemology and of presenting them as a sort of "empirical science". <<Le positivisme juridique – writes

approvingly Michel Troper – se caractèrise avant tout par la volonté de construire une science de droit sur le modèle des sciences de la nature>>.[24] Now, the assumed centrality of "facts" and the claim to build law (legal doctrine) as a kind of empirical science have a strange effect on the view of law as "man-made", that is as conventional, artificial, changeable, unstable therefore. Facts which deserve scientific treatment cannot be unstable and highly contingent. The result is that for much legal positivist doctrine there is a shift in the idea of law now conceived as having the same ontological density as nature, and a temptation becomes visible of equating laws of nature with State laws. The following statement by Vittorio Emanuele Orlando, the founding father of Italian public law, is good evidence of such development: <<We draw a distinction between the legal and the political order: the former refers to the study of natural and necessary relations, the latter to relations which are modifiable according to the conscious performance of subjective aiming. In this way constitutional law differentiates itself from politics>>.[25]

Orlando thus, by seeking a secure ground for his "science" of constitutional law, is induced to state that constitutional law is something very different from politics, from political fights and agreements, since it is stable, objective, permanent, that is, quite the opposite of the subjectivity and volatility of politics. Accordingly, constitutions cannot any longer be conceived as acts of politics, as political events, nor can they be considered as agreements. Constitutions – in this view – are given back the pre-modern meaning of political order "nature" or "essence". For the legal positivist usually so much worrying about formalities and procedures a constitution loses its sense of a "formal" establishment and acquires that of "material order", that is, the "nature", the "reality" of the formation which to the positivist's eyes really counts: the State. At the end of the day for legal positivism "constitution" is equivalent to the "material constitution" of the State,[26] its "scientific" notion is for him neither that of a "constitution of free countries" nor the one of "constitutional" or "representative" State, nor that of "constitutional monarchy", but simply "State law". Constitutional law here is equivalent to public law.

This conclusion trivialises the notion of constitution and connects it to the concrete political context in a realistic mood. By drawing such a conclusion legal positivism becomes a good companion to all those antiliberal doctrines which oppose the notion of constitution as a foundational act of self-determination, the historicist, evolutionary concept of a constitution embedded in the traditions of the given country. It is Burke's, not Paine' view that the legal positivist in the end assumes as his own. In this context, in the framework of the positivist approach, constitution is not a central qualifying notion, since it is conceptualized as the State "nature" or "structure" or else "history" The only possible constitution will be a "material" one. Accordingly, whatever State will be given the dignity of being "constitutional", since it cannot be denied a "nature", "structure", or "history".

The material concept of a constitution in this way is much more formal than the notion of "formal constitution", in that it is much less substantively informative. It is in the end an empty notion, since there is no State, no body politic, which could not be said to possess such a constitution. The outcome of this trivialization is by-passing constitutional law as a specific legal discipline and focusing instead on "State law".

II. 2. Legislation and Sovereignty

As a matter of fact for the legal positivist the epochal legal event has not been formal constitutions proclaimed in the American and French revolutionary process but rather the invention of that new kind of political command called, law, "la loi", and more specifically the event of its systematization in a code. It is the *code*, not the constitution, the legal positivist's bible. For him it is the code the "real" constitution, the relevant formal document supporting the whole legal order, since it is the systematic, rational and in principle complete, collection of State laws. And these, the laws, are the fundamental legal *sources*. This they are for a very simple reason: it is not the constitution but the laws, which express State "essence", that is its power, sovereignty, ultimate and final supremacy. A formal constitution's main task indeed is power limitation, the taming of sovereignty, not its sanction and celebration. Sovereignty is bound and civilized through a constitution recognizing fundamental rights and prescribing separation of powers. Such civilization process is unconceivable for the legal positivist, for whom taming sovereignty can only mean exercising a superior, higher power, which will be then defined as the "real", "proper" sovereignty. Constitution are thus seen in the best of cases as a kind of noble lie: a kind of a morality without legal consequences or an act of self-limitation by the sovereign through which the sovereign paradoxically retains his dignity and ultimate power.

In this respect the case of John Austin's analytical jurisprudence is quite telling. Austin's sharp distinction between law and morality is not so much dictated along the line of the separation of "is" and "ought", since positive morality certainly belongs to the "is" domain and nevertheless is not dignified as "proper law", because it lacks an imperative backing. For Austin a true law in fact is only a command and a command is an intimation of a wish to do or refrain from acting backed by the threat of a sanction (an evil inflicted in case of non-compliance).

What distinguishes law from (positive) morality therefore is not their respective epistemological quality ("objective" in the case of law, "subjective" as far as morality is concerned), but rather that only law is made entirely of laws "properly so called" and especially of those true laws which derive from political superiors, from the sovereign's final will. Political superiority, sovereignty, we have – according to Austin – only if the following two conditions are satisfied. (i) There must be a tradition, a habit, of obedience to the political superior. (ii) There must not be any political dependence of the "political superior" in question on any other political actor, a "superior" more superior to the said superior.

Law is here depicted as the true form of an order backed through a menace. Permissions or law without sanctions or with "positive" sanctions (rewards) are not considered "proper" laws. Accordingly, there are only "duties", no rights, and judges are merely thought of as officials subordinate to the political superior's will and expression of wish. Now, particularly relevant are the consequences of this approach, in so far as political and constitutional theory is concerned. Austin's fundamental point here is that a political society is in any case a hierarchical order: <<A given society [...] is not a society political, unless the generality of its members be in a habit of obedience to a determinate and common superior>>.[27] And <<in order that a given society may form a society political and independent, the superior habitually obeyed by the bulk or generality of its members must not be habitually obedient to a certain individual or body>>.[28] From this perspective there might be some difficulty to distinguish family authority and political power, private and public. Indeed, Jeremy Bentham, Austin's main philosophical reference, explicitly draws a similarity between the family and the "perfect political society", in so far as both base in principle on a "state of perfect subjection".[29] The only difference here is that subjection in the family, since it is rooted in children's natural weakness, is temporary, that is, <<incapable of continuing for ever in virtue of the principles which gave it birth>>.[30]

The political sphere is in essence seen as a fractured body, in short a class society, a society of "superiors" and "inferiors". <<An independent political society is divisible into two portions: namely, the portion of its members which is sovereign or supreme, and the portion of its members which is merely subject>>.[31] Now, an implication of such a view might be that political equality, democracy, government of the people by the people, is sheer nonsense, "nonsense upon stilts" – to use the well-known expression that Jeremy Bentham adopted to mark down human rights – which to him indeed are "anarchical fallacies".[32]

Political superiority is a good that cannot be redistributed along liberal or egalitarian criteria. <<The sovereignty – argues the positivist Austin – can hardly reside in all the members of a society: for it can hardly happen that some of those members shall not be naturally incompetent to exercise sovereign powers>>.[33] Only a few can have full political competence, since by nature human beings do not have equal wisdom and talents. This is the reason why every political society, every State, <<every supreme government is a *monarchy* [...] or an *aristocracy*>>.[34] No true democracy is conceivable within such positivist jurisprudential framework; democracy can only be an aristocracy, when the proportion of the sovereign number to the number of the entire community is not small but large.

But if true democracy is unconceivable, the same holds as far as constitutionalism is concerned. In fact, <<sovereign or supreme power is incapable of legal limitation, whether it resides in an individual or in a number of individuals>>.[35] Separation of powers is <<too palpably false>>.[36] As a matter of fact, constitutionalism in general as a limitation to sovereignty is branded a logical contradiction. <<A monarch or sovereign number bound by a legal duty were subject to a higher or superior sovereign: that is to say, a monarch or a sovereign number bound by a legal duty, were sovereign and not sovereign, supreme power limited by positive law is *a flat contradiction in terms*>>.[37] This idea again echoes Bentham's teaching according to which supreme power cannot be bound through rules or obligation: <<the word duty [...] – he says –, if applied to persons spoken of as supreme governors, is evidently applied to them in a sense which is figurative and improper>>.[38] Constitution and constitutional laws accordingly cannot be true laws; they will have a much higher essence and impact. <<Against a monarch properly so called, or against a sovereign body in its collegiate and sovereign capacity, constitutional law – claims Austin – is positive morality merely, or is enforced merely by moral sanctions>>.[39]

The whole is crowned by a utilitarian downgrading of freedom and by imperativist reductionism which lead to a position quite close to an expression of contempt. Political liberty cannot be a principal end, since it is merely <<a mean to that furtherance of the common weal, which is the only ultimate object of good or beneficent sovereignty>>.[40] And political liberty at the end of the day is only an appeal to duty and obedience, in that it <<is coupled with a legal right to it:

and, consequently, political liberty is fostered by that very political restraint from which the devotees of the ideal liberty are so fearfully and blindly averse>>.[41] In short, wherever one turns around in the precinct of a political society, one can only be confronted with power (as "might"), duty (as subjection to an impending menace), to constraints and inequality of natural talents and social conditions: a picture – I would like to add – hardly favourable to a constitutional State.

Now, the image which XIXth century legal positivist doctrine as a whole offers of the law is not very much different from the one propagated by Austin's "analytical jurisprudence". In this respect the German line represented by Gerber, Laband and Jellinek, the three founding fathers of continental European public law, is congruent with the approach taken by British jurisprudence.

II. 3. The Rise of German Public Law

The history of German modern public law begins – one might say – with a bold statement made by Friedrich Carl von Gerber, a Prussian private lawyer: <<State authority is will power by a subject conceived as an ethical organism [*Die Staatsgewalt ist die Willensmacht eines persönlichen gedachten sittlichen Organismus*]>>.[42] It is an application and expansion of the so-called *Willensdogma*, the "will dogma". That is, the will theory as a fundamental doctrine of private law, and especially of contract law, is now applied and adapted to the domain of public law.[43] Accordingly, the State is conceived as an individual subject endowed with a will of its own. Such will, which in the case of private law is labelled "autonomy", is in the domain of public law called *Staatsgewalt*, "State power". This "State power" finds its holder not in the king as such, but rather in the State itself conceived as a corporation, a "legal person". The State is real not so much in the king's person, as it exists in its own right and not merely as a fiction or a mystical body but as an entity based on a natural foundation (the people). Its will is not the outcome of a legal or theological construction (as it is, for instance, in the medieval doctrine of the king's two bodies); indeed Gerber believes it is a real will rooted in the spirit (*Geist*) of the State's essence, which is the people, the *Volk*.

The legal expression of *Staatsgewalt* – says Gerber – is *Herrschaft*, dominion: <<Die Aeusserung der Staatsgewalt ist Herrschen>>.[44] To such expression of State will – domination – the entirety of people are subject. Now, to be faithful to the people's spirit, which is its own foundation, the State will should be *sovereign,* that is, should derive from the people's spirit itself. In other words, the State will to be sovereign should not be subject to a power superior and external to its own structural, ontological foundation. Sovereignty – stresses Gerber – has nothing to do with king's rights or with monarchical prerogatives. <<Mit dem Begriffe des Monarchenrechts im engerem Sinne steht der Begriff der Souverainetät an sich in gar keiner Relation>>.[45] This latest statement actually marks a paradigm shift in the German State doctrine, giving rise to an impersonal view of the State, now detached from the very person and the rights of the king. The king in this perspective becomes an "organ", an "official" of the State, not its owner or – as it were – its holder.

Here then we face an important difference with respect to Austin's jurisprudence. Sovereignty is no longer a quality of one or several given persons, but the attribute of a collective entity which to act as such needs the law. A State and a State will are possible – in this view – only in the form of law. The problem here, as in any imperativistic doctrine, is how to combine political will considered in terms of domination and command with the limits that are intrinsic to the legal instrument, the law. In Gerber's perspective a constitution certainly is not the answer to such a problem; a constitution in fact according to him is nothing more than the ordering of State agencies ("organs") and it cannot as such be seen as a constraint set to those agencies' action. A constitution is not a rule controlling State activity; it is rather the *normality* – as it were – of such activity. <<One cannot properly define a State constitution in the narrow sense, that is as the system of State agencies and legal expressions, as a constraint to State power>>.[46] The solution is to be found elsewhere, in a doctrine of *State purposes*. Indeed, these only can offer the sought for limits to State action. We eventually reach the following conclusion: <<State power is no absolute will power. It should only serve State purposes and exist solely for them>>.[47] Such State purposes are culturally relative and find a determination through the *Volksgeist*, the so often appealed to "Spirit of the People".

Laband and Jellinek shared Gerber's dilemma: how to maintain a full *Staatsgewalt* as domination and absolute power and nevertheless have access to some kind of legal restraint. The question is acute after the foundation of the Second Reich, the unified Germany, not so much with regard to constitutional guarantees as with reference to the federal structure of the Reich.

The Second Reich, gloriously proclaimed in Versailles in 1871, is a federal State, endowed with full sovereignty. Nonetheless, in the Reich the previous States do not disappear: kings, princes, dukes, archdukes and freetowns, they all yet keep their ancient statutes and symbols. But how can they be sovereign, that is "States", within a larger, fully sovereign State? And in case they are not sovereign, do they still deserve to be called "States"? The solution offered by Laband and Jellinek is the doctrine of State self-limitation, whereby it is then possible to distinguish between (i) *sovereignty* and (ii) *sovereign rights*.

In Paul Laband's most famous treatise, *Das Staatsrecht des Deutschen Reiches*, we read the following statement: <<There is no dimidiated, divided, diminished, dependent, relative sovereignty, but only either sovereignty or not sovereignty. Nevertheless, an entity which does not have any sovereignty features, and therefore is subject to a superior legal power in some respect, can in spite of this hold sovereign rights on free human beings and their groupings, thus be a State power>>.[48] But what is in this view the difference between "sovereignty" (*Souveränität*) and "sovereign rights" (*Herrschaftsrechte*)? This is is explained by Georg Jellinek in his monograph *Gesetz und Verordnung*. The sovereignty here is conceptualised as a negative attribute: the fact that the State as a legal (collective) personality does not suffer any (legal) limitation. It does not however determine which concrete powers and competences the State actually owns in a specific context. <<The concept of sovereignty says only in negative terms that no external legal constraint binds the State in the determination of its competences; however, it can never define in positive terms the State action's contents>>.[49] By an act of self-limitation the State defines in detail to which ends its action has to be directed. In this way it gives rise to sovereign powers and competences (*Hoheitsrechte*), which are constrained within the law (produced by the self-limitation move).

The solution therefore to the conflict between a sovereignty in principle unbound and absolute on the one side and concrete, well-defined and legally constrained *Hoheitsrechte* on the other, is distinguishing a specific sovereignty from a potential one. Sovereignty implies that a State may potentially hold whatever legal power. However, exercising a legal power means to specify a context within which it is to be exercised; and by so doing sovereignty becomes restrained. <<We get the concept of sovereign rights, whenever the State through its self-determination focuses its own action on specific issues of the common life. A sovereign right is sovereignty concreteley constrained. Accordingly, it is intrinsic to the notion of sovereignty that the State potentially holds all sovereign rights, that is, that there is no good valuable for the people's community that would be in principle foreign to sovereignty. However, the State factually holds only those sovereign rights which it in concrete issues claims>>.[50]

The State in a concrete situation will hold only those legal powers that are the outcome of a specific (therefore legal) self-limitation. Sovereignty in short means the possibility of exercising all conceivable legal powers, without however being equivalent to the sum of concrete valid legal powers. This conceptual stipulation thus makes it possible to have a federal State holding full sovereignty and subordinate federate entities, which can still be given State dignity and prerogatives.

The said conceptual solution is also important for another purpose: the shaping of the State as a "constitutional" order, at least in the narrow sense of a "legal" State. A State in this perspective is "legal" by an act of self-limitation, which however does not require a constitution as an act external or previous to State activity itself. Such a solution renders a "constitution" a matter of course, since it implies that any State has a constitution and therefore is a "constitutional" State. Constitutions according to such a view do not possess a specific legal function nor a specific legal efficacy. They are either equated with "material constitution" (the fact of the working legal order) or with normal legislation or with a programmatic (if not rhetorical) declaration without direct legal effect. The "real" constitution, which is in any way related to the factual mode of State functioning, is thus said to change through the mere exercise of State power: <<Durch die Art der Ausübung staatlicher Macht wandelt sich die Verfassung>>.[51]

We are here not very far from Lassalle's famous, critical and somewhat cinical view of a constitution as the concrete power relations within a given community.[52] The only relevant difference perhaps is that while Lassalle conceives of constitutions as relational situations emerging from social conflict, Jellinek's view is more faithful to the idea that connects a organic compact sovereignty with a constitution as its – as it were – deep grammar. So that a constitutional change need not being conceptually linked with a notion of legality: <<Theory ascribes unlimited will power to the sovereign State. Hence, it can change its constitution, dissolve it, replace it with a different one, as it feels like. And this not only through the means of law>>.[53]

II. 4. Legal Positivism and Constitutionalism

What is in conclusion the relationship of legal positivism with the idea of a constitution? First of all, the proclaimed scientific ("positivistic") approach to law pushes towards an understanding of the constitution in descriptive terms. This has as a consequence that constitutions are not given a strong normative status and are more or less seen in terms of a concrete factual situation, usually defenseless, exposed to whatever incursion that legislation may deem appropriate.

Second, the seemingly neutral State-centered definition of law (as a State monopoly of social control, or as political command and violence) is inclined to present the constitutions either as "positive morality" (someting non-legal) or as a law without a special status with regard to ordinary legislation. Accordingly, the notion of (legal) State, *Rechtsstaat*, takes the upper hand. Constitutionalism henceforth becomes fundamentally equivalent to "legalism" or to the "rule of law", and the latter is thematised as a "self-limitation" of State sovereignty, that is a series of disciplinary or administrative procedures or controls internal or intrinsic to the State machinery. "Rule of law" (*Rechtsstaat*) in the German public law means paradigmatically administrative jurisdiction. Democracy (government of the people by the people), constitution in a strong sense (as an act of self-institution) and fundamental rights (as individual entitlements independent from legislation) disappear from the province of public law. Fundamental rights are suggestively replaced by "public subjective rights" actionable not before ordinary judges, but exclusively in front of administrative courts, and such *subjektive öffentliche Rechte* are often conceptualized as "Reflexrechte", a reflex of legislative supremacy.[54]

This development is due in many aspects to the political reaction to French Revolution perceived as the harbinger of anarchy and subversion. Human rights are accordingly marked as "nonsense upon stilts" and catalogues of civic freedoms as "anarchical fallacies". Democratic constitutionalism is widely rejected within legal positivist doctrines, because it is seen as a formidable threat to monarchical regimes (the only really appropriate way to express the idea of "political superiority"). And as an alternative to democratic constitutionalism, three main strategies are worked out: (i) liberal, (ii) legalist, and (iii) traditionalist. (i) For the liberal strategy (adopted mainly in post-revolutionary France) a constitution means a monarchy limited through a charter formally conceded by the king to the people by which the former promises to limit his own prerogatives and to safeguard and respect a few civil and political rights. *Gubernaculum* (government) and *iurisdictio* (law concerning individual entitlements and private agreements) are here kept separate through some form of parliamentary control. The king's power is "neutral" (a "pouvoir neutre") with respect to civil society interests and parties. Such neutrality must at the same time assert the primacy and intangibility of monarchical prerogatives. These may be exercised in a neutral way only in so far as they remain opaque to civil society and indisposable by citizens.

(ii) In the legalist strategy there is no need of an explicit constitutional charter. Here the fundamental guarantee is offered through the procedural form given to State acts and by the conceptual configuration of the State as a collective legal subject. In the best case some sort of jurisdiction internal to the executive power is envisaged. In such a case, though public administration is not subject to ordinary *iurisdictio*, there will be an internal procedure established by which administrative agencies are hierarchically checked and eventually censured.

(iii) Traditionalism finally opposes the liberal formal *Konstitution* the communitarian and historical *Verfassung* – an opposition which we find explicitly expressed in Hegel's legal philosophy. This strategy is common to political romanticism. However, we are usually confronted with two versions of such an approach, a moderate and a radical one. For the moderates a constitution is a collective practice which nevertheless allows for individual rights and parliamentary control such as it would be, for instance, in the British case. Burke's proposals could perhaps be ascribed to this moderate model. For the radical view on the other side *Verfassung* is a deeper communitarian practice, which bases on *Stände*, organic and corporative aggregations, and on monarchical prerogatives planned to work as a unifying and crowning moment of socal hierarchies. Stahl's *Rechtsphilosophie* could represent a good example of a theory defending this second view.

Nevertheless, there is – it cannot be denied – a convergency between the new (democratic) understanding of the constitution as an instituting act, a process *ex nihilo* (that is, produced not from tradition but from principles) and the arising doctrine of sovereignty, which sees the State as an act of self-affirmation and an expression of an unbound, somewhat nihilistic power. This convergency makes it possible to interprete legal positivism (which as a theoretical position – as we saw above – centres around an absolute notion of political supremacy) as the general theory of law most congruent to modern (democratic) constitutionalism. However, to render this interpretation plausible, the self-instituting act or the "constitutional moment" is to be conceived in the existential terms of self-affirmation and not in the discoursive mood of public deliberation. Deliberation, internally bound through the arguments upon which it is based, should be replaced by sheer decision. *Auctoritas, non veritas, facit legem*, authority not truth makes the law – this the motto most cherished and repeated by the legal positivist. But discussion and deliberation are in fact not oriented and guided through authority, but through a search for the better argument, that is, for the truth however provisional, probable and fallible.

The hidden link between legal positivism and modern constitutionalism is thus given by a romantic concept of a constitution, by the idea of a general will thought not so much as a process of universal and discursive (deliberative) decision as rather the instant, "existential" intuition of a homogeneous collective life. That no democracy can be possible without a strong "*demos*" (a thick cultural and national unity, that is, an "*ethnos*") is the thesis which at the end of the day seems to render legal positivism compatible with a democratic constitution.

III. FROM STATE LAW TO CONSTITUTIONAL STATE, OR, FROM HERRSCHAFT TO "DISCOURSE"

III. 1. Normativity and Facticity

XIXth century legal positivism led to two main outcomes. They are both products of a process of radicalization and – so to say – of purification. Legal positivism featured as a sort of hybrid or compromise of two rough materials: on the one side, the legal form, rule or norm, or – if you like – normativity; on the other side, the social and political context, power, or – if you like – facticity. Now, once these two poles are assumed in their pure form, they tend to put in question the compromise reached by legal positivism and to make themselves mutually free and independent. Thus, facticity radicalized leads to a positivism of social facts and regularities, which is very well represented by institutionalist and realist doctrines. Normativity radicalized on the other hand finds one of its best expressions in the so-called "pure theory of law", a theory admitting only rules and their formal relations as pieces of the legal order.

The Italian public lawyer Santi Romano already at the beginning of last century showed that the formalistic liberal State with a few interventionist competences on economy and society at large and a minimal footing on it was no longer a working machinery for the emerging mass society. In a series of articles written before the First World War, he announced the forthcoming crisis of liberal State and culture, and tried to offer new formulae for State reform. Its main idea was to let the materiality hidden by the positivist doctrine of law be clearly exposed and recognised. However, in doing so he curiously once more reaffirmed the notion of political power, which was already more or less explicitly presupposed by legal positivism even in its most formalistic visions. Vindicating the materiality of law in this perspective thus means a kind of amnesia about the counterfactual, ideal reference of law, seen now as fully congruent with the given social landscape. This view favours once again a position preaching the priority of State perrogatives over the legal checks, though admitting the possible plurality of different legal systems. However, such plurality is not operationalized in a pluralist concept of political order. This is rather conceived on the one side as a system among many (Mafia being suggestively one of them), which one has to choose among. On the other side, it is perceived as pluralist as well within its own borders, in the sense that it is allowed for forms of corporatism and hierarchical social distinction. Constitutionalism is not reserved for a special legal order (an "institution"). Nor did it denote a special character or trait of such an order. In the alternative between a constitution seen as the supreme norm, the "master rule" of the system, and a constitution conceived as unitary principle intrinsic to the single order, Romano chooses for the second, while nevertheless conceding that there might be a plurality of legal systems all effective within the same social territory.

Constitution for Romano is the fundamental structure of any legal order. <<We use the expression "constitutional law" or that other equivalent of "constitution" to designate that part of every institution, that is, of every legal order, which is its essential structure and which is the basis of all its other parts [...] In short: constitutional law, or a constitution, is the State supreme order>>.[55] Therefore, every State has and cannot but have its own constitutional law. Constitutional law is State law, or rather, its essential core. <<The State by definition is a legal order [...] and one cannot therefore conceive of it in any of its forms outside the law>>.[56] All State expressions are legal acts. In such a configuration of State activities there is no room for a specific "constitutional moment" or for a control on the constitutionality of legislative acts, as was the case for the traditional XIXth century positivism.

Santi Romano is defending a "material constitution" theory, an idea of constitution as given through the concrete social structure. Costantino Mortati's work, centring *expressis verbis* around this notion and using it as an alternative to liberal constitutionalism, will indeed develop several suggestions already offered by the Sicilian lawyer. Romano's doctrine as a matter of fact may also in turn be interpreted as a more sophisticated reformulation of views that are typical of German political romanticism. If we take, for instance, Friedrich Julius Stahl's work on philosophy of law, we are confronted with an idea of constitution as the articulation and differentiation of human society, whereby the State comes to existence as an "institution": <<Gliederung der menschlichen Gemeinschaft, durch welche der Staat als Anstalt besteht>>.[57] Here the essential words are *Gliederung* and *Anstalt*. A constitution is only possible – says Stahl – if a community is structured in organic units, which are spontaneously displayed along a hierarchical scale.

A constitution is something connected not with any political order but only with a special form of this endowed with stability and a hierarchical structure, that is an "institution", an *Anstalt*. The two notions, *Gliederung* and *Anstalt*, converge into one which presides over Stahl's view of a constitution: hierarchy, both social, as a principle of society as a whole, and political, as the overarching criterion in the relationship between government and citizens.

While democratic constitutionalism implies a claim for an equal civic competence, thus opening the way to a struggle for political equality at large and a principle of equal concern, romantic thought asserts that a constitution could only take place in the framework of a pluralist (in the sense of driven by unequal membership) social reality. Now, there is – I think – the justified suspicion that Romano's view, though no longer captured by an anti-modernist nostalgy, nevertheless shares the same prejudice against political equality, which is the distinctive mark of Stahl's romantic philosophy of law. In any case, Romano also does not allow for a conceptual distinction between State and constitution, in so far as his doctrine makes the latter collapse into the former.

This suggestively is also the point where Hans Kelsen fails to render justice to modern constitutionalism. Kelsen's attempt to build a "pure" science of law is well known. This attempt is mainly based on two theoretical pillars: first, a concept of rule not as a command or imperative but as "hypothetical judgment"; second, a notion of the legal system as a "dynamic order", a hierarchical structure of rules, the ones empowering the production of all others, culminating in a master rule, the so-called *Grundnorm*, which however, no longer is a positive, posited rule but merely a presupposed norm, an epistemological device meant to allow lawyers to conceive legal rules as a unitary system. This doctrine *prima facie* seems to bring about a full normativistic deconstruction of the State. This is now conceived solely as an agglomeration of norms without an internal substance or a proper ontological dignity. However, once we read Kelsen's theses with more attention, that first impression quickly evaporates and we see a different pattern in front of us.

<<Staatsfunktion ist Rechtsfunktion>>, State function is law function – writes Kelsen in his most representative public law treatise, the *Allgemeine Staatslehre* published in 1925.[58] The State exists – he says – in so far as there is a permanent process of production of rules and a concretization of these. This is made possible through the working of a dynamic order closed at its summit by a fictitious master rule. Such a rule according to him is the real constitution in a logical sense. What we usually call "constitution" is such only "in the sense of positive law";

but this is not able to provide for a unitary principle of legal order. In particular – he adds –, since the positive constitution can be changed and is actually often changed, such positive regulation is not able to offer stability and identity to the State. Such permanent identity can only be given by a constitution as a rule which has not to endure the contingencies of political fight and historical developments: that is, a pure logical or epistemological rule. Such a rule has no substantive content except for the empowerment of those officials or "organs" that produce the historical constitution, whatever its substance might be. <<Indeed a "constitution" [*"Konstitution"*], that is, the constituting moment of a concrete State legal order, the foundation of its unity, rests on the presupposed, not enacted ground rule [*Grundnorm*]. The latter can be called a "constitution" [*"Verfassung"*] from the point of view of legal logic. For the first act of legislation, yet not justified through a prior positive enactment, is backed by that rule. *This, the ground rule, is the foundation of State identity*>>.[59]

It is the need for a State identity beyond any political form that claims the necessity of an abstract, nearly empty notion of (logical) constitution – to be considered as the really supreme permanent master rule of the legal order. This is also the reason why Kelsen easily (too easily, in fact) disclaims any contractualist foundation for constitutionalism. Contractualism – according to the Austrian jurisprudent – is exposed to the most serious reproach: that it is a natural law doctrine. To affirm that a constitution means a basic people's agreement or a deliberation is branded as a natural law thesis, since it refers the supreme source of the law not to a normative figure, but to a special event, a *Tatbestand*, violating the purity of the legal normative domain. Natural law in this view is curiously seen as a kind of triumph of facticity over the normativity of the pure legal form (the norm).

This approach, however, leads to disruptive consequences for constitutional law. In particular Kelsen by so much overstressing the constitution in the logical sense against a positive constitution is then induced to claim that the constitution as a written, formal document is a remnant of natural law ideas, an expression of the view that legal order and State base on a material agreement, then enshrined in a charter to which an aura of sacrality is ascribed. Knowing how much Kelsen connected natural law with a notion of "ideology" the conclusion of his argument might well be that a constitution is essentially an ideological device. He thus comes to his final statement: from the positive law angle, the utility and opportunity of getting such a formal, sacral document are really doubtful, <<seine Zweckmäßigkeit ist [...] mehr als zweifelhaft>>.[60] An astonishing statement indeed for someone who is likely to have been the drafter of quite a number of formal constitutions.

III. 2. Normativism, Institutionalism, Decisionism

In 1934 Carl Schmitt published a booklet, *Die drei Arten des rechtswissenschaftlichen Denkens*, where he singled out three main types of legal doctrine: normativism, institutionalism and decisionism. However, writing in a historical context in which law was openly contempted and used in the best case as mere *instrumentum regni*, it was of the past that the German public lawyer was speaking. And the past to which he more or less explicitly referred was the turbulent years of the Weimar republic. In fact, those years were decisive, first of all because the Republic's breakdown produced the Third Reich monster and the *untergang* of Europe in the second World War. But they were fatal in another sense too. They proved beyond any reasonable doubt that traditional legal doctrine and especially legal positivism in its narrow XIXth century version, could not cope with democracy and its defense. Legal positivism proved inadequate to offer a concept of law, which could be logically congruent with democratic ideals and supportive of these. In particular, legal positivism was unable to react properly to the rise of mass societies and the Social State without endangering liberal culture. Nonetheless, the Weimar republic gave rise to a rich debate and to a dramatic confrontation about the notion and interpretation of constitution, whose outcomes were later (after the end of World War Two) taken seriously and pondered to find out a better solution for a reform of the liberal State. This is why it is advisable to dwell on the Weimar constitutional debate for an understanding of contemporary European constitutionalism. In that debate we shall find outlined in tragically pure form the intellectual options available.[61]

We should first spend a few words on the structure and wording of the Weimar constitution, issued in 1919. As a matter of fact, we are confronted with a constitution of a new type, deeply distinct from XIX century constitutional documents. First of all, the Weimar constitution is the explicit product of a constitutional moment, of an institutional act external to government itself and refereed to people. <<The German people [...] – we read in its Preamble – have given this constitution to themselves>>. The Weimar constitution is not "octroyée", a gracious concession, in the way for instance of the *Statuto albertino*, the first constitution of the Italian unitary State issued in 1848.

The second relevant feature of the Weimar constitution is that it contains as an essential part of it and not just as a preliminary declaration a list of intense fundamental rights. The third innovative feature was furthermore the mention of equality as a legal principle not merely reducible to the formal equality before the law. Equality in the law accordingly acquired again – after its decline following the decay of French democratic ideals – a pivotal position in the system of legal principles. We should also add that the Weimar constitution allowed for the building of elements of constitutional justice or judicial review around the institution of a *Staatsgerichtshof*, whose powers however remained a matter of doctrinal controversy.[62]

In the Weimar republic we are confronted with three main constitutional doctrines beside legal positivism and Kelsenian normativism. To single out these we can follow up to a certain point Carl Schmitt's categories. We have first to do with an institutionalist view, quite popular in the twenties of the last century because of its romantic origins and undertones. We then find a decisionist approach, curiously often combined with a communitarian ideological background. And finally, there is also a sort of Platonist constitutional theory, according to which political institutions are deductions of a higher moral order, which however can only be perceived by and known to a limited group of *Gebildeten*, of enlightened and virtuous statesmen. This last theory was defended for instance by the philosopher Leonard Nelson, without however having much impact on the Weimar constitutional debate. Such an approach nevertheless was deeply embedded in the *Zeitgeist* and absorbed and then – as it were – dispersed in the air the latter's antidemocratic effluvia – once more disqualifying the conceptual independence of a constitution "deduced" from the superior notion and reality of the State.

Institutionalism's most refined representative was Rudolf Smend, an admirer of Rudolf Kjellèn's view of State as *Lebensform* and of Theodor Litt's phenomenological nationalism. A constitution for him is an act of *Selbstgestaltung*, of self-production of a social body. However, such *Selbstgestaltung* was not conceived in deliberative terms as an act of understanding and agreement among plural concepts of good life around a possible overlapping consensus. A deliberative strategy Smend would have labelled as "contractualist", therefore "individualist", *ergo* "mechanical". Constitutional *Selbstgestaltung* for him is rather a process of integration (and his theory therefore is an "Integrationslehre"), where this process is a kind of irrational merging together of people around a collective myth. An integrative device according to Smend is, for instance, marching behind a flag or acclaiming a leader seen as a reflection of our culture and ethnic identity. Parliaments may also have integrative effects, but only if deprived of their deliberative and discursive character, and if assuming the character of a laboratory for the production of myths and a depository of charisma.

Of the three doctrines mentioned, decisionism seemed the one closer to a democratic world-view and the most apt for a better understanding of modern constitutionalism. This because of its overt voluntarism and its explicit reference to a foundational constitutional moment, is a "pouvoir constituant", which would render justice to the ideal of government of the people by the people. There are nevertheless at least two problems with decisionism, if this is taken as a reference theory for the modern constitutional State. First, while recognizing the foundational intent of the constitution, its intrinsic originalism, it is incapable of seeing constitutional rules as a workable system of limits. Since a constitution is an act of independent will, though it structures and subordinates future legislation, it is assumed that it cannot order the will whose expression it actually is. The constitution is conceptualized as the outcome of a supreme constituting power upon which no restraint can be laid. A "pouvoir constituant" is always behind the constitutional arrangement, ready to change this whenever it may feel like it. A constitution, accordingly, could hardly guarantee stability and security to social and political relationships without repudiating the primacy of the original "pouvoir constituant". Fundamental rights depend – as it were – on the constituting power's whims and cannot offer a secure basis for controlling legislation.

A further problem with decisionism's is that it – in the line of positivistic tradition – ends by affirming the State's supremacy against the dignity of constitutional chartering. Since the decisionist "pouvoir constituant" by making up the constitution affirms itself as an existential collective entity, this must have a prior existence with regard to the constitution itself. Now, this entity endowed with such a strong will of self-affirmation is but the (national) State, as the only possible collective subject to which political homogeneity and effective will can be ascribed. This explains why at the end of the day, for the decisionist view (according to Schmitt, for instance), the hard core of a constitution is not the part enschrining fundamental rights but the provisions dealing with State form and security.

III. 3. "Wille zur Verfassung", Will of Constitution

Of the three main doctrines competing in the arena of the Weimar constitutional law none, however, was apt to offer a credible defense for a democratic constitutionalism. On the contrary, quite a few of them were openly meant as a criticism of the liberal State and were holders of more or less explicit authoritarian plans of reform. Both Smend's communitarianism and Schmitt's decisionism ended by eschewing and considering obsolete the question of political power's limits. Moreover, they imbued their respective theories with a strong anti-individualistic pathos, which made it quite difficult to think of the constitutional moment also in terms of the vindication of counterfactual individual rights. Platonism in its turn, by reinterpreting political action in terms of (moral) knowledge, flatly denied the necessity of any constitutional moment as distinct from a technical assessment and did not articulate proposals for a serious separation of powers. Finally, formalist normativism and legal positivism, by claiming to be "scientific" and neutral, could not provide a strong normative justification for the democratic State. They were condemned to repeat Ödön von Horváth rhime: <<es ist alles halt relativ>>, everything is indeed relative.[63] If any State is a legal and constitutional State, there will of course be very little room for any critique of (unconstitutional) attempts to reshape the present State order in authoritarian terms. In any case, for such approaches there is no room for a non-relative, objective response founded on value-laden concepts.

The German crisis leading to Hitler's seizure of power is terrible evidence of the permanent failures and shortcomings of the Weimar constitutional doctrines. Now, it is precisely upon a serious attempt to overcome those shortcomings and contradictions upon which contemporary European constitutionalism is founded. The tragic experiences of Fascism and totalitarian States are fundamental to a new perception of constitutional law. This is again, as it was in its origins, related to a kind of natural law view. When dealing with the constitution – we read in the perhaps most influential treatise of democratic Spain's constitutional law – <<the question is establishing *within* the legal order a rule fulfilling functions previously ascribed to natural law>>.[64] Human beings have a dignity the law cannot deny – this is an essential acquisition around which are centred all European constitutions drafted after the Second World War. Human dignity is not negotiable or subject to trade-offs: this seems to be the meaning of article1 of German *Grundgesetz*. Article 15 of the 1978 Spanish Constitution provides that torture will be "en ningún caso", *in no case*, allowed. This is a right moreover granted to "todos", to *every human being*, not only to Spanish nationals. Doubtless, here we are before an "absolute", undefeasible and universal human right.

Rights and their protection are seen as the hard core of the constitution. A second element that is stressed and which asks for guarantees is the intangibility of the constitution itself or better of its essential contents, its *Wesensgehalt*. Constitutional provisions for rights should now be entrenched against the malleability that legal positivism attached to constitutional rules usually considered as more or less equivalent to ordinary laws. Constitutional law needs to be neatly differentiated and defended – as it were – from ordinary law. Legalism cannot be equated with constitutionalism.[65]

In the new democratic State there is a relevant shift in the sense of a constitution. In the XIXth century liberal States' legislative power was not subordinated to significant constitutional constraints also because in the "sense" of the constitution there was a limitation of effective political power in that specific historical context, and such effective power was yet held by the executive, by the king. So that the constitution's main task was a limitation of the king's executive power, implemented by way of intense competences assigned to a distinct power, legislation. Limiting legislation in that historical situation would have meant hindering the very device whose functioning was conceived as the real constitutional constraint for the monarchical principle. Now, however, that the monarchical principle has dissolved, it is precisely legislative power that is the rising danger for constitutionalism; so that it is legislation that has to be especially put under control.[66]

Finally, a constitution – as becomes apparent in the German *Grundgesetz* and in the Italian republican constitution of 1948 – is not only a rule whose main task is coordinating State agencies. It is rather a programmatic agreement according to which an entire society makes a special commitment for its future. A constitution is a long-term common project for a better form of life. Its programmatic aspect takes here a different meaning from the one that legal positivism was disposed to attach to it. For a constitution to be a "programme" does not now mean that it has no direct legal effects. It means on the contrary that its legal effects are of a non-deontological nature, nor only limiting political power but also and above all, prescribing to it an end to be maximized and a means to reach that end. This change of normative status is well mirrored – I believe – in the doctrine of fundamental rights as commands of optimization defended – at least with respect to German constitutional law – by Professor Robert Alexy[67]. A constitution thus has now not so much a deontological as a teleological character.

The central consequence of this new approach and of a powerful revival of natural law ideas as this is witnessed within contemporary constitutional law and legal philosophy is – if you will allow me the expression – a conceptual and in a sense an institutional, "withering away" of the State. This effect is more or less distinctively perceived by the most distinguished European constitutional lawyers of the second half of XXth century. Costantino Mortati for instance, once a Fascist public lawyer and the great theorist of "material constitution",[68] is obliged to adapt this notion (originally coined to serve the authoritarian regime's purposes) to the new political developments. While in a Fascist context "material constitution" coincided with the Fascist monopolistic party structure and power claim, in the new post-war democratic republic it is meant both to reflect and justify political and social pluralism. "Material constitution" here is the outcome of the interplay of various groups within a pluralistic public sphere. Such interplay prevails over rigid, formal, legal forms and over the traditional State form itself. The pre-political nature of the latter dissolves when confronted with the heath of political parties' and unions' interplay. The constitution in short is the bedrock of a legal order, not of the State. Mortati moreover acknowledges the constituting character of the constitutional moment, which the constitution is then asked to hand down, transmit and safeguard. His definition of a constitution is perhaps the best and shortest presentation of contemporary European "thick" constitutionalism as distinct from its XIXth century "thin" positivistic version. There are according to the Italian scholar three "constitutive elements of the concept of constitution": (i) a people not as subject to an external supreme political power but as the <<unique holder of a power of producing in a unilateral way the constitutional order>>; (ii) a solemn and formal procedure of drafting and writing down the constitutional charter as the supreme rule governing State agencies; (iii) the overarching aim of safeguarding individual freedoms.[69]

A similar approach is also taken by Konrad Hesse, probably the most influential German constitutional lawyer after 1945. His theory of *Wille zur Verfassung*[70] is in a sense not very far from Costantino Mortati's later pluralist interpretation of a "material constitution". As it happens, in Mortati's terminology, a compromised notion is here redeemed through bold reconceptualization. Hesse takes Nietzsche's controversial *Wille zur Macht*, a source of decisionistic and antidemocratic views, and reshapes it in a way that makes it possible to use a voluntaristic attitude to oppose precisely those constitutional tendencies within which *Wille* was most claimed and instrumentalized. Mortati's "material constitution" is another case of the same retorsive strategy.

"Wille zur Verfassung" means that it is true that a fundamental decision has to be taken, that it is a decision to live in a public sphere of shared understanding, and that this is the existential ground for the State.[71] Such a decision however, need not be incompatible with democracy and interpreted as a decision whose only actor could be a pre-constitutional subject, the State. A pre-constitutional State – this is the argument – which is active before the constitution is given, would not do justice to the foundational sense of the constitutional moment, that is the "Wille zur Verfassung". A State can be necessary and even unavoidable or indispensable as an element of the constitutional order. But on the one side its borders do not coincide with those much broader ones of the constitutional order (which clearly comprises civil society as distinct from State):[72] and, on the other side, the State can be necessary only as the outcome of a constitutional moment. <<There is as much State as is produced by the constitution>> – writes Peter Häberle,[73] adding then that the State is not a "primary element" of a constitutional order.

In short, within a constitutional order there is first a constitution and only afterwards and eventually shall we have a State. This is why a legal philosopher of Ulrich Klug's caliber can boldly state that the fundamental principle of the constitutional rule of law is "anarchy".[74] "Anarchy" here – it must be stressed – is not meant as an apolitical and lawless situation, chaos, a moment where everyone is a fiend, "lupus", to the other, that is, the opposite of a "civil condition", the collapse of "civility". Klug's "anarchy" is rather thought of as "civility" in its pure and idealized form, a collective order where political participation is widely realized and nobody commands and rules over the others. Such "anarchy" in short is very close to Habermas' ideal speech situation where participants acknowledge each other's full normative dignity and reach agreement without coercion.

Democratic constitutionalism is a law of "fundamental rights". It is the protection and the improvement of such rights that justifies the access to the legal domain and the use of specific legal instruments (which are connected in the end with force and coercion). However, the use of law and the coercion connected to it should not contradict the contents and the free exercise of fundamental rights. Otherwise, they would lose their normative justification and their democratic relevance. Most fundamental among fundamental rights and presupposed by these is autonomy (which is the parallel to constitutional moment on the individual scale). If this is so, then autonomy cannot overtly be denied through the introduction of law as a means of coordination. Otherwise, the originalism of the constitutional foundation would be contradicted. On the contrary, coordination within the constitutional order means – as it were – the socialization of autonomy and a reproduction of the constitutional moment's originality. But autonomy socialized, extendend to the community – so runs Klug's argument – is nothing less than self-government, absence of political domination, *anarchy*. This is why, according to Habermas, neither contractualism nor the communitarian search for prepolitical roots could work as an appropriate foundational model for the constitutional State. The element of collective interaction would be missing. <<Neither the social contract nor the assurance of a common cultural heritage offers an appropriate model for the process of constitution-making. [...] A more appropiate model is that of public discourse in which free and equal participants come to an agreement about which rights they must mutually recognize if they want to legitimately regulate their common life by means of positive law>>.[75]

In the democratic constitutional State we are thus confronted with an apparent paradox, that the law, an institution related to coercion, is rendered instrumental to the implementation of collective autonomy, that is of "anarchy". The conflict between law and autonomy however becomes less strident, if we conceive of law as a tool, which is capable of making people free. It would do so, since an individual subject only to law would no longer be dependent on masters and bosses and their whims and arbitrary will. Freedom as independence from another man's will is not injured, indeed is promoted by a general standard applied to all and everyone and not disposable to anybody. This, following a distinguished tradition which opposes men's to laws' rule, is stressed by Hayek: <<When we obey laws [...], we are not subject to another man's will and are therefore free>>.[76] The law as the rule of law is a universal prescription, the command of nobody.

Nonetheless, the coercive dimension of legal institutions can hardly be denied. Contemporary constitutional law accordingly requires strong limitation not only of traditional *Herrschaft*, domination and power, but also and foremost of coercion and violence. Law, once constitutionalized, rendered "constitutional", is therefore required to be fully civilized, thoroughly human, "mild", "diritto mite" – as this is intelligently labelled by the Italian constitutional judge Gustavo Zagrebelsky.[77] What was before, in the *Rechtsstaat*, forced into unity is now eventually separated. This separation takes place particularly on three levels: (i) separation of rights and legislative rules; (ii) separation of justice from positive law; (iii) separation of principles from rules. What legal positivism through its reductionism united, is in the end exploded as an immanent contradiction, where however, one term is to gain the upper hand: rights over the statutes, justice over law, principles over rules.[78] A constitution – says Zagrebelsky following Schmitt's *Verfassungslehre* but leading to different conclusions – is not equivalent to constitutional laws or rules. It is rather the outcome of an exceptional situation, a constitutional moment, where <<the political actors' will converge on a common purpose: to issue principles beyond everyone's particular interests to make possible everyone's living together with everyone>>.[79] In material terms it is something quite close to the original position envisaged by John Rawls to build up a concept of justice acceptable to individuals who gather as citizens.

A constitutional law is a "mild law" first in the sense that it is open to justification and refers to argumentation and discourse, to a "civil conversation". But it also mild in the sense that within its province – which is essentially discursive – the use of force and coercion is reduced as drastically as possible, in order to make it possible for collective autonomy, for "anarchy", to daily express and reproduce the foundational "Wille zur Verfassung". A "will of constitution" in fact is eminently a will of discourse – and this abhors violence and coercion. Here, therefore, criminal law can only be "minimal" and punishment will be mainly reeducation to citizenship.[80] The death penalty, for instance, cannot but be banned, since it, beyond being in our cultural context an unusual and cruel punishment, would represent the most serious infringement of the "anarchy" requirement laid upon the constitutional rule of law, that is, the overwhelming and overarching respect for permanent individual and collective autonomy. The death penalty as much as torture will be an extreme violation of the cruelty ban intrinsic to modern constitutionalism. Nothing more than the ban on torture has an "archetypical" relevance for our liberal understanding of the rule of law.[81] Indeed – says Professor Zagrebelsky – <<the sense of law and constitution is [...] to hinder naked power>>.[82]

The incompatibility between fundamental rights and a traditional notion of State sovereignty is stressed by another influential German constitutional lawyer, Martin Kriele. His position is clear. After a critique of Hermann Heller's notion of sovereignty (the latter thematized in a paradoxical Schmittian mood as the legal capacity of violating the law[83]), his conclusion is the following: <<In short, in the constitutional State there is no sovereign>>.[84] A position which is echoed by Italian scholarship, when this dares to affirm that in the constitutional State sovereigns are only values, not subjects or agencies.[85] Fundamental and human rights – says Kriele – do not allow for the embarrassing and menacing presence of an almighty centre of power: <<Only where there is no sovereign, can we have human rights as rights>>.[86] Otherwise, they will be, in the best case, "Reflexrechte" – to use Gerber's terminology – pale reflexes of duties and obligations laid upon citizens by State agencies. Once rights are taken seriously – as is recommended by Ronald

Dworkin[87] – a constitution cannot but be subservient to them. the constitutional discourse and its interpretation would be have to be translated in strong normative terms. Holding a right does not mean only having a sphere of autonomy and power over one's own scope of agency, but also and perhaps more fundamentally "being right", raising a claim of rightness, claiming to be right. And such claim cannot be satisfied through just legalistic considerations; it will require some sort of moral reasoning – which if it is thought to be generally binding should exceed the mononological mood, ask for others' voice, and be institutionalized before public fora and by procedures available to citizens.

This priority of rights (especially as "claims to be right") over rules and duties changes the constitutional landscape and the very meaning of the constitution. This now – as is forcefully argued by John Rawls – <<is seen as a just political procedure which incorporates the equal political liberties and seeks to assure their fair value so that the processes of political decision are open to all on a roughly equal basis>>.[88] This is why it would quite paradoxical to a rights-based critique of constitutional rights. If rights are to be secured against the changing mood of the sovereign, they are embedded in a constitution, or better, it is the very sovereignty that would have to be reshaped as a constitutional arrangement, a political province defined or delimited by rights. An informal dialogue among citizens, representatives and officials will not do without substantive and procedural rights allowing a civil conversation, and in the end without some more or less thick "forms", which would institutionalize, that is, project over time and stabilize in space, that very dialogue.

Once invested by constitutional law (and rights), the old wild beast, the Hobbesian sovereign, the State, Leviathan, the cold monster feared by Nietzsche's Zarathustra, will hopefully be tamed. The State will undergo a process of civilization, if not of "extinction". If it should still be of use among humans, this will happen in a new capacity, that – as it is said ironically[89] – of a nice house pet. This process releases an immediate effect on how lawyers and citizens will think and operate about the law. This is now imbued with principles and values and is also the outcome of a deliberative decision-making. Its application and transformation in case law, in a ruling for the concrete case, in *Fallsnormen* – to use a German expression – will have to take into account the novel civilized dimension of law-enactment. By virtue of the constitutional rule of law natural law, requirements have been incorporated into the positive legal system. In such an institutional setting legal "validity" – says Professor Ferrajoli – is no longer equivalent to the "being in force" of a rule.[90] This is also due to the fact that public authorities under contemporary conditions have to cope with an increasing intricacy of the social texture and the fact of pluralism. Conditional regulations do no suffice any longer to orient social life and to protect citizen's fundamental interests. Purposive and teleological provisions, "programmes", cannot be avoided. Promoting the common good is now openly perceived as the the State's paradigmatic task. In such context – as Ronald Dworkin remarks – <<government has become too complex to suit positivism's austerity>>.[91]

If the law "invested" by a constitution has undergone a further process of "civilization" and thus become "mild", "mild" likewise will have to be its enforcement. Reasoning about the law will have to take seriously those principles and procedures that the law purports to reflect and project. In a constitutional State legal validity refers to principles of justice and is open to judicial review. In short, under constitutional conditions legal reasoning will be obliged to go beyond a positivistic black-letter law exercise. As pointed out by a distinguished Italian scholar, <<after constitution's entering into the legal order systematic interpretation [...] has become insufficient>>.[92] We will need in addition a dimension of *justification*. Interpreting the law has acquired a clearly perceptible axiological, moral dimension.

NOTES

1. See his seminal contribution *Constitutionalism: Ancient and Modern*, Cornell University Press, New York 1947. And cf. P. Barile and M. Fioravanti, <<Costituzioni>>, in *Enciclopedia delle scienze sociali*, Vol. 2, Istituto della Enciclopedia Italiana, Roma 1992, pp. 548 ff., especially section one.
2. King James I and VI, *Political Writings*, edited by J. P. Sommerville, Cambridge University Press, Cambridge 1994, p. 191.
3. In the following I rely on Dieter Grimm, *Die Zukunft der Verfassung*, Suhrkamp, Frankfurt am Main 1991, chap. 4.
4. M. Dogliani, *Introduzione al diritto costituzionale*, Il Mulino, Bologna 1994, p. 181.
5. E. Burke, *Reflections on the Revolution in France*, ed. C. C. O'Brien, Penguin, Harmondsworth 1986, p. 120.
6. Th. Paine, *The Rights of Man*, Everyman Library, London 1954, p. 182.
7. *Ibid.*, p. 184.
8. *Ibid.*
9. *Ibid.*, p. 186.
10. See *ibid.*, p. 191.
11. *Ibid.*
12. *Ibid.*, p. 45.
13. E. Sieyès, *Que'st-ce que le Tiers Etat?*, Presses Universitaires de France, Paris 1989, p. 65.
14. See H. Arendt, *On Revolution*, Penguin, Harmondsworth 1973, p. 184.

15. E. Sieyès, *Op. cit.*, p. 67.
16. *Ibid.*, p. 68.
17. *Ibid.*
18. See E. Sieyès, *Dire sur la question du veto royal*, in Id., *Ecrit politiques*, ed. by R. Zapperi, Editions des archives contemporaines, Bruxelles 1994, p. 231.
19. Cf. M. J. C. Viles, *Constitutionalism and the Separation of Powers*, Clarendon, Oxford 1967, pp. 21 ff.
20. For a similar view in the American constitutional thought as manifested in the *Federalist Papers*, cf. B. Ackerman, *We the People*, Vol. 1, *Foundations*, Cf. also G. Rebuffa, *Costituzioni e costituzionalismi*, Giappichelli, Torino 1990, pp. 59 ff.
21. Cf. H. Arendt, *Op. cit.*, p. 46: <<It was only in the course of the eighteenth-century revolutions that men began to be aware that a *new beginning* could be a political phenomenon, that it could be the result of what men had done and what they could consciously set out to do>>(italics mine).
22. E. Sieyès, *Préliminaire de la Constitution. Reconnoissance et exposition raisonnée des droits de l'homme et du citoyen (lu les 20 et 21 juillet 1789, au comité de constitution)*, in Id., *Ecrit politiques*, p. 198.
23. Cf.W. J. Waluchow, *Inclusive Legal Positivism*, Oxford University Press, Oxford 1994.
24. G. Burdeau, F. Hamon, and M. Troper, *Droit constitutionnel*, 25th ed., Librairie générale de droit et jurisprudence, Paris 1997, p. 36.
25. V. E. Orlando, *Principii di diritto costituzionale*, 5th ed., Barbera, Firenze 1909, p. 39.
26. Cf. *ibid.*, pp. 44-45.
27. J. Austin, *The Province of Jurisprudence Determined*, ed. by H. L. A. Hart, Weidenfeld & Nicholson, London 1954, p. 196.
28. *Ibid.*, p. 212.
29. J. Bentham, <<A Fragment on Government>>, in Id., *A Fragment on Government with An Introduction to the Principles of Moral and Legislation*, ed. by W. Harrison, Blackwell, Oxford 1948, p. 42.
30. *Ibid.*, p. 40
31. J. Austin, *The Province of Jurisprudence Determined*, p. 216.
32. See J. Bentham, <<Anarchical Fallacies>>, in *The Works of Jeremy Bentham*, ed. by John Bowring, Vol. 2, Edinburgh 1843, pp. 491 ff.
33. J. Austin, *The Province of Jurisprudence Determined*, p. 216.
34. *Ibid.*, p. 218.
35. *Ibid.*, p. 223.
36. *Ibid.*, p. 235.
37. *Ibid.*, p. 254. Italics mine.
38. J. Bentham, <<A Fragment on Government>>, p. 108.
39. J. Austin, *The Province of Jurisprudence Determined*, p. 259.
40. *Ibid.*, p. 270.
41. *Ibid.*, p. 271.
42. C. F. von Gerber, *Grundzüge des deutschen Staatsrechts*, 3rd ed., Bernhard Tanchnitz, Leipzig 1880, p. 19.
43. Cf. O. Jouanjan, *Une histoire de la pensée juridique en Allemagne (1800-1918)*, Presses universitaires de France, Paris 2005, pp. 213 ff.
44. C. F. von Gerber, *Op. cit*, p. 21.
45. *Ibid.*, p. 22.
46. *Ibid.*, p. 33.

47. *Ibid.*, p. 31.
48. P. Laband, *Das Staatsrecht des Deutschen Reiches*, 5th ed., Vol. 1, Mohr, Tübingen 1911, p. 73.
49. G. Jellinek, *Gesetz und Verordnung. Staatsrechtliche Untersuchungen auf rechtsgeschichtlicher und rechtsvergleichender Grundlage*, Mohr, Freiburg i B. 1887, p. 200.
50. G. Jellinek, *Op. ult. cit.*, p. 2OO.
51. G. Jellinek, *Verfassungswandlung und Verfassungsänderung*, Häring, Berlin 1906, p. 34.
52. See F. Lassalle, *Über Verfassungswesen* , Rede am 16. April 1862 in Berlin, Europäische Verlagsanstalt, Hamburg 1993, p. 23: <<Thus we have now seen, gentlemen, what a country constitution is, namely: the concrete *power relations* existing in a country [Wir haben jetz also gesehen, meine Herren, was die Verfassung eines Landes ist, nämlich: die in einem Lande bestehenden tatsächlichen *Machtverhältnisse*]>>(italics in the text).
53. G. Jellinek, *Op. ult. cit.*, p. 3.
54. Cf. M. La Torre, *Disavventure del diritto soggettivo. Una vicenda teorica*, Giuffrè, Milano 1996, chap. 3.
55. S. Romano, *Corso di diritto costituzionale*, 4th ed., CEDAM, Padova 1933, p. 9.
56. *Ibid.*, p. 10.
57. F. J. Stahl, *Die Philosophie des Rechts nach geschichtlicher Ansicht*, Vol. 2, 5th ed., Mohr, Tübingen 1878, p. 205.
58. H. Kelsen, *Allgemeine Staatslehre*, Springer, Wien 1925, p. 248.
59. <<Doch liegt die "Konstitution", d. h. die Konstituierung der einzelstaatlichen Rechtsordnung, die Begründung ihrer Einheit, eigentlich in der als Verfassung im rechtslogischen Sinne bezeichneten, nicht gesatzten, sondern nur vorausgesetzten Grundnorm. Denn auf ihr beruht der erste, noch durch keine positivrechtliche, d.h. hier: gesatzte Norm bestimmte Akt der Gesetzgebung. *In ihr – der Grundnorm – ruht auch die Identität des Staates*>>(*Ibid.*, p. 249; italics mine).
60. *Ibid.*, p. 253.
61. On that somehow tragic, but nevertheless rich and fruitful discussion about contrasting models of constitutional order, cf. M. La Torre, *La crisi del Novecento. Giuristi e filosofi nel crepuscolo di Weimar*, Edizioni Dedalo, Bari 2006.
62. Cf. M. Stolleis, <<Judicial Review, Administrative Review, and Constitutional Review in the Weimar Republic>>, in *Ratio Juris*, Vol. 16, June 2003, pp. 266 ff.
63. Ö. von Horváth, *Italienische Nacht*, Suhrkamp, Frankfurt am Main 1995, p. 11.
64. I. de Otto, *Derecho constitucional. Sistema de fuentes*, Ariel, Barcelona 1987, p. 22. Italics in the text.
65. Cf. R. Dreier, <<Konstitutionalismus und Legalismus – Zwei Arten juristischen Denkens im demokratischen Verfassungsstaat>>, now in *Konstitutionalismus versus Legalismus? Geltungsgrundlagen des Rechts im demokratischen Verfassungsstaat* (Archiv für Rechts- und Sozialphilosophie, Beiheft No. 40), ed. E. E. Dais et al., Franz Steiner, Stuttgart 1991, pp. 85 ff.
66. Cf. R. Bin, *Capire la costituzione*, Laterza, Roma-Bari 2002, chap. 1.
67. See R. Alexy, *Theorie der Gründrechte*, First edition, Nomos, Baden-Baden 1987, now translated into English as *A Theory of Constitutional Rights* (Oxford University Press, Oxford 2002).
68. For a general assessment of Mortati's approach, cf. M. La Torre, <<The German Impact on Fascist Public Law Doctrine. Constantino Mortati's Material

Constitution>>, in *Darker Legacies of Law in Europe*, ed. by Christian Joerges and Navraj Ghaleigh, Hart, Oxford 2003, pp. 305 ff.
69. C. Mortati, *Costituzione (dottrine generali)*, in *Enciclopedia del Diritto*, Vol. 11, Giuffrè, Milano 1962, p. 143.
70. See K. Hesse, *Die normative Kraft der Verfassung*, Mohr, Tübingen 1959.
71. See G. Zagrebelsky, *Princîpi e voti. La Corte costituzionale e la politica*, Einaudi, Torino 2005, p. 126.
72. See K. Hesse, *Grundzüge des Verfassungsrechts der Bundesrepublik Deutschland*, 17th ed., Müller, Heidelberg 1990, p. 10.
73. P. Häberle, <<Lo Stato costituzionale europeo>>, in *Sovranità, rappresentanza, democrazia. Rapporti tra ordinamento comunitario e ordinamenti nazionali*, Proceedings of a Conference Held in Naples, 25-26 June 1999, Jovene, Napoli 2000, p. 52.
74. See U. Klug, <<Die geordnete Anarchie als philosophisches Leitbild des freiheitlichen Rechtsstaates>>, in Id., *Skeptische Rehtsphilosophie und humanes Strafrecht*, Vol. 1, Springer, Berlin 1981, pp. 88 ss.
75. J. Habermas, <<Remarks on Erhard Denninger's Triad of Diversity, Security, and Solidarity>>, in *Constellations*, Vol. 7, 2000, p. 523.
76. F. A. von Hayek, *The Constitution of Liberty*, Routledge & Kegan, London 1960, p. 153, and cfr. R. Dworkin, <<Hart's Postscript and the Character of Political Philosophy>>, in *Oxford Journal of Legal Studies*, Vol. 24, 2004, p. 30.
77. See G. Zagrebelsky, *Il diritto mite. Legge diritti giustizia*, Einaudi, Torino 1992.
78. See *ibid.*, pp. 49 ff.
79. *Ibid.*, p.156.
80. L. Ferrajoli, *Diritto e ragione. Teoria del garantismo penale*, Laterza, Roma-Bari 1990, pp. 325 ff.
81. This point is convincingly stressed by J. Waldron, <<Torture and Law. Jurisprudence for the White House>>, in *Columbia Law Review*, Vol. 105, 2005, pp. 1681 ff.
82. <<Il senso del diritto e della costituzione è [...] impedire il bruto predominio>> (G. Zagrebelsky, *Princîpi e voti.*, p. 116).
83. On Heller's radical doctrine of sovereignty, cf. M. La Torre, *La crisi del Novecento. Giuristi e filosofi nel crepuscolo di Weimar*, chap. 2.
84. M. Kriele, *Einführung in die Staatslehre*, 2nd ed., Westdeutscher Verlag, Opladen 1981, p. 116.
85. See G. Silvestri, <<La parabola della sovranità>>, in *Rivista di diritto costituzionale*, 1996. Cf. also for a similar view L. Ferrajoli, *La sovranità nel mondo moderno. Nascita e crisi dello Stato nazionale*, Laterza, Roma-Bari 1997.
86. M. Kriele, *Einführung in die Staatslehre*, 2nd ed., p. 116.
87. See R. Dworkin, *Taking Rights Seriously*, 2nd ed., Duckworth, London 1978.
88. J. Rawls, *Political Liberalism*, Columbia University Press, New York 1993, p. 337.
89. Suggestively, it is once more a Post-war German constitutional lawyer that in this way forestalls the perfection of State power submission to the public sphere (see E. Denninger, *Der gebändigte Leviathan*, Nomos, Baden-Baden 1990, pp. 27-29) .
90. See L. Ferrajoli, *Diritto e ragione*, pp. 347 ff. Cf. G. Bongiovanni, *Costituzionalismo e teoria del diritto*, Laterza, Roma-Bari 2005, pp. 142 ff.
91. R. Dworkin, *Justice in Robes*, Belknapp Press, Cambridge, Mass 2006, pp. 211-212. Cf. M. La Torre, *Il giudice, l'avvocato e il concetto di diritto*, Rubbettino, Soveria Mannelli 2002, chap. 2.
92. A. Falzea, <<La costituzione e l'ordinamento>>, in *Rivista di diritto civile*, 1998, p. 276.

CHAPTER 2

LEGAL REASONING AND THE CONCEPT OF LAW

I. RHETORIC AND PRACTICAL REASON

I. 1. Two Paradigms of Right Reasoning

Until the Eighteenth century an important place in a lawyer's training was reserved for education in reasoning about the rules or principles of law. This reasoning was indeed understood more as rhetoric, as the art of the orator, as the capacity to exercise persuasion. Nonetheless, the less pragmatic, more formal aspect of legal discourse was not neglected. Little treatises on "legal logic" burgeoned, generally, though not only, applications of Aristotelian logic to the structure of the arguments used in legal disputes.[1] And it may be recalled that Giambattista Vico was a teacher of rhetoric, *professor eloquentiae*, in the Law School of Naples University, though as we know he never succeeded, to his great vexation, in landing a post teaching civil law. Rhetoric was, however, a qualifying subject at the time in the curriculum of the law student.

Everything changed in a way I do not hesitate to term dramatic first with the paradigm shift in philosophy during the XVII century. After Descartes and Hobbes, not to speak of Galileo and Newton, reasoning is equated with mathematical calculus, "reckoning". Eloquence and rhetoric are therefore expelled from the domain of reason and knowledge. *Ratio* is now opposed to *oratio*. Reasoning and knowing accordingly centre around the notion of a "law", either to be discovered or to be applied.

Such a great shift is then ratified and expanded with the assertion of Enlightenment ideology and the great codifications, especially the French one. Indeed the Prussian code (*Allgemeines Landrecht*) was still very indulgent towards the corporative social structure and plurality of legal orders handed down by the class State,[2] and the Austrian one still left ample room for so-called natural reason, i.e., assessment in accordance with extra-positive principles (recall in this connection Article Seven of the ABGB, the 1811 Austrian civil code, written by Franz von Zeiller, a Kantian jurist much criticized for his "philosophical" attitude by the historicist Friedrich Carl von Savigny). It was, then, the French codification and the Enlightenment ideology it was nourished on, so to speak, that made the difference.

This is not the place to dwell on the history of the French codification and its difficult gestation, on the drafts by Cambacerès and Portalis. Suffice to recall that thanks to the elimination of the original Article Nine in the Portalis Draft, which provided for recourse to the equity where the law was silent, the dogma of the completeness of the legal system was asserted.[3] Nor should it be forgotten that in 1793 the Convention had decreed the abolition of Law Schools, an extreme manifestation of maximal trust in the clearness and exhaustiveness of the legislator's work and of suspicion of the jurist as interpreter of the law, whereby interpretation was seen as the bending of the rule's proper meaning. Napoleon's reform of legal education only added a militaristic touch to the model of a lawyer absolutely subject to the legislator's wording.[4] *Stulta sapientia quae vult lege sapientior esse* – this is the permanent device of Napoleonic professors of law.

Note that when speaking of the legal system in Enlightenment, legal positivist language, what is meant is exclusively the set of statutes explicitly issued by the legislative authority, that is, by the representative of popular sovereignty. The order's completeness here means, then, completeness of the system of laws. Put in other words, the Enlightenment and the Napoleonic codification marked a move from a theory of law centred on arguments, however heterogeneous, frequently mutually contradictory and unsystematized, to a theory of law centred around the notion of "source". What made headway was what a British scholar, Joseph Raz, has called "source theory"[5], and Ronald Dworkin has termed "conventionalism".[6]

But if there is a source, some sort of fact, from which the law springs, its application becomes primarily a question of finding the source itself. The judge's role is thus conceived – in line with Enlightenment suspicion of the figure of the judge and desire to make it the mere "mouthpiece of the law" – as that of a sort of natural scientist. In this perspective the judge's activity becomes eminently cognitive; he is regarded as using theoretical reason, not practical reason, that is, "descriptive" statements, not prescriptive evaluations. It was believed that the judge should operate solely in a syllogistic fashion, with as major premise rigorously the law, and as minor premise the fact, the conclusion being the verdict.[7]

So strong was the model of the syllogism[8] – a syllogism, I repeat, seen essentially as a purely cognitive operation – that the separation of powers itself and the rule of law were conceived of as a consequence of the model. Kant, but Condorcet before him too, affirms that judicial power is to legislative power as the conclusion of a syllogism is to its major premise.[9] The novelty in this model is however not so much the importance given to the syllogism. That is something not even such a confused, lax jurist as Manzoni's Azzeccagarbugli could do without. Use of the syllogism is in a certain sense a platitude. To speak is already to function syllogistically, at least where a term with an inevitably general extension – a meaning – is applied to a specific object, thus denoting the latter through the term. (If I call *this* table "table", I am operating syllogistically with the term "table", reaching the conclusion of designating the object in front of me as "table").

It is not, then, the syllogism as such that is the novelty in the Enlightenment and legal-positivist model. The novelty lies in what it is held ought to constitute the major premise of the syllogism, and in the qualities attributed to it. The major premise is the law, and this is already regarded as clear, its meaning as evident, as unambiguously given by the letter of the law itself. The novelty lies further in the epistemological, let us say, quality attributed to the judicial syllogism: it is conceived of as an essentially cognitive operation, as a theoretical rather than practical syllogism. Very suggestive in this connection is a passage from one of the founding fathers of legal positivist dogmatics, Paul Laband: <<Legal decision consists of a given case's subsumption under valid law; like any other logical conclusion it is independent from will. There is no freedom of the resolution whether the consequence should take place or not; it is produced – as it were – by itself, by intrinsic necessity>>.[10]

I. 2. Theoretical versus Practical Rationality

At this point I feel it needful to mention one fundamental distinction in philosophy and theory of knowledge: between theoretical rationality and practical rationality, or, if you will, between two different models of reason. Very approximately, we may say that theoretical reason is the set of arguments that justifies descriptive statements, assertions about states of affairs. Practical reason consists instead of a set of arguments that justifies prescriptive or normative statements, preferences, value judgements or norms. This distinction obviously has meaning only if it is assumed that descriptive and normative statements are not semantically and epistemologically homologous; that is, if it is assumed that the meaning and rightness of a value statement are not deducible from the meaning and rightness of a descriptive statement, and *vice versa*.

Theoretical or descriptive reason or rationality can be reduced to two series of arguments: (a) the basically deductive formal ones, founded on certain principles and logical operations; (b) the material ones, basically inductive, founded on empirical observations and data from experience. Formal arguments serve to develop material or substantive arguments. They are, then, auxiliary in relation to the latter. This means that theoretical rationality, at least in the sphere of empirical knowledge, is fundamentally based on experiential data. Within the province of the so-called formal sciences, mathematics for instance, one might by contrast do without such experiential data or observational situations of empirical events. Here, principles and logical operations suffice.

But practical reason, the reason that justifies value judgements or deontic statements, does not precisely coincide with theoretical reason. This is because experiential data and logical operations are not enough to supply us with indications of preference and guides to action. There is a need for a further type of premise, for criteria or normative principles.

Having quickly clarified the sense in which I use the terms "theoretical reason" and "practical reason", I shall now move to the conclusion of this first section. We have seen that it was with codifications and legal positivism that the syllogistic model, or better a theory of law centred around the notion of source, became what dominated legal epistemology on the European continent. But in the last few decades this model has, after a century of ups and downs, fallen into deep crisis. This is motivated by two principal factors: (i) one eminently theoretical, (ii) the other more contingent and historical.

(i) The great theoretical problem with what I here for brevity's sake call the "syllogistic model" is that it does not fit the reality of the operations performed by the judge in applying the law. The law cannot be applied mechanically, above all because it is never absolutely clear as a far as its relevance to contingent circumstances is concerned. What is applied is not the abstract "law in the book", but instead a provision of law which is often constructed by gathering, combining and breaking down various legal texts,[11] and reconstructed by attributing a meaning to these materials. These accordingly have first to be interpreted, and only then handled logically. Understanding and interpreting are not just subsumtion, thought they are not disconnected from it. Nor are they a matter of sheer decision. All this of course is a highly reflective, not just a mechanical process.

Then comes the fact to apply the law to. This has to be regarded as legally relevant. This is a decision that cannot be derived simply from applying the law to the fact, since the reconstruction or indeed construction of the legally relevant fact often precedes consideration of what provision is appropriate to the facts. A legally relevant fact is something more than an empirical fact. Evidence and its rules here play a decisive role in the perception and presentation of the fact.

The decisive problem that explains why the syllogistic model is (theoretically) in crisis is that even where a clear provision is available, appropriate to the case under consideration, and the factual elements have been adequately classified and tested, it is not always possible to reach a single correct answer. The syllogism allows various conclusions, all formally (logically and legally) correct. However, among these various possible conclusions there should be one which looks more convincing, though this may happen not through logical inference, but because it is supported by better arguments. For the norms, from their generality and abstractness, often lend themselves to multiple concrete manifestations, and yet we are called upon to reach one right conclusion. On the other hand, it is hard to be sure that all the factual circumstances relevant for constructing the minor premiss have been brought into consideration. Besides, the "facts" of the case, the minor premiss of the legal syllogism, take their shape, that is, are properly reconstructed, all through the judicial process with reference to an appropriate rule. It is the applicable rule that gives "facts" their profile.[12]

In short, there are no easy cases for the judge. <<In some cases – as pointed out by Micheal Oakeshott – the meaning of *lex* in relation to the contingent situation is more readily concluded than in others, but in no case can it be concluded without reflection. There is no 'plain case' in the sense of a dispute which settles itself or one which can be settled in a merely 'administrative' act>>.[13] These difficulties worsen still further in those legislations, like our contemporary ones, where special laws abound, and codifications take on even the character of residual or auxiliary provisions, in which moral and political principles are explicitly adopted in constitutions and other legal documents.

(ii) The syllogistic model further faces more contingent problems deriving from the evolution of contemporary legal systems. Two aspects of this evolution have just been mentioned: the proliferation of *ad hoc* statutes, the so-called "motorization of legislation", and the move from the rule of law in which the "fundamental" is the principle of legality and hence the reservation of law (for some areas like individual "rights"), to the constitutional State, in which rights are taken to be a "material" hierarchically superior to the law, and the principle of equality before the law is reinterpreted as a principle of reasonableness or substantive rationality.[14]

In this context of problems the most important crisis factor is undoubtedly the growing mass-juridification of our legal systems, in turn a response to the growing decline of the law. The latter, understood as a general norm and abstract rational expression motivated by a legitimate instance of popular sovereignty, is in deep crisis. This is so because it is no longer so general and abstract, but increasingly particular and concrete, an *ad hoc* law or "mini-law". And it is increasingly less justified and rational because the instance producing it has lost much of its legitimacy because of its inability to pursue the general interest in a transparent fashion. We are seeing what has been called the "juridification" of social life, or also, in Habermas's words, the "colonization of the life-world", but this over-production of laws and decrees, this instrumental and "situational" use of law, does not enhance the legislator's prestige. The mass production of laws necessarily escapes discussion of principles or pondered public debate, obeying instead more corporative, not to say clientelist, logics. The "public reason" thus driven out of legislative assemblies is often transferred to courtrooms, and democracy – in order to escape the corrupt and corrupting logics of part clientelism and technobureaucratic opacity – tends to become, so to speak, "judicial".[15]

It is today the judge that is put forward as the new centre of the legal system, no longer the legislative power, like it or not. And in the judge's view central importance inevitably attaches to the procedure whereby the decision is arrived at. Here, the law is not enough, other criteria of choice have to be resorted to.

To be stressed is the growing part played by constitutional law in many democratic systems. But constitutional law by its nature operates not so much with laws as with principles and rights. These are often balanced using argumentative operations that are more complex than a mere either-or. Constitutional justice, in order to justify its own decisions, must then use argumentative strategies much more highly structured than in the syllogistic model.[16]

Moreover, in the presence of the possibility of constitutional review of a law, it may also be considered that over and above the differences between centralized and diffused systems, every judge (whatever be the organ or instance he belongs to), insofar as she may accept a finding of unconstitutionality, or ask for it to be made, assumes a power of assessing the constitutionality of norms, and thus in a way herself becomes a "guardian of the constitution". The argumentative style proper to constitutional justice consequently spreads throughout the whole judicial system. Here, then, is a further reason for the rebirth and the prospering of theories of legal reasoning turned towards determining a broad spectrum of criteria for the rightness of a judicial decision.

II. LEGAL REASONING REDEEMED

II. 1. Rehabilitation of Practical Reason: Topics

Since the Second World War, two pieces of research have foreshadowed the new theories of legal reasoning: Theodor Viehweg's topics and Chaim Perelman's "nouvelle rhétorique". There are at least three main ways in which topics may be understood: (a) as a technique of searching for premises in practical discourse, in discourse directed towards taking a decision, in which, accordingly, legal discourse would only be one element; (b) as a theory of the content of the premises of practical discourse; (c) finally, as a theory of the use of those premises. In the first case, topics suggests collecting and classifying the various types of argument used in legal discourse, so as to arrive at a sort of catalogue of *topoi.* These, as Professor Alexy rightly notes,[17] are however fairly inhomogeneous: ranging from principles like *lex posterior derogat priori* to the interpretative technique of referring back, say, to the legislator's intentions.

From the viewpoint of the theory of the content of the premises of practical discourse, topics denies that they can be true or false, and trusts to the concept of likelihood or plausibility. As a theory of the use of premises in practical legal discourse, topics prescribes the rule of considering the various viewpoints, and is based on the principle that debate is "die einzige Kontrollinstanz", the sole check on the correctness of decisions.

Topics, just as is the case with rhetoric, concentrates too much on the pragmatic side, on the effects or "results" of reasoning. Putting it better, while rhetoric is a technique aimed at reaching certain effects on an audience, namely persuading it, topics is a technique directed to securing particular results on the speaker: *inventio*, the finding by oneself of the arguments one needs in a speech or piece of discourse. It is – in Cicero's words – *ars inveniendi* (*Topica*, 2,6). Topics is, then, oriented to the conduct of the orator, *viz.* whoever has to or wishes to put forward or articulate a discourse or an argument, that is, the utterer of a linguistic communication, partly irrespective of the presence or reactions of his audience, or of the recipients of the message. What matters – at least in topics as developed starting from Cicero's work – is that the speaker should in fact have at her disposal the arguments, whatever be their value (truth or rightness); just as rhetoric is basically interested in the orator's actually persuading her audience, irrespective of the formal quality of her theses. Thus, topics ends up being hard to deal with from a viewpoint of logic and argumentation,[18] and is reduced to a sort of apology for the orator, just as rhetoric often degenerates into a sort of audience psychology.

Moreover, topics, by starting from *topoi*, or *loci*, from generally accepted "commonplaces", before any further epistemological check on their content, risks becoming a bearer in the theoretical and normative sphere of traditional concepts without reflexive verification, and hence of prejudices,[19] and in the artistic sphere of ideas of no originality at all, of canons, not just without the artist's creativity and inventiveness, but even often incompatible with them. It is certainly no coincidence that the term "commonplace" has taken on a highly negative colouration in the last few centuries. While for Aristotle a *topos* is not yet a reason, being only a place from which one could subsequently develop an argument, this difference is blurred in Cicero's rhetorics where the "place" and the content and the justification of an argument are finally made to coincide. *Locus*, *sedes argumenti*, *argumentum*, and *ratio* end up being one and the same.[20]

Aristotle's "topos" is a heading under which one can collect and find several enthymemes, that is, rhetorical arguments, or syllogisms based on only probable premises (see his *Rhetoric* 1403a and 1355a). Though, as both Aristotle and Cicero say, rhetoric is a counterpart of dialectic, that is, of the argumentative practice of dialogical discourse (see *Rhetoric* 1354a, and cf. Cicero, *De oratore*, 114), it is so in so far as to hold an argument people sometimes accuse or defend themselves and reach a conclusion on concrete issues, while dialectics aims to obtain general inferences. In any case, both dialectics and rhetorics are said to deal with issues that are not subject to strict demonstration, that is, to reasoning whose premisses are incontrovertibly true. Topics' purpose – says Aristotle just at the outset of his treatise on this subject – <<is to discover a method by which we shall be able to reason from generally accepted opinions about any problem set before us and shall ourselves, when sustaining an argument, avoid saying anything self contradictory>>(*Topica* 100a18-21).[21] There are no possible irrationalistic motives involved in such process. Topics here is the technique of *right* reasoning moving "from general accepted opinions".

"Topics", in the version sketched out by Viehweg, is less engaged with the idea of a "right" or "reasonable" argumentative proceeding. A sort of communitarianism lurks behind it: arguments to be valid are to be "common places", that is, *common* to a shared contextual view rooted in a concrete, particular *community*. And it is *intuition* whereby they are reached. However, in spite of its latent romanticism, Viehweg's approach has two important merits. The first is that of subjecting to criticism the traditional mode of proceeding of so-called legal science based on "institutes", in short, on a doubtful ontology, on an essentialism according to which there are, behind legal concepts, substances that the lawyer can "distil" and then "combine" anew. <<For here very often a creation of legal language is presented as something extralinguistic, as an object which is merely mirrored by legal language. In this way one sometimes creates independent fields of objects, which were meant to be discovered and accordingly described by legal thought, while they were produced by the latter. In the German legal doctrine it was Ihering who delivered the most blatant instances of this kind>>.[22] It is this criticism, more or less explicit, that sparked off the recent argumentative revolution in legal knowledge, which prefers to speak of "arguments" and "reasons" rather than of "sources", and of "principles" rather than of "institutes". This is, if you wish, the revenge of "philosophers" like Franz von Zeiller over "historians" like Friedrich Carl von Savigny. The other important merit is that of stressing the procedure of balancing, of weighing "pros and cons", as typical of practical reasoning and of legal argumentation in particular.

II. 2. The "New Rhetoric" School

More articulate is Chaim Perelman's theory. After an initial period when he defended rigidly non-cognitivist metaethical postulates, and trusted in order to "test" the rationality of practical decisions purely to formal justice, summarized in the principle of treating like cases alike, he then sought, starting from the ancient tradition, to reconstruct techniques enabling us to go beyond the determination of dissent, the sole end-point of radical non-cognitivism. This gave birth to the "new rhetoric". It too, like topics, starts from the Aristotelian idea of *endoxa*, that is, the thesis that the premises of practical discourse can be founded only on probable or likely statements, or ones accepted by general opinion.

In Perelman too, as in Viehweg, it is discussion as such that is the founding element of practical argumentation. Perelman's theory is, however, more articulated than Viehweg's. In particular, it escapes the latter's typical defect of being insufficiently analytic in reconstructing arguments.

Perelman starts from a close critique of the dominant doctrine in both philosophical and legal spheres, which tends to equate theoretical reason and practical reason, that is, to deny the independence of the latter and reduce it to the former. His explicitly polemical objective is the <<conception of reason and of reasoning born with Descartes, which has marked the last three centuries of Western philosophy>>,[23] and conceives reasoning as a binding discursive procedure.

Perelman's *Leitmotiv* is that formal logic is incapable of yielding fruit in practical reason, and that nonetheless there is a practical reasoning distinct from the theoretical discourse of the scientist. It is a discourse equipped with its own internal rationality criteria, in no way condemned to decisionism or reduced to a mere beating of fists on tables, as authoritative representatives of logical neopositivism and of analytical philosophy try to make out, in the sphere of legal theory too (e.g., Alf Ross[24]).

Perelman's basic concept is that of the *audience*. The audience is the set of subjects that the speaker wishes to influence by his argumentation. The object of argumentation is to secure audience support for the speaker's theses. Accordingly, rhetoric <<has as its object the study of discursive techniques likely to promote or enhance the acceptance by minds of theses offered for their assent>>.[25]

The audience is accordingly decisive in characterizing an argument. <<The notion of audience is central in rhetoric. For a discourse cannot be effective unless it is adapted to the audience that is to be persuaded or convinced>>.[26] An argument may be convincing or not, depending on the audience it is addressed to. This, according to Perelman, implies that the fundamental rule of argumentation is suitability of the discourse to the audience, whatever that may be.

Put this way, it would seem that Perelman's theory is nothing but a strategic theory of argumentation aimed at securing consensus irrespective of the quality of the thesis under discussion and of the arguments employed. But it is not always so. For Perelman, in fact, the criterion of the rationality and objectivity of all argument lies not in support from a specific audience, as an expression of a given situation, but only in acceptance by the universal audience.

Perelman, however, is ambiguous on the composition of this audience.[27] Initially, in his 1958 *Traité de l'argumentation*, he states that the universality of the audience is only that of a particular community or historical culture and in any case depends on the speaker's psychological representations. Subsequently, the Belgian scholar seems instead to maintain that the universal audience consists of all rational beings, of all human beings, or still more simply, of all.[28]

Equally, while in the 1958 treatise he maintained that it was persuasion (of the audience) that was the criterion of the rationality of argument, in subsequent works he has distinguished clearly between persuasion and conviction. Now it would seem to be conviction rather than persuasion that is the criterion for argumentative rationality. On this last view, not every effective argument (which persuades a certain local audience) is also valid (convinces the universal audience). <<It will, then, be said that appeal is made to reason, using convincing arguments that should be accepted by any reasoning being>>.[29] Nonetheless, later on Perelman takes care to specify that the audience is defined <<instead, as the whole

set of those at whom the effort of persuasion is directed>>.[30] One may, thus, address oneself to various audiences. The universal one is the audience only for the philosopher; the jurist by contrast has to refer to a specific context and a specific social community.[31]

Perelman has also denied that the argumentative model he sketches out is necessarily monological. The "new rhetoric" he proposes would not, then, exclude dialogical argument, and thus the exchange of roles between speaker and audience, and a conception of impartiality and formal justice no longer based solely on the generality or universality of the speaker's statements, but also on the possibility for the audience to require reasons of the speaker, and hence to change from mere passive recipient of the message into active participant in a discourse.[32]

II. 3. Philosophical Hermeneutics

Hermeneutics as a special methodology was revived by Protestant reformation. Basing on the principle "*sola scriptura, sola fidei, sola gratia*", one of its tenets – as is well known – was the "free interpretation" of scriptures, meaning by this that the believer is able to grasp the sense of the Biblical message only through her own personal endeavour. Contrary to Catholic theology, Luther claimed that the Bible was to be read first literally, without referring to the tradition. Grammatical interpretation had to get the upper hand over for instance allegory and especially over subsequent dogmatics. History or tradition here is assumed as interpretive criterion only in so far as it is embedded in the grammar of a particular language. In this way, and somehow paradoxically, Luther's religious protestantism and secular humanism agreed on a similar methodological approach. Humanism in fact required philological rigour whenever approaching classical Greek or Roman texts. There is also a striking family likeness between the literality-centred or philological approach and the so-called "*mos gallicus*" in legal studies which were to prevail in the XVI century. "*Mos gallicus*", as opposed to "*mos italicus*", meant a greater attention to the philological or linguistic side of old Latin documents reporting Roman law[33]. Here understanding is equated with taking the position of the original addressee of a message, of the original reader.

A further step in the progress of hermeneutics is represented by Spinoza's philosophy of language. In the fourth chapter of his *Tractatus theologico-politicus* the great Dutch thinker proposed a more differentiated approach. In the Bible, what was not immediately understood through a normal reading had to be interpreted by reference to author's original intention. Allegory thus could not be excluded, so that the question of sense or meaning (*sensus*) had to be carefully distinguished from the question of truth. For a statement to have a meaning did not imply its being true. History had to be conceived not only as embeddedness in a language but also as the original context within which the statement, the text, had been produced.

The contextual foundation of interpretation was later very much developed by German romantic philosophies, especially by Schleiermacher. His paradigm for an object to be interpreted is poetry or an act or product of art, so that discourses are conceived as similar to a poetic or artistic expression. Hermeneutics and aesthetics converge. Here we find an equivalence between poetry and rhetoric, according to which discourses are not so much truth-oriented as rather forms of artistic invention and expressions of inner feelings and sentiments. Accordingly, the act of understanding, interpretation, should not be oriented to the discourse subject matter but rather to the contextual psychological situation of its production. It is only by an act of congeniality and invention that discourses could be interpreted. Rhetoric and understanding are very much connected. Indeed understanding and interpretation are the reverse of rhetoric and its operations.[34]

According to Schleiermacher interpreters should attempt to assume the same place of speakers and text writers and by an act of sympathy feel the same as the author of the speech to understand or of the work to interpret. Only by this congeniality between interpreters and author, where the former take the stance of the latter, could one reach a correct interpretation. Discourses are very much like poems, and these are a product of genius. Thus, it is only by a renewed act of intellectual imagination that discourses or texts could be really and deeply understood. Schleiermacher's problem – as it is pertinently pointed out by Hans-Georg Gadamer[35] – is not history's obscurity, but the opaqueness of the other's life experience. Only through feeling could we raise the veil hiding the dimension of "otherness", of what "you" are and mean. Since what you *say* is but what indeed you *are*. Interpretation thus is made possible thanks to empathy and divination – which however means that, since any understanding is an act of interpretation, understanding is somehow an exceptional event. And an exceptional event might be open only to exceptional beings.

Moreover, the act of interpretation here has an epistemological privilege over the author's stance. By interpreting one is able to understand the work to interpret better than its author. In fact, while the author's production, if genuine, is in some degree an unreflective operation, interpretation has to explicitly consider that production's implicit background. For instance, language rules are immediately applied by the issuer of a message or the author of a poem or a story, while the interpreter will be called to assess their use. The author's psychology in addition is something which brings about the author's work, while it is not taken into account in the productive act. The interpreter on the contrary can assess the sense of that work against its psychological background, which in the context of interpretation is not so much a motive as a *reason* of the work's general meaning. Said in different terms, the interpreter sees things that the author could not look at. There is – this is Schleiermacher's conclusion – a clear epistemological superiority of the interpreter over his own subject matter.

Such a position's shortcomings are evident. In Romantic hermeneutics there is first a stubborn rejection of methodic strategies for interpreting. Since interpretation here is an *art*, not a technique, hermeneutical methodology should in the end look "mechanical". Interpretation – as we have seen – is considered a matter of genius, hence something that cannot be taught or tested.

Schleiermacher's hermeneutics is especially poor as far as legal practice is concerned, where interpretation should be conceived as a matter of course and must be submitted to justification and control. In this domain a Romantic psychological approach is insufficient for an additional reason. Usually law-givers are not "artists", and their products can hardly be considered performances of genius. In law, in the production of legal "artifacts", there is a strong institutional element, which should be decoupled from exalted geniality. Moreover, in the law there is often no clear ascription of *one* author of legal provisions. Not seldom rules are the outcome of customary collective practices, not of volitive individual creativity. And even when laws are the result of deliberation, the latter can hardly be referred to the well-articulated will of fully distinguishable "subjects". Intersubjective deliberation is hardly a psychological expression of one collective body or entity that could be encapsulated from individual contributions and arguments. More often than not, laws are a matter of negotiation, compromise, concessions, universalization of individual views that in this way lose their original occasionalistic point. In short, even when we have in front of us an explicit (collective) deliberation, this cannot easily refer to an explicit (individual) volitive act.

Schleiermacher's work in any case is fundamental in connecting interpretation and understanding (*Verstehen*), though he maintains interpretation within its traditional precincts: linguistic communication and text reading. It is only thanks to Johann Gustav Droysen, a historian, the author of a famous and beautiful biography of Alexander the Great, that the province of interpretation is expanded well beyond philological questions. *Verstehen* is now raised to a basic cognitive category together with *Erkennen*, reserved for philosophy and theology, and *Erklären*, a function of natural science. Knowledge thus has three main modalities: knowing (*Erkennen*), explaining (*Erklären*) and understanding (*Verstehen*). The latter modality has to do with cultural artifact and human action in general, not just with language. Now, history is seen as the pradigmatic expression of human action and therefore a privileged subject matter for understanding and interpretation.[36]

Gadamer believes that Schleiermacher's theoretical shortcomings could be remedied and overcome by taking into account what two other great German philosophers have taught us. On the one side, we could remedy to psychological romanticism by adopting Wilhelm Dilthey's historicist and holistic approach – which is very much indebted to Droyen's generous reconceptualization of *Verstehen*. Dilthey's problem is less that of interpreting texts and works of art than that of history as a special knowledge, which is not justifiable through natural, empirical sciences. In this domain the relationship between a subject and an object is thoroughly different: the subject is a part of her object. In such perspective, thus, interpretation is a kind of historical knowledge, and psychology will no longer do, for there is not a strong cleavage between author and author's work and creation. Interpretation is the understanding of a totality, which cannot be the task of a single subject or individual disconnected from that totality itself. Nevertheless, Dilthey's hermeneutical paradigm is still the romantic one: <<das Verstehen – he says – ist ein Wiederfinden des Ich im Du>>,[37] understanding is finding one's own self in the second person perspective. There is however one important difference: that undertanding is now extended to the whole of the historical experience. The second person, "Du", is immediately referred to as a third person societal perspective. Genius is rooted in <<a community of ideas, inner life, and ideals in a concrete time and context>>.[38] Good psychology thus will have to jump to "Geisteswissenschaften", to the sciences of culture, especially to history. According to this view life ("Erleben") and history, or the past, as well as words and signs, have a "meaning" in the proper sense, which is there to be grasped through "interpretation" and hermeneutical sensibility and expertise.

Gadamer's other reference and source of inspiration is Heidegger's powerful metaphysics. Heidegger – as is well known – brings about an ontological turn of the Cartesian "*cogito*" perspective. This is now immediately translated in terms of "being". In such a view the "being" par excellence takes the shape of a Cartesian self no longer haunted by sceptical doubts. It is a "being here", *Dasein. Sorge*, "care", is her main and primordial business and interpretation or understanding is something connatural to it. According to Heidegger's understanding thus is *Sein*'s original mode – which means that interpreting acquires a fundamental, ontological centrality. Now, according to this approach, interpretation's ontological specificity, or, if you like, its special phenomenology is given by the so-called hermeneutical circle.

Understanding is not a passive situation; it is rather a project by which the interpreter takes care of a particular object. This is approached through a kind of preliminary assessment of its merits– which has then to be confirmed by the explicit hermeneutical operation. Interpreters operate thanks to a *Vorverständnis*, a "pre-understanding" of what they set out to interpret. They are ruled by <<Vorhabe, Vorsicht und Vorgriff>>, by planning, caution and anticipation.[39] A pendular going to and fro between "pre-understanding" and the object to understand should take place. In a similar way interpretation develops within two diverse temporal dimensions. Two different times, contexts, or "horizons", converge in the interpretive act: an object's context, which is somehow rooted in the past, and an interpreter's context, which is in the present. The act of understanding requires the merging of these two dimensions, a "fusion of horizons". Here we are reaching the core of Gadamer's philosophical hermeneutics. By interpreting one's starting point is one's own *locus standi*, one's own actual status, which cannot but comprise one's own *Vorurteile*, "pre-judgments", "prejudice". These however are seen as an ontological, not as a psychological event. Gadamer's move indeed is a rehabilitation of tradition: in interpretation we could not do without prejudices, that is, well-established common places and widespread dominant views, irrespectively of their truth or normative justification.[40]

Tradition is central in Gadamer's approach, according to which that is the site – as it were – of "prejudices", that is, of much "pre-undestanding", thus of that *Vorverständnis* which sets in motion the "hermeneutical circle" that expresses the phenomenological situation of interpretation. Tradition furthermore is central because understanding a subject is not just a subjective event but a fundamental moment of the subject matter's *Wirkungsgeschichte*, of its relevance in time, and at the same time of the "history" of such relevance. Interpretation accordingly can never be a discovery of the *mens auctoris*, of an author's original intentions and purposes. "originalism" cannot but be bad hermeneutics.

Comprehension, understanding – in this perspective – does not consist in a communion of souls, or of an individual act's divination, nor is it based on empathy or sympathy: it is rather participation in a common or better communal practice. Comprehending – which here amounts to the same as interpreting – is not a merely psychological or sentimental state of affairs: it is mainly a kind of institutional fact. Accordingly, it would seem that Gadamer defends a strong traditionalist and communitarian view. However, his communitarianism is much weakened through his pointing out a few normative assumptions that rule hermeneutical practice.

Here the fundamental assumption is that of *Vollkommenheit*, "perfection".[41] This is *prima facie* the outcome of a coherentist, holistic theory of meaning. Meaning – it is said – and consequently understanding presuppose an "accomplished unity of sense". When reading a text, for instance, we assume and anticipate that it is perfectly meaningful. Such expectation moreover implies that we take seriously the statements made in the text according to the expected hermeneutical character of the text considered and that we are oriented by their possible truth. Understanding first of all is an understanding about the issue or subject matter of the hermeneutical object. Thus, the assumption of perfection leads to two different but related expectations: (i) the expectation of an accomplished, or of a "perfected" meaningfulness; (ii) the expectation of the truth of what is to be understood. Now, these two expectations lead to a more general claim raised by the interpreter driven by, and acting according to, the two mentioned expectations. This is a *claim* to *correctness, Anspruch auf Richtigkeit.*[42]

Every interpretation – says Gadamer – cannot but raise a claim of rightness, though – he adds – there is no interpretational rightness in itself, since interpreting is an historical experience rooted in an ever changing traditional setting. Nonetheless, interpreting as a phenomenological event cannot do without that claim. In such a perspective all understanding acts are governed by the ideal of a *right understanding*.

In a contrary move to Gadamer's view – I would like to remember – Emilo Betti, a distinguished Italian private lawyer, sharply opposes a cognitive, historical, against a normative, legal, interpretation. Whereby the former would base on the "object" (typically the meaning of a past event or action), while the latter is focused on its "subject" (one's practical question).[43] Now, it is important to remark that to Betti's point Gadamer replies by explicitly stressing the unity of the different kinds of interpretive acts. For according to the German philosopher, every interpretation basically is a situation of understanding that is guided by the ideal of the right understanding.[44]

By referring to a rightness claim Gadamer's hermeneutics is allowed to go well beyond a traditionalist stance. That reference in fact introduces the necessity of some normative requirements for the interpretive act. Now, quite surprisingly, such requirements are eventually shaped as openly *universal* and *counterfactual*. As a matter of fact any text to interpret – according to Gadamer – should be taken seriously as raising a claim to *truth*, a *Wahrheitsanspruch.*[45] We reach here a point where Gadamer's philosophy meets with Perelman's idea of an universal audience and might be seen as anticipating Habermas' proposal of an ideal speech situation as the foundation of communication and understanding.

Hermeneutics, however, runs the risk of being unprepared to offer an articulate methodology for legal reasoning. Its main device indeed is that of transforming *topoi*, traditional and contextual points of view, in general principles of law. This might be perhaps practicable and successful in a society with a strong communitarian ethos, though *topoi* – as it has been remarked – are too opaque to be really informative. Be that as it may, under conditions of "post-metaphysical",[46] cultural pluralism there are few undisputable normative commonplaces. As a matter of fact – says Habermas – <<in a pluralistic society in which various beliefs compete with each other, recourse to a prevailing ethos developed through interpretation does not offer a convincing basis for legal discourse>>.[47] In a similar vein Josef Esser objected to the *Interessenjurisprudenz* (heralded by Philipp Heck) that "interests" as such, even if socially dominant, are yet to be transformed into "values" or "principles" to become operative in the judicial solution of a case.[48]

In particular, we might say that hermeneutics based on prejudices and very little else is inappropriate to render the justificatory enterprise which judges and lawyers are called to enter into in the context of a *constitutional* political order. Textual "fit" is not sufficient to make citizens aware of judicial decisions' legitimacy claims. The principled core of their ruling should be somehow exposed in order to satisfy those claims and to make also possible widespread understanding and criticism by citizens. A modern constitution – as we have seen in the previous chapter – is not "just" a text or a source; it is an enterprise and a foundational discourse. It is not an "*auctoritas*" only to be "interpreted" and not to be questioned; it is rather the memory of a practice, which in order to be still binding needs to be somehow repeated or "rehearsed". Now, such practice is eminently a discussion about basic principles of justice.

In the constitutional State, legislation itself is subject to the rule of law. Accordingly, it is not sheer decision, possibly instruction by a commander-in-chief but the outcome of principled deliberation reasonably acceptable to all concerned. In a constitutional polity citizenship prevails over sovereignty, or better sovereignty should be read and enforced through citizenship. Applying legislation cannot in its turn be a decisionistic fiat. Adjudication has to dig out the sense and the justificatory point of the relevant law and so direct its enforcement to such end or in such light. A mere reference to a dominant tradition as much as to a given text here will not do. In short, constitutionalism as a legal legal order will require constructivism, not historicism, as the most appropriate methodology for the interpretation of its own rules.

III. CONTEMPORARY DOCTRINES

III. 1. Neil MacCormick's Formalist Model

Viehweg's and Perelman's pioneering work has been followed by reconstructions or proposals for models of legal reasoning. The latter are, by comparison with these first two attempts, marked by greater trust in the resources of formal logic, or else less suspicion of theoretical reason. While in Perelman and in Viehweg one sometimes notes a certain antirationalist pathos,[49] this is no longer the case for the major contemporary theories of legal reasoning, both MacCormick's and Alexy's and Ronald Dworkin's; the first two being undoubtedly more formalist, the last more "communitarian", or if you wish, antiformalist.

Behind the syllogistic model of legal reasoning there is in general, maintains MacCormick, the "validity thesis". The Scots scholar puts this as follows: <<Legal systems have criteria, sustained by 'acceptance' in the society, satisfaction of which is at least presumptively sufficient for the existence of a rule as a 'valid rule' of the system>>.[50] These criteria in essence correspond to what H. L. A. Hart calls a "rule of recognition", a rule that supplies us with criteria whereby we "recognize" the other rules as forming part of a particular legal order and hence as valid. Yet the "rule of recognition" too has to be "recognized", in a different sense from the one in which the other rules may be said to be recognized as valid: it must namely, to be "recognized" as such, first and foremost be effective, *de facto* observed and applied. Yet this is sufficient only from a purely external viewpoint, say that of an ethnologist studying the norms of a particular community and seeking to offer a survey of them. From the internal viewpoint, of someone operating within the legal system for which a particular norm is the "rule of recognition", the ascertainment or "recognition" of its being "recognized", viz. practised and observed as a "rule of recognition", is not enough. Since this rule has to justify other rules and ultimately practices, it has to possess such a normative character as to justify ought statements: that is, it must be legitimate.

To be such, the "rule of recognition", continues MacCormick, has to be screened against reasons like: (i) it is good for legal decisions to be predictable and hence to adopt objectively or intersubjectively recognizable criteria (hence the "rule of recognition"); (ii) it is good for judges to confine themselves to applying the law and not producing it (making law), so as to secure greater guarantees of public and private liberties through separation of powers. And the presence of a rule of recognition as a public criterion enables the law and its application to be distinguished. For were the law not objectively recognizable, depending accordingly on the mere interpretation of whoever is applying it,[51] the distinction between the norm and its application would dissolve, and with it that between legislation (production of norms) and jurisdiction (application of norms). (Not to mention, one might add, the very reason for the existence of the norms: what use could a norm ever be if its meaning were reduced in everything and for everything to the mere act of application?) Only if the norms (and their meanings) pre-exist application can application be separated from the production of the norms themselves and be checkable by reference to them, so that the norms can maintain their function (their main one, if not the only one) of guiding human conduct. A further reason to screen the "rule of recognition" against would then be the following: (iii) the constitutional order of which the "rule of recognition" is the expression is a just order and therefore to be complied with (along with the norm in question).

Deductive justification (on the basis of a particular norm taken as "valid") thus comes about within the framework of the legitimacy of a particular institutional order. This, for MacCormick, is a first fundamental limit of the syllogistic model: that for better or worse it has to start from some sort of assumption of a political and normative nature. That is always there in any legal order and in whatever political system.

But in his view there are two other limits present especially in hard cases. The first is that of "interpretation", the second that of "relevance". The norms are expressed through linguistic statements, that is, in order to be communicated and apprehended, they have to be formulated in linguistic expressions. But language is often vague and ambiguous: accordingly, to derive meaning from it it has to be "interpreted". <<Only if no issue of interpretation arises, or after any that arises has been settled, does the deductive phase of argument proceed>>.[52] By syllogism alone, which is nothing but the deduction of a conclusion from a major premise combined with a minor premise, one cannot, where normative syllogisms are concerned (that is those deriving from a norm as the major premise),[53] either produce or interpret norms (the major premises). It is to the production of norms that the "validity thesis" is directed, with the associated reference to the legitimacy of the recognition norm. To interpret the norm, assuming that the language is in any case "open-textured", one must have recourse to hermeneutic criteria outside the deductive justificatory model. Assuming that the logical structure of a norm can be reduced to the pattern "if p then q", and that the problem of interpretation means answering the question "what does p mean: p' or p" or even p'''?", the problem of "relevance" is to know whether the norm "if p then q" applies, that is, is relevant, to the state of affairs under consideration. In this case, MacCormick goes on, one may ask the question: <<Does the law in any way justify a decision in favour of this party against that party in this context?>>.[54]

In the hard cases produced by problems of interpretation and relevance, a first guiding criterion is that of formal justice, according to which like cases must be treated alike, and hence the decision of a case oriented on a general, or universal, or universalizable, criterion. <<Any justification of a decision in such areas of dispute must involve the making of a 'ruling' which is (in the strict logical sense) 'universal', or 'generic', even though the parties' own dispute and its facts are irreducibly individual and particular, as must be the order or orders issued to them in termination of the dispute>>.[55] But these "rulings", these general or universal rules, whereby the decision of the hard case is justified, must in turn be justified.

We then move on to what the Scots scholar calls "second-order justification". <<Second-order justification must therefore involve justifying choices; choices between rival possible rulings. And these are choices to be made within the specific context of a functioning legal system; that context imposes some obvious constraints on the process>>.[56]

The guiding criteria for this sort of "second-order justification" are basically: (i) <<making sense of the perceptible world>> and (ii) <<making sense within the given legal system>>,[57] that is, the legal principles must at this level be compatible with knowledge of the structures of the empirical world, and be consistent with the set of principles, norms and values that constitute that particular legal order. In particular, <<making sense of the world>> refers to the consequences that the rules have on reality. The rules active at the "second level" must accordingly be assessed for their consequences.

As far as <<making sense within the legal system>> goes, this means that the criteria identified must (i) be logically compatible (or not contradictory) with the system's valid norms and (ii) be "consistent" or "congruent" with the general principles and values of the legal system under consideration. "Consistency" or "congruency", "coherence", means that the manifold rules of a legal system must "make sense" if considered as a whole.[58] This is possible as far as certain specific sets of norms are concerned thanks to rules of a still more general nature (the "principles"), of which the norms in question can be regarded as representing an emanation. A principle is accordingly the rationalization of a specific norm. The principles then play a twofold role: justification and explanation. "Justification" is when a norm can be subsumed under a principle P, assessed as such as positive or good, so that norm N can consequently likewise can be assessed as positive or good. "Explanation" is when there is doubt as to the intrinsic meaning of norm N, and its being subsumed under principle P supplies the key to understanding the meaning of the norm; one application of this mode of procedure is analogy, a very common procedure in legal reasoning.

Neil MacCormick, in short, reconstructs the theory of legal reasoning on the basis of the idea of formal justice. Anyone raising a legal claim in relation to certain circumstances, says MacCormick, and asserting that this claim is legitimate, also implicitly asserts the position that that particular claim is legitimate in any other circumstance similar to the one giving rise to the claim.

The principle of formal justice, that what is equal (in every essential aspect) should be treated equally, is for the Scots scholar the *Grundprinzip*, the fundamental principle, of legal reasoning. He sees this principle as acting in two directions. In one direction, it is assumed by anyone raising a legal claim, claiming a certain right, for instance; in the other, the principle of formal justice is seen as leading, in legal reasoning, to a principle of still more general scope: the principle of universalizability.

A legal decision will be correct, in this view, only if it is capable of being universalized, that is, can also be applied consistently in the future to similar cases. <<Treating like cases alike is possible – it is stressed – only given the enunciation of general norms as principles of decision, which supply criiteria of likeness between different cases. But if the norms of the system are not <<coherent>> in the sense here outlined, cases which are similar in principle may end up being decided quite differently simply because they fall under different rules>>.[59] In this sense every legal decision, even when it has to do with questions of fact, turns round a point of law. The criterion of "coherence" obviously does not rule out the possibility of deductive justification of legal decision. MacCormick accordingly does not question what was earlier called the "syllogistic model". He merely seeks to integrate it, complete it and refine it. Formal justice in short is supplemented by a "coherence" test concerning the whole of the system as a reasonable set of practical requirements. "Coherence" is actually here a test also for the fact finding moment, in the sense that all propositions of fact involved must be mutually consistent and "make sense" as a holistic piece of explanation.[60]

It should further be specified that a decision's capability of being universalizable here represents only a necessary, but not also sufficient, condition for its correctness. In addition to the principle of universalizability, recourse has to be had to consequentialist considerations about the acceptability of the decision itself, that is, its practical consequences for the parties. For MacCormick, however, universalizability and consequentialism have to be combined: a decision acceptable only to the parties in question but not for all others who might be in the same position, that is, a decision acceptable to the parties in question but inconsistent with the legal order would, for the Scots scholar, have to be rejected.[61]

III. 2. Dworkin's Interpretive Turn

Ronald Dworkin – as is well known – identifies three chief conceptions of law. The first two are those he calls "conventionalism" and "pragmatism". Conventionalism is roughly the equivalent of what Raz calls "source theory".[62] The fundamental idea here is that there are social conventions that once and for all determine what the law is, and the judge thus merely has to "find" these. Nonetheless, Dworkin's "conventionalist" recognizes that his conventions are not complete, so that in certain "hard cases" the judge cannot have recourse to any "source" in deciding, and has to base himself on a discretionary choice.[63] "Conventionalism" is, then, a decisionist variant of "source theory", fairly faithfully reproducing the image of the "reformed" legal positivism proposed by Hans Kelsen and H. L. A. Hart. For both, the judge is no mere applier of norms, but has considerable powers to produce norms.

Pragmatism is instead an instrumentalist conception of law, seen solely as an instrument towards certain ends, over and above any faithfulness to texts, forms or procedures. What counts here is a certain "policy", an objective to be reached, in relation to which the legal means proves particularly appropriate and to which, so to speak, it can be bent. Whereas conventionalism looks back to decisions taken in the past, intending in general to reproduce them, pragmatism does not have these concerns for historical continuity, and instead looks forward to the objectives to be achieved. Using some old terminology of Niklas Luhmann's, we might say that "conventionalism" represents or is moved by a "conditional programme", that is, lays down the conditions for certain conduct, and that "pragmatism" is a "purposive programme", sets the objectives to be pursued by legal activity irrespective of constitutive or regulatory conditions. To explain the difference between pragmatism and conventionalism, Dworkin uses the figure of a legal right. While for conventionalism, which is a non-sceptical theory, there are rights that the subject can claim by referring to legal texts and judicial precedents, <<pragmatism, on the contrary, denies that people ever have legal rights; it takes the bracing view that they are never entitled to what would otherwise be worse for the community just because some legislature said so or a long string of judges decided>>.[64] According to the "pragmatist", norms and rights are merely, so to speak, the servants of a better future; as such, they have no strength or value of their own.

To these two conceptions, regarded as unsatisfactory particularly because they do not take norms and rights sufficiently seriously, and trust to judicial decisionism, Dworkin counterposes the conception of law as "integrity". This asserts that the law is basically an interpretive practice guided by the fundamental principles of a certain community, aimed at supplying the "best possible theory" of these. This "integrity", note, is not the tradition of a particular legal order, but its strong normative content (political and moral): it is a synchronic rather than diachronic principle. <<It insists that the law contains not only the narrow explicit content of these decisions but also, more broadly, the scheme of principles necessary to justify them>>.[65]

Now, this "integrity" has a specific content, given by three principles, namely "fairness", "justice" and "due process of law".[66] "Fairness" is the procedure that enables political power to be distributed in the most just way possible. "Justice" has instead to do not so much with procedures as with the outcomes of political decisions. It is mainly a criterion for redistributing goods and rights. "Due process" is a procedure for assessing when a subject has breached the laws laid down by the political decisions.[67]

Once the concept of law as "integrity" is accepted, Dworkin derives three consequences, namely (a) that the law is an interpretive (reconstructive) practice, (b) that this practice is guided by principles, and (c) that it therefore aims – as normative, "principled" practice – at the "one right answer", i.e., the justification for its choices, and accordingly at the assertion that its choices are "justified". Dworkin further derives from the concept of "integrity" a number of interpretive criteria that should guide the judge's action. As a matter of fact, "integrity" is the discursive translation of a deontological model of judicial virtues, "Justice Hercules", previously proposed by Dworkin himself. Hercules – in Dworkin's words – is <<a lawyer of superhuman skill, learning, patience and acumen>>,[68] who is able to fully grasp the normative features and assumptions of the legal order in question. By the notion of "integrity" such a deontological and rhetorical figure is eventually transformed into an institutional set of operationalizable criteria. Now, Judge Hercules or "integrity" within Dworkin's innovative doctrine play the role of Kelsen's *Grundnorm* or of Hart's "rule of recognition"[69]: they offer an ultimate foundation to the legal system.

The basic requirement of "integrity" is fairly obviously that of the "best possible theory" implicit in the robust normative point of view thought as pivotal for giving parties their "right". The American scholar preliminarily identifies three stages in any interpretive practice. A first pre-interpretative phase in which the rules and criteria to refer to for identifying a particular practice are identified. Second, a stage of *interpretation* in the strict sense, presenting the reasons why a particular practice is considered in a particular way, or particular meanings are ascribed to it. Third, a post-interpretative stage, in which the practice interpreted is reconsidered in the light of the reasons established at the interpretive stage. Interpretation thus amounts to a sort of "reformation", however minimum and imperceptible, of the object interpreted.[70] The theory of interpretation then becomes eminently a theory of argumentation.

If one starts from a conception of law as "integrity", the central aspect of the judge's activity is interpretation. At this level, two further stages of the judge's argumentative operations must be distinguished: "fit" and "justification". The criterion of "fit" allows us to make a first selection among the available interpretations: only those should be accepted that take account of, or are consistent with, the "fit", the set of norms, principles and values that make up that particular order. However, since the mesh of this first sieve is still rather broad, it is likely that more than one interpretation among those available will pass the test of "fit". There then has to be a further selection: "justification".[71] We have here not to do with the best political theory and the ideal legal system, but more modestly with <<the best justification that can be provided for the community's actual legal history>>.[72] "Justification" differs according to the relevant judicial sphere and according to the legal system concerned. It will thus be different, for instance, according to whether one has to do with "common law" or with interpreting statutes. In the latter case – which is of more interest to "continental lawyers" – the criteria of justification identified by Dworkin number three: "fairness", "textual integrity" and "legislative history".[73] "Fairness" can be understood here as a sort of criterion of "reasonableness" or "constitutionality"; "textual integrity" corresponds to our grammatical and systematic interpretation; and "legislative history" represents the criterion of recourse to the legislator's will.

In analogy with literary criticism there are – says Dworkin – three possible strategies for legal interpretation. (i) A proposition of law can be considered "true" if it is laid down by a lawmaker or such that it would be inconsistent for the lawmaker to deny it. (ii) Further propositions of law are assertable as true if it is unlikely that a lawmaker would deny them. (iii) Eventually there is a third way: further propositions of law are to be considered as true if they provide a better fit than their negation with propositions of law already established because they explain in a more satisfactory way that law is what it is or that lawmakers made the law that they made.[74] Dworkin's favourite way is this third one. <<A proposition of law – he argues – is sound if it figures in the best justification that can be provided for the body of legal proprositions to be settled>>.[75] Now, the quality of the best justification is judged through two "dimensions". (a) The first is *fit*, that is coherence with the valid legal materials, a hermeneutical property. (b) The second dimension, however, is genuinely normative, political and moral. <<The second dimension – the dimension of *political morality* – supposes – he adds – that, if two justifications provide an equally good fit with the legal materials, one nevertheless provides a better justification than the other if it is superior as a matter of political or moral theory; if, that is, it comes closer to capturing the rights that people in fact have>>.[76] Constitutional rights thus provide the bedrock for the justificatory exercise. Such rights have overwhelming significance and efficacy, in so far as the law is the outcome of a community of principles, where people acknowledge each other an equal dignity and political competence. A "system of rights" – Habermas would later write – implies a relation of mutual normative presupposition.[77]

Constitutionalism in this way is directly and conceptually connected to legal interpretation. Suppose we are members of a political order in which we are not given rights – what would legal reasoning be like in such context? Wouldn't it be significantly different and no longer ruled by the dimension of justification? But – one might object – if this dimension is contingent, an interpretation oriented by the"one right answer"requirement should not be considered as an essential feature of law and legal practice. Dworkin's reply here is not powerful: he only points out that in case justification did not play a role in legal reasoning we would not be within the practice of a community of principle. We would thus be ouside the scope of law as this concept and practice we know and have learnt through ours societies' moral and institutional evolution.

Be that as it may, the requirement of legal certainty is by no means ignored by Dworkin, whatever many of his critics may say. It might even be maintained that he is obsessed by it, to the point of supplying a veritable catalogue of rules of legal argumentation. And this is confirmed by the interest that constitutes the guiding theme of all his work: rejection of the idea of the judge's verdict as a discretionary decision. From the viewpoint of legal theory, for Dworkin the central question in relation to a judge's decisions is not whether they are "judicial", i.e., decisions by a judge exercising her functions, but whether these decisions are right. Just as, one might add, from the epistemological viewpoint the central question regarding linguistic statements about a particular state of affairs is not whether they are "linguistic", but whether they are true. This obviously takes no relevance away from the preliminary question of identifying a particular event as a judge's decision (or a linguistic statement), for the solution of which the criteria identified by an empiricist, legal positivist methodology (in particular, recourse to a "norm of recognition") may prove very useful.[78]

Accordingly, retorting to those asserting that legal decisions constitute a special case of practical decision that legal decisions are "judicial" and hence, different from other types of practical decision (especially the moral kind) and that the decisions of judge Hercules (the ideal judge in Dworkin's picture) are just as "legal" as those of the lowest magistrate[79] amounts to upholding a thesis that the theorist of the "special case" in no way intends to dispute. Legal decisions cannot, in the latter's view, be reduced to specifically moral decisions, since they too constitute a special kind, though a different one, of practical decision. On the other hand, what is at stake here (in attributing to judicial decisions the quality of being a "special case" of practical decision) is not the descriptive qualification of an event (the decision in question) and hence its "legality", but the normative description of that event (the "rightness" of a decision), as the only thing that can justify a normative conclusion (the provision in the judicial verdict).

The theory of argument and interpretation developed by Ronald Dworkin might at first sight seem very far away from MacCormick's theory. While MacCormick is a legal positivist and (moderately) non-cognitivist, Dworkin appears in the opinion of many as the renewer of a sort of more or less sociologizing natural law approach. He is even labelled a "Pre-Benthamite" by the Scot, because of confusing the two dimensions of expository and censorial jurisprudence.[80] While Dworkin defends the idea of the "one right answer", MacCormick does not abandon Hart's thesis of the discretionary character of judicial decision at least in hard cases,[81] which is on the contrary fiercely disputed by the American scholar.[82] Rights and discretion – it is suggested – contrary to what Dworkin believes, are different legal techniques, in that discretion is rooted in "judgement-independent operative facts", a common eventuality in law.[83]

Properly considered though, Dworkin and MacCormick are much closer than might appear. For Dworkin – as I have just said – there are three main guiding criteria for the rightness and fairness of the legal decision.

(i) First, it must be aimed at placing a certain norm in the "best light" possible. If a norm is applied, it is applied, from the viewpoint of the one applying it, in the best possible way. In the same way, if a play is put on, it is interpreted from the actor's viewpoint according to what is the best possible probable interpretation. Just as it would be pragmatically contradictory to play a Mozart piece deliberately badly, in the same way it is, for Dworkin, contradictory to apply a legal provision in accordance with a meaning that is not the best possible. However, this does not mean that there is only one right answer for every case. <<No judicial decision – says Dworkin – is necessarily the right decision>>.[84] <<I do not claim (indeed I deny) – he adds – that the process of decision will always yield the same decision in the hands of different judges>>.[85] The "one right answer" thesis only implies that adjudication is aimed to "discover" rather than to "invent" the parties' rights and is thereby bound to a strong requirement of truth or correctness. This first assumption thus is more or less equivalent to the less stringent factual claim that <<there is *often* a single right answer to complex questions of law and political morality>>.[86]

(ii) The judge must further follow two other criteria, integrity and fit (or "consistency"). The criterion of fit is that a judge has the obligation, as he puts it, to interpret the legal story as it comes to him already told, not to invent a different story, even if a better one. The decision must thus be consistent with the legal order enforced; it must, so to speak, constitute another link in an already existing narrative chain, and therefore extend that chain in a direction that suits ("fits") the one already taken by the story, that is, the series of verdicts and legal decisions handed down.

(iii) But the decision must also aim at the criterion of integrity. This is not so much the historical consistency of the legal order, but represents the decision's content of formal justice. A decision meets the criterion of integrity if it meets the principle of treating like cases alike. Integrity in short amounts to universalizability.[87] But fit as coherence and integrity as universalizability are the criteria on which, as we have seen, MacCormick also builds up his proposals.

Moreover, the thesis of the one right answer does not for Dworkin, at least the later Dworkin, mean that for every case there is already one single possible right decision. It means instead that for whoever is taking a legal decision, it represents the one right answer for the case in question.[88] But this position is fairly similar to MacCormick's other idea that any legal decision turns round a point of law, and therefore, as such, has an intrinsic claim to rightness. <<It makes sense – adds the Scots scholar – to demand that judges strive for 'correctness' in their decision making and seek the best decision within the limits of the law and the bounds of practical reasonableness. Dworkin's 'right answer thesis' is an overstatement, but an overstatement of a point that is all-important to make>>.[89]

III. 3. Discourse Theory

I come finally to professor Alexy's theory of legal reasoning. He develops in the legal sphere ideas of Jürgen Habermas's and gives an analytical content to Gadamer's thesis of interpretation's claim to rightness. Alexy, like Habermas, starts from the assumption that ideas and concepts have a discursive origin. One speaks, or thinks too, only because one is in and has been incorporated into a context of discourses from which our socialization takes its origin. But this transcends individual cultures. The discursive practice Habermas and Alexy refer to is universal, that is, independent of local contexts.

These two authors then hold that they can identify a series of transcendental principles, that is, ones implicitly assumed by any participant in a discourse, and even by any speaker. Anyone uttering a statement, or performing a speech act, is *ipso facto* said to put forward the claim, or to assert, that (i) her linguistic utterance is sincere (that is, fits what the speaker really thinks), (ii) is correct or "happy" (fits the social norms governing that act and is appropriate to the specific situation in which it is uttered), and finally (iii) is true or valid (that is, universally acceptable to subjects affected or "interested" by the statement itself).[90] All of these claims can come about and be met only in discursive situations. These implicit claims then become still stronger in the case of judicial decisions, where the claim to rightness takes on the features of a veritable claim to justice. For it would be inconceivable and hence, performatively contradictory, for the judge to add to his verdict after reading the measure, <<and this is unjust>>.

Alexy counterposes four alternative models: (a) the decision model, (b) the deductive one, (c) the hermeneutic one and (d) coherence. The first maintains that in reality there is no discourse or argumentation that is valid in law, and indeed that judicial experience sanctions an opposite situation from that of discussion. This is a radical decisionist model, the paradigmatic representative of which might be regarded as one brand of American legal realism.[91]

The second model is the one we earlier called the "syllogistic model", on which I do not feel it necessary to add anything further. The third is the one proposed by Gadamer and Betti: here adjudication is eminently seen as a matter of interpretation, of ascribing a meaning to linguistic entities. Such ascription is then conceived as predetermined by cultural assumptions made by interpreters in approaching their task. Alexy recognizes its importance, but regards it as too self-satisfied. Ascribing meanings in the law is not just a question internal to a text or a linguistic situation. It will have practical consequences on human affairs; therefore it has a clear moral impact. Now an action having such moral relevance could not escape the question of its *justification*. Argumentation in law accordingly needs good reasons to enforce a special reading of a principle or rule.

All the hermeneutic problems, in particular those raised by the so-called hermeneutic circle in its various parts, can and should thus be solved using adequate criteria of argumentative rationality. The theory of *interpretation* must accordingly, for Alexy, inevitably come down to a theory of *argumentation*.

The fourth model criticized by Alexy is the one known as "coherence", coherence with the normative order. An order, says the German scholar, is never complete. Accordingly, coherence alone cannot be enough. A model of legal reasoning centred on coherence must necessarily prove insufficient.

Alexy's alternative is a procedural model. Discourse, any discourse, presupposes principles for conducting discourse itself. (This is significantly adumbrated in Viehweg's own topics, at first sight the expression of a "realist", anti-rationalist and anti-normativist *Weltanschauung*. For Viehweg writes: <<When anyone speaks, he has to be able to justify his discourse>>[92]). The point is, then, for Alexy, to make explicit what is implicit, and universalize it. Universalization is in turn a transcendental (implicit) requirement of discourse on norms, values and principles.

Asserting that something (a piece of behaviour) is just, or that A is a valid norm, implies a claim to the validity or rightness of the statement and hence, the anti-sceptical thesis that there is a "right answer". (This is put similarly by Dworkin: <<So there is no important difference in philosophical category or standing between the statement that slavery is wrong and the statement that there is a right answer to the question of slavery, namely that it is wrong. I cannot intelligibly hold the first opinion as a moral opinion without also holding the second>>[93]). The idea of the validity claim, continues Alexy, in turn contains the idea of being universally valid for all cases like the one in question. However, in order for this claim to validity and universality to be legitimate, it must satisfy the principles that can be derived from the normative – procedural – nature of our practical discourses.

The rules of practical discourse for Alexy have two principal types: (a) rules on the structures of arguments (for instance, the consistent use of predicates, or linguistic clarity), or else (b) rules on the procedures employed for the discourse (for instance, the rule that any speaker can take part in a discourse). For the German scholar, practical discourse is distinguished from legal discourse because the latter is tied to certain substantive limitations: for instance, legal discourse by contrast with practical discourse cannot go on endlessly but instead has specific time-limits. Nonetheless, with adjustments and additions, legal discourse according to Alexy represents a special case of practical discourse.[94]

It is very important to stress that the substantive limitations imposed on legal discourse, drawn from the practice of discourse in general, are according to Alexy – as is the case according to Dworkin – embedded in the *constitution* of the democratic State. What a constitution represents is much more than a simple management schedule for State agencies; it is rather a body of fundamental rights – which mainly embody the normative requirements of practical discourses. Discourse theory thus becomes in the legal domain, first a doctrine of the connection of law and morality, and second, a doctrine of constitutional rights as defining the entire scope of public affairs. A revived and reinforced constitutionalism is therefore the outcome of a view of legal practice as argumentation and discourse.

Alexy's work is the standard version of discourse theory in law. However, by a somewhat surprising move, Jürgen Habermas, the founding father of discourse theory in philosophy, takes distance from Alexy's views. Alexy – following Dworkin – neatly and strongly distinguishes between "rules" and "principles". Constitutional rights are then reconstructed not as "rules", but rather as "principles", a kind of normative proposition whose application conditions are underdetermined and do not necessarily conflict each other when considered for the solution of a concrete case. While rules are to be applied through an "either ... or" logic, principles rely on weighing or balancing. Alexy's novel contribution to the theory of principles is that these are given the shape of "optimization commands", that is, of prescriptions that aim to maximize a particular good.[95] Accordingly, principles assume the purpose of a teleological device. Now, Habermas objects that such reconstruction severely plays down constitutional rights' deontological character. Indeed it makes possible for balancing (the specific mode of application of rights) to overcome rights' normative core. In this way deontic requirements become vulnerable to policies and other consequential considerations of aggregative utility: which is the very outcome that Dworkin's view of rights as "trumps" (entrenchments against utilitarian algorithms) was intended to avoid. By conceptualizing constitutional rights as teleological prescriptions – claims Habermas – the normative "firewall" against unprincipled policy measures – which is the sense of constitutional rights – finally crumbles down.

Habermas, moreover, points out the necessity of a more articulate discourse theory. Following Klaus Günther, he proposes to distinguish between a justification and an application discourse in law. "Justification" would only contribute to found the *validity* of a legal norm; it could not however assess the rules' appropriateness for the case at hand. To decide a case we would thus need a further effort than just a justificatory enterprise. While justification rests on a universalizability test, application – claims Günther – is geared by *coherence*.

What Günther and Habermas have here in mind is on the one side a revision of Dworkin's hermeneutic of "integrity", by on the other side conceding to realist and functionalist approaches that legal norms might conflict at the level of validity (and justification). Legal realism in its manifold versions has one common obession: that legal materials are far from being a coherent, gapless system of rules and directives. Now, Günther and Habermas say that this may be true as far as norms that are not "rules" (with clear and predetermined "if" conditions of application) are concerned. Indeed, since most valid legal norms are not "rules" in such sense, conflicts and contradictions are unavoidable. The realist nonetheless is wrong when she drives her assumptions to the extreme by claiming that not only the context of justification but that also of application is intrinsically plagued by tensions and incoherences. This is contested by Habermas and Günther, who insist that appliclation is geared through a powerful adequacy requirement.

A ruling for a case will be appropriate and fitting only if it has taken into account all the relevant features of the case. And this is accomplished when the "history" – as it were – of the case is seriously considered. This would put in motion the paradigmatic understanding of that case within a concrete legal community. Valid legal rules are thus seen as mere *prima facie* valid rules, which compete for the best possible application decision. A contradiction affecting the level of valid legal rules would not put in question the rationality of judicial discourse and of a legal system in general, since it is just a *prima facie* contradiction – which in the discourse of application will have to be overcome to make a decision possible.

Legal certainty is translated from a doctrine of valid rules into a standard of concrete rulings, and this is done thanks to a procedural shift from the "right norm" to correct process. <<Procedural rights – says Habermas – guarantee each legal person the claim to a fair procedure that in turn guarantees not certainty of outcome but a discursive clarification of the pertinent facts and legal questions>>.[96] This, however, will become a very complex search for appropriate arguments. Legal norms, being only *prima facie* valid, would be disposable by parties and judges. Conflict solutions would depend on the contextual situation of understanding. Complexity and the danger of ideological distortions might thus increase to a too high degree to be managed without an additional stability factor. Günther and Habermas hence rely on "paradigms", that is on established views or dominant doctrines, to build up "coherence" in the concrete ruling. <<In actual practice the complexity of this task is reduced by the paradigmatic legal understanding prevailing at the time>>.[97] Such a solution however, seems to reinstantiate a "topical" mode of reasoning through commonplaces or hermeneutic "preunderstanding", a return indeed to that traditionalist interpretive strategy previously criticized by Habermas in his critical assessment of Gadamer's approach. Habermas, with some embarrassment, acknowledges that <<it is admittedly somewhat ironic that legal certainty increases precisely in virtue of an element that, although moderating the ideal demands on legal theory is the most susceptible of ideological distortions>>.[98]

By disarticulating legal discourse in two different and somewhat unrelated moments Habermas and Günther believe to be also able to re-establish a conceptual separation between law and morality. While a justificatory discourse, aiming to assess norms validity, would be imbued with moral considerations, this is not the case of application discourse that takes place within cognitive arguments concerning facts, "fit", and past legal history. A trascendental universalism leads to moral discourse, while legal reasoning would be driven by a contingent community of interpreters. <<Interpretive communities are established and enfranchised to give an authentic coherent interpretation of the law, which then leads to a definite decision>>.[99] Nonetheless, application discourses, though based on a <<highly contextualistic interpretation of the situation>> and taken from <<the particular participant perspectives>>, cannot do without some connection with the justification context that has produced valid legal norms. <<In application discourses – continues Habermas – the particular participant perspectives must simultaneously preserve the link with the universal-perspective structure that stands behind presumably valid norms in justification discourses>>.[100]

Much sympathy notwithstanding, Habermas does not fully follow Günther's strategy. Actually, this once more makes legal reasoning a "special case" of moral discourse, this time however of its application moment: it – in Habermas' words – <<conceives legal argumentation as a special case of moral discourses of application>>.[101] This is again a *Sonderfallthese* – which ignores what for Habermas is the real point of disagreement with Alexy's views: legal validity derives from much more than moral discourse requirements and a legal validity that satisfies the requirement of the ideal discursive situation is necessarily bound to a specific political horizon: constitutional democracy. Alexy's mistake would then be his silence or ambiguity about the relevance of a special institutional setting (*constitutionalism*) for the rationality of legal discourse.

In any case, Habermas' acknowledgment of the value of universal claims also within contextual legal reasoning is unequivocal and allows to reconnect legal decisions to those fundamental rights and reasons, which legislation is based on in a constitutional State. Under constitutional conditions law-giving and adjudication have the sense of re-producing and – so to say – rehearsing the foundational moment of constitution making; and they do so by sharing and then making explicit the same discursive structure embedded in the universality requirements of general acceptability; a fact – we may remember – which is stressed by Dworkin when he insists on constitutional State being a "community of principles". By virtue of such reference to "integrity" and universal pragmatics, constitutionalism is not taken out of the courtroom. At the end of the day – and this is what matters most here – for both Alexy and Habermas constitutionalism could not be prevented from being operative and effective within adjudication too.

IV. LAW AS DISCOURSE AND CONSTITUTION

IV. 1. Morality Reconnected to Law

I would like to stress the impact or influence of theories of legal reasoning on positive law and legal practice. A first influence is methodological in nature. Theories of reasoning and argumentation help to make legal practice itself more argumentative, to enrich its dialectic and make it an object of apposite reflection. Legal theory thus becomes the silent prologue to any legal dispute.

I see further influences on two issues. The first is the very concept of law. <<The very idea of law as arguable – says Neil MacCormick – leads us at once to consider the rhetorical character of law>>.[102] My contention is that here the converse also holds. The rhetorical character of legal argumentation at once leads to the very idea of law as arguable. If reasoning about the law is an argumentative and discursive enterprise, its subject matter and outcome are also given an argumentative and discursive character. If to get the law I need argumentation, that means that the law is arguable. The theories of legal reasoning, by highlighting aspects of legal decision that are external to the law as just will or text or fact, call into crisis the formalist, legal positive (statist and static) concept of law. They open up a broader, more liberal, more pluralist and dynamic notion of the "legal". One could now calmly assert, as Guido Calabresi does, that beliefs, ideals and modes of thought are an integral part of our law.[103] What is here asserted is more or less equivalent to what Robert Alexy calls a "three-level model", a "Regel/Prinzipien/Prozedur Model".[104] This is an image of law no longer obsessively dominated by the idea of the rule, of the norm, with a central role instead assigned to principles, which Alexy defines as "optimization precepts" of the values they express and where practices as a procedural moment also count as particularly relevant.[105]

Such theories, then, since they hold that legal decisions are the outcome of non-legal (not located in texts or "sources" of law) criteria of rightness, and that these are instead justified by more general or stronger normative practices (like Alexy's and Habermas's ideal speech situation), end up referring to ethical criteria. This goes some way to bridging the gap between law and morality dug by modern legal positivism. In particular, on a prospect that favours the discursive or communicative element over the decisional or instrumental one, the very concept of law loses much of its more truculent features as a coercive order. Violence is shaded out of the picture of the essential features of the phenomenon of law, and the more human features of rights and the "right" are clearly asserted. It is then not so much the monopoly of violence as its domestication that is imposed through the form and institution of the State. Constitutionalism – I would thus contend – might be a conceptual consequence of self-conscious legal argumentation.

Theories of legal reasoning further contribute to changing our perception of the State based on the rule of law. This is no longer a State where judges and administration are subject only to law, but also and especially one, where jurisdiction and administration are governed by procedures able to satisfy exacting principles of argumentative correctness. Once the law is conceived of as argumentative practice, the rule of law will be the political form that best reflects, or gives most space to, this practice.[106] The law projects itself as a foundational discourse about the law itself. Such discourse, doubtless, is very much related to some sort of constitutional enterprise or "moment".

Law here is not just the command or decision of an autocratic and all-powerful sovereign, but what the citizens and subjects concerned agree that it is. And they agree what law is not just through agreement or compromise, but through agreement *around principles and substantive reasons*. Law conceived as argumentation is thus submitted – as it were – to a process of constitutionalization and materialization. It is now the outcome of the discourse *and the reasons* of the people involved. It is no longer a simple matter of will. Decision here is not just an existential gesture, but one moment of a much more complex deliberation. The rule of law becomes the law of a constitution.

Ronald Dworkin explicitly disputes the positivist conception of the rule of law, in which the "law" in question is understood purely formally, so that the State's action is right and just as being conducted in respect for the legal forms prescribed by statute, by law in the formal sense, that is, by what the American scholar calls the "rule book".[107] To this conception Dworkin counterposes a "rights-based rule of law", one founded on fundamental rights and hence, a substantive conception of the rule of law. State conduct, in order to meet the principles of the rule of law, cannot be just formally correct and, like Kelsen's *Stufenbau*, respect the hierarchies of competences laid down by the legal order. A legal order that respects the rule of law cannot, à la Kelsen, be just a "dynamic" order in which the norms are linked to each other according to relationships of *Ermächtigung*, or empowerment delegations, or in which – à la Hart – no obligations are addressed to the law-giver but eventually disabilities.[108] It must instead, if we still wish to follow Kelsen's terminology, be a "static" order, in which, that is, the norms are linked with each other according to relations of logical or argumentative inference, so that the State's individual action, the "individual norm", but also the legislator's "general norm", can be interpreted as a deduction or else a plausible conclusion from the material content expressed by fundamental norms of the system, from its principles. Moreover, this is what is practised in States with "rigid" constitutions and hence, forms of constitutional justice in which the individual norm can be reviewed in relation to the constitution's substantive principles and perhaps abrogated should it, though issued in conformity with the hierarchy of State powers, not fit the principles of the constitutional order, or not be deducible from them.

Moreover, a common doctrine in constitutional interpretation does not limit principles constitutionally in force to those explicitly expressed in the written norms of the constitutional text. Is it, for instance, often asserted that the part of the constitution devoted to fundamental rights, and even the form of government, are not subject to constitutional amendment, even though there is no specific norm that sets such limits. It is also maintained that the fundamental principles stated in the constitution are not necessarily a closed list, but rather have an exemplary role, showing what the system's highest values are.[109] These can then be derived from the constitutional text as a whole, from its "sense", and hence from the State's political structure and normative ideals of reference, and thus – à la Dworkin – from the "best theory" of that particular polity, its "integrity" as a community of principles.

Dworkin's "rule of law" proposal is not, however, only "non-formal", substantive, but also "non-negative", i.e., positive.[110] That is, the American scholar, having tied the "rule of law" down to a material concept of justice (as, by the way, Hayek also does[111]), does not believe that the substantive justice in question ("integrity") is purely negative, as, for instance, Hayek himself believes, and has more recently been said by Joseph Raz;[112] that is, he does not believe that it is solely a matter of defending negative freedoms of individuals. What is rather at stake in the idea of justice evoked here as a basis for the rule of law is an exacting equality requirement, which may on certain occasions entail an active attitude by the State in social life.

This attitude finds a counterpart in Alexy's complex, articulated theory of fundamental rights, as being first and foremost expressed by principles: that is, the norms that guarantee fundamental rights are said to have the nature of principles. These rights can then be balanced against each other and asserted even, irrespective of any explicit action by their bearers.[113] The fundamental rights, being the product of principles, need not necessarily take the form of *Abwehrrechte*, rights protecting individual freedom from undue interference by the State, hence establishing a duty of abstention on the State's organs. They may also have as their content positive actions of the State.[114]

IV. 2. A "Deliberative" Model of Democracy

The normative model of democracy also changes. This is explicit in such authors as Carlos Nino and Jürgen Habermas, who refer unambiguously to theories of practical discourse in their respective views of the modern constitutional State.[115] Democracy is no longer defined as the system in which popular sovereignty prevails and is expressed but as the institutionalization or, putting it with Dworkin, the "best" political theory of the rules of practical discourse, especially of its three fundamental rules. Which according to Alexy are: (1) that anyone able to speak may take part in the discourse; (2) that anyone may question any statement in a discourse; (3) that no-one may be barred from exercising rights deriving from the foregoing rules.[116] Democracy here is a mutual practice of recognition and a *deliberative* enterprise: not an oligarchic game or competition of élites, but neither the existential self-affirmation of a homogenous national community.

This *inter alia* seems to confirm the centrality of freedom of expression among the fundamental rights: <<Political freedom is the necessary and natural consequence of everyday human speech>>.[117] Political freedom and democracy, that is, have a "discursive" hard core that theories of argumentation as normative reconstructions of practical discourse (such as, notably, Robert Alexy's one) serve to highlight.

Similar consequences have been explicitly drawn by Alexy himself in a work later than his *Theory of Legal Argumentation*, dedicated specifically to the concept of law: *The Argument from Injustice*. Here the German scholar offers us a definition of the concept of law that in a certain sense represents the point of arrival of his whole legal-philosophical thinking: <<The law is a system of norms that (1) lays claim to correctness, (2) consists in the totality of norms that belong to a constitution by and large socially efficacious constitution and that are not themselves unjust in the extreme, as well as the totality of norms that are issued in accordance with this constitution, norms that manifest a minimum social efficacy or prospect of social efficacy and that are not themselves unjust in the extreme, and, finally, (3) contains the principles and other normative arguments on which the process or procedure of law application is and/or must to be based in order to satisfy the claim to correctness>>.[118] Claim to rightness, principles, further normative arguments and their final justificatory bedrock, that they are not instantiating gross or extreme injustice, are now all embedded in the concept of law, together with the more traditional notions of norm, legal order (or constitution) and social efficacy.

The theory of discourse – I would like to stress – has the further advantage of being able to provide a foundation for democracy and tolerance on a non-relativistic basis. One is democratic and tolerant, in this view, not because all opinions are equivalent, a position that condemns democracy and tolerance to unjustifiability and ends up turning against itself; we are so rather because discussion, discourse, dialogue, require the plurality and liberty of opinions in order to happen, and because discussion, discourse, dialogue, are "objective" goods, that is, are not relative to the subject. One is democratic and tolerant, one accepts others' opinions (in the sense of granting full freedom of expression to them), because this is required by the procedural rules of ideal discourse and this is an analytical and normative reconstruction of the deep structure of actual discourses, deriving from the "universal pragmatics". In short, it is assumed, as one Spanish political thinker of the Baroque period said, that <<where there is a dispute [...] it is necessary that there be defenders of all opinions [*donde se disputa* [...] *es fuerza que haya valedores de todas opiniones*]>>.[119] Accordingly, the democratic constitutional State will not be neutral to whatever opinions or lifestyles citizens may hold: though it is *prima facie* respectful towards all opinions, not all opinions will be judged equivalent. Discourse itself and its normative requirements are the threshold.

The theories of legal argumention thus have a direct impact on our conception of power and of politics. They lead us to consider political experience as not so much a fight to the death between irreconcilable adversaries, a friend-foe ruthless relationship in the terms of Carl Schmitt's political realism, or a *magnum latrocinium* in the sombre tones of a Dürer etching, as a public space in which solutions to the community's problems are debated and adopted in accordance with criteria acceptable to an audience that is tendentially universal. In this sense therefore, the argumentative approach to legal reasoning leads to a notion of law no longer seen as the monological command of a political superior addressed to a body of inferiors. Law from this perspective will rather be considered as a constitutional setting within which citizens discuss and rule on their own major common issues. Argumentative paradigms, by making it possible for discourse and principles to act as proper legal instruments, can thus help determine and strengthen a concept of law which no longer needs violence as a definitional character or precondition. It would also help to conceptualise democracy as a political regime where principles and rules have the upper hand over interests and decisions.[120]

NOTES

1. See e.g. C. Regneri, *Demonstratio logicae verae iuridica* (1638), ed. by G. Kalinowski, CLUEB, Bologna 1986.
2. Cf. G. Fassò, *Storia della filosofia del diritto*, new ed. by C. Faralli, Vol.3, Laterza, Roma-Bari 2001, pp. 10-12.
3. Cf. N. Bobbio, *Il positivismo giuridico*, 2nd ed., Giappichelli, Torino 1979, pp. 79 ff.
4. <<C'est véritablement à une conception militaire que nous avons affaire>> (J. Bonnecase, *La pensée juridique française de 1804 à l'heure présente*, Vol. 1, Delmas, Bordeaux 1933, p. 234).
5. See J. Raz, *The Authority of Law*, Oxford University Press, Oxford 1979, chapter 3, and J. Raz, <<On the Autonomy of Legal Reasoning>>, in *Ratio Juris*, pp. 1 ff. Vol. 5 (1992).
6. See R. Dworkin, *Law's Empire*, II ed., Fontana, London 1986, pp. 14 ff.
7. Read the famous fourth chapter of Cesare Beccaria's *Of Crimes and Punishments*. For German doctrine on the subject, at any rate as far as nineteenth century goes, see R. Ogorek, *Richterkönig oder Subsumtionsautomat? Zur Justiztheorie im 19. Jahrhundert*, Vittorio Klostermann, Frankfurt am Main 1986, passim.
8. On this see L. Gianformaggio, *Modelli di ragionamento giuridico. Modello deduttivo, modello induttivo, modello retorico*, in *La teoria generale del diritto. Problemi e tendenze attuali (Studi dedicati a Norberto Bobbio)*, ed. by U. Scarpelli, Giuffrè, Milano 1983, pp. 131 ff.
9. Read I. Kant, *Metaphysische Anfangsgründe der Rechtslehre, Metaphysik der Sitten*, Erster Teil, ed. by B. Ludwig, Felix Meiner, Hamburg 1986, § 45, p. 129.
10. <<Die rechtliche Entscheidung besteht in der Subsumtion eines gegebenen Tatbestandes unter das geltende Recht, sie ist wie jeder logische Schluß vom Willen unabhängig; es besteht keine Freiheit der Entschließung, ob die Folgerung eintreten soll oder nicht; sie ergibt sich – wie man sagt – von selbst, mit innerer Notwendigkeit>>(P. Laband, *Das Staatsrecht des Deutschen Reiches*, Vol. 2, Mohr, Tübingen 1911, p. 178).
11. See what is written in this connection by G. Tarello, *L'interpretazione della legge*, Giuffrè, Milano 1980, pp. 31-32.
12. Cf. J. Esser, *Vorverständnis und Methodenwahl in der Rechtsfindung. Rationalitätsgarentien der richterlichen Entscheidungspraxis*, Athenäeum, Frankfurt am Main 1970, pp. 50 ff.
13. M. Oakeshott, *On Human Conduct*, Clarendon, Oxford 1975, p. 133.
14. In this connection I wish to recall the words of an outstanding jurist, the late lamented Francisco Tomás y Valiente, judge of the first constitutional court of democratic Spain: <<Legal reason is the projection of practical reason. It never operates in a vacuum. It proceeds from a universe of values, principles and concepts developed in positive law and seeks to solve problems posed by the interpretation of norms (the supreme one being the Constitution) or by the doubtful classification of individual situations arising in social reality in the framework of the normative system. The constitutional judge has to solve problems that in the last analysis consist in a conflict among various ways of understanding and applying the Constitution. The Court, as constitutional organ of the State, solves political problems through legal argument: it is legal reason that is its instrument, not the reason of (or of the) State, or of the Government or of this or that party>>(F. Tomás y Valiente, *A orillas del Estado*, Taurus, Madrid 1996, p. 266).

15. For a comparative perspective on this phenomenon see C. Guarnieri & P. Pederzoli, *La democrazia giudiziaria*, Il Mulino, Bologna 1997.
16. For the Italian case see R. Bin, *Diritti e argomenti*, Giuffrè, Milano 1992.
17. See R. Alexy, *Theorie der juristischen Argumentation. Die Theorie des rationalen Diskurses als Theorie der juristischen Begründung*, 2nd ed., Suhrkamp, Frankfurt am Main 1991, pp. 39 ff. Cf. also J. A. García Amado, *Teorías de la tópica jurídica*, Civitas, Madrid 1988, pp. 364-365.
18. Recall Viehweg's insistency in rejecting the possibility of articulating *topoi* in logical chains: <<Long inferences are incompatible with their function; thus the logical weight of concepts' and sentences' structures which they make up remains always quite small [*Lange Folgerungen vertragen sich nicht mit ihrer Funktion, das logische Gewicht der von ihnen aufgebauten Begriffs- oder Satzgefüge bleibt deshalb stets gering*]>> (Th. Viehweg, *Topik und Jurisprudenz. Ein Beitrag zur rechtswissenschaftlichen Grundlagenforschung*, 5th ed., Beck, München 1974, p. 38).
19. Something closer to topics is, accordingly, the hermeneutic proposal of someone like Gadamer, so proud of rehabilitating – against the Enlightenment – the notion of "prejudice": see H.-G. Gadamer, *Wahrheit und Methode. Grundzüge einer philosophischen Hermeneutik*, 6th ed., Mohr, Tübingen 1990, pp. 281 ff.; on this see *infra*, section II. 3, and Jürgen Habermas's critical observations in the third chapter of his *Zur Logik der Sozialwissenschaften* (5th enlarged ed., Suhrkamp, Frankfurt am Main 1982, pp. 271 ff.).
20. See e. g. Cicero, *Topica*, 2, 8. Cf. J. A. García Amado, *Teoría de la tópica jurídica*, pp. 69-69, and M. Kriele, *Theorie der Rechtsgewinnung*, 2nd ed., Duncker & Humblot, Berlin 1976, pp. 141 ff. It might be that we have here to do with a more general difference in the attitude towards rhetoric of two different cultures. For the Greek rhetoric is a particular form of wisdom or reasoning, while for the Roman it is just *eloquence*, a technique subsidiary and instrumental to wisdom and reasoning whose purpose is that these (wisdom and reasoning) be not "silent" and "powerless", that is in order to give them an additional external efficacy. Rhetorics as eloquence thus is a means to make wisdom capable to influence and direct *others'* minds and behaviour.
21. Aristotle, *Topica*, English transl. by E. S. Forster, LOEB Classical Library, Harvard and London 1976, p. 273.
22. <<Denn hier werden sehr häufig Produkte der Rechtssprache als außersprachliche, von der Rechtssprache lediglich abgebildete Gegenstände vorgestellt. Auf diese Weise schuf man zuweilen selbständige Gegenstandsfelder, die das Rechtsdenken anzutreffen vermeinte und dementsprechend beschrieb, obgleich es sie selbst herstellte. In der deutschen Jurisprudenz hat der geniale Ihering die krassesten Exempel dieser Art geliefert>> (Th. Viehweg, *Topik und Jurisprudenz*, 5th ed., pp. 113-114).
23. Ch. Perelman, L. Olbrechts-Tyteca, *La nouvelle rhétorique. Traité de l'argumentation*, Vol. 1, Presses Universitaires de France, Paris 1958, p. 1.
24. See A. Ross, *On Law and Justice*, Stevens & Co., London 1958, p. 274.
25. Ch. Perelman, *Logique juridique. Nouvelle rhétorique*, Librairie générale de droit et de jurisprudence, Paris 1976, p. 105. See L. Gianformaggio, <<La nuova retorica di Perelman>>, in *Discorso e retorica*, ed. by C. Pontecorvo, Loescher, Torino 1981, pp. 110 ff.
26. Ch. Perelman, *Logique juridique. Nouvelle rhétorique*, p. 107.
27. Cf. R. Alexy, *Theorie der juristischen Argumentation*, pp. 203 ff.

28. None can fail to note the closeness of the idea of "universal audience" to Peirce's one of a <<community without definite limits, capable of an indefinite increment of knowledge>>(C. S. Peirce, *Collected Papers*, ed. by ch. Hartshorne and P. Weiss Vol. 5, 2nd ed., Belknap, Cambridge, Mass. 1960, p. 311).
29. Ch. Perelman, *Logique juridique. Nouvelle rhétorique*, p. 107.
30. *Ibid.*, p. 122.
31. See *ibid.*, p. 123.
32. See Ch. Perelman, *Cinq leçons sur la justice*, in Id., *Droit, morale et philosophie*, Librairie générale de droit et de jurisprudence, Paris 1968, p. 54.
33. Cf. F. Wieacker, *Privatrechtsgeschichte der Neuzeit* 2nd ed., Vandenhoeck & Ruprecht, Göttingen 1967, pp. 206 ff.
34. See F. D. E. Schleiermacher, *Hermeneutik und Kritik*, ed. by M. Frank, Suhrkamp, Frankfurt am Main 1977, p. 76: <<The connection between hermeneutics and rhetoric consists in that every act of understanding means the reversal of an act of speech, in so far as one has to become aware of which thought was the one that the speech laid upon [*Die Zusammengehörigkeit der Hermeneutik und Rhetorik besteht darin, daß jeder Akt des Verstehens die Umkehrung eines Aktes des Redens ist, indem in das Bewußtsein kommen muß, welches Denken der Rede zum Grunde gelegen*]>>.
35. See H. G. Gadamer, *Wahrheit und Methode. Grundzüge einer philosophischen Hermeneutik*, 6th ed., pp. 188 ff.
36. Cf. H. Schnädelbach, *Philosophie in Deutschland 1831-1933*, Suhrkamp, Frankfurt am Main 1983, pp. 148 ff.
37. W. Dilthey, *Der Aufbau der geschichtlichen Welt in den Geisteswissenschaften*, Suhrkamp, Frankfurt am Main p. 235.
38. *Ibid.*, p. 256.
39. See M. Heidegger, *Sein und Zeit*, 17th ed., Max Niemeyer, Tübingen 1993, p. 150.
40. See H. G. Gadamer, *Wahrheit und Methode*, pp. 275 ff.
41. *Ibid.*, p. 299.
42. *Ibid.*, p. 401.
43. See E. Betti, *Zur Grundlegung einer allgemeinen Auslegungslehre*, Mohr, Tübingen 1988, pp. 43 ff. To the cognitive and normative types, Betti adds a third kind of interpretation: the one consisting in an artistic performance in music or drama.
44. See H.-G. Gadamer, <<Emilo Betti und das idealistische Erbe>>, in E. Betti, *Op. ult. cit.*, p. 95.
45. See H. G. Gadamer, *Wahrheit und Methode*, p. 302.
46. This is one of Habermas' favourite expressions and is used to mark the conventional, post-religious, and post-foundationalist Weltanschauung that constitutes the "fact of pluralism" of contemporary Western societies. See J. Habermas, *Nachmetaphysisches Denken. Philosophische Aufsätze*, Suhrkamp, Frankfurt am Main 1988.
47. J. Habermas, *Between Facts and Norms*, Polity Press, London 1998, p. 200.
48. J. Esser, *Grundsatz und Norm in der richterlichen Fortbildung des Privatrechts. Rechtsvergleichende Beiträge zur rechtsquellen - und Interpretationslehre*, 4th ed., Mohr, Tübingen 1990, p. 4.
49. For instance when Viehweg rules out the possibility of topics having anything to do with the syllogistic model, or in general with deductions of a formal-logical nature: <<Topic is a technique of problematic thought developed from rhetoric. It deploys an intellectual structure which is clearly different from deductive-systematic reasoning even in details [*Die Topik ist eine von der Rhetorik entwickelte Techne des*

Problemdenkens. Sie entfaltet ein geistiges Gefüge, das sich bis in Einzelheiten hinein eindeutig von einem deduktiv-systematischen unterscheidet]>>(Th. Viehweg, *Topik und Jurisprudenz*, V ed., p. 14).

50. N. MacCormick, *Legal Theory and Legal Reasoning*, Clarendon, Oxford 1978, p. 62.
51. A position brilliantly defended in Italy by Giovanni Tarello. See G. Tarello, *Il "problema dell'interpretazione": una formulazione ambigua*, in Id., *Diritto, enunciati, usi. Studi di teoria e metateoria del diritto*, Il Mulino, Bologna 1974, pp. 389 ff.
52. N. MacCormick, <<Smashing the Two-Way Mirror>>, in *Anti-Foundationalism and Practical Reasoning. Conversations Between Hermeneutics and Analysis*, ed. by E. Simpson, Academic Printing & Publishing, Edmonton, Alberta, Canada 1987, p. 210.
53. There are also those who deny the possibility of the normative syllogism, excluding the applicability of logic to norms. This, as we know, is the case for the "later" Kelsen (see H. Kelsen, *Allgemeine Theorie der Normen*, Manz, Wien 1978). In this view one is therefore constrained to deny the very possibility of legal argument, and hence to uphold radically irrationalistic, decisionistic theses. Behind judicial decision there are, on this view, not reasons but *motives*, sociological, psychological or even physiological causes (say indigestion), unreflexively determining the judge's conduct.
54. N. MacCormick, *Legal Theory and Legal Reasoning*, p. 69.
55. *Ibid.*, p. 100.
56. *Ibid.*, p. 101.
57. *Ibid.*, p. 103.
58. See also N. MacCormick, <<Coherence in Legal Justification>>, in *Theorie der Normen. Festgabe für Ota Weinberger zum 65. Geburtstag*, ed. by W. Krawietz et al., Duncker & Humblot, Berlin 1984, pp. 37 ff.
59. N. MacCormick, <<Formal Justice and the Form of Legal Arguments>>, in *Etudes de logique juridique*, Vol. 6, 1976, pp. 114-115.
60. See N. MacCormick, <<Coherence in Legal Justification>>, and Id., <<The Coherence of a Case and the Reasonableness of Doubt>>, in *The Liverpool Law Review*, Vol. 2, 1980, pp. 45 ff.
61. MacCormick's is, then, not so much a "consequentialism of the act" as a "consequentialism of the rule": see N. MacCormick, <<On Legal Decisions and their Consequences: From Dewey to Dworkin>>, in *New York University Law Review*, 1983, pp. 240 ff.
62. For a similar use of the term "conventionalism", see L. Strauss, *On Natural Law*, now in Id., *Studies in Platonic Political Philosophy*, ed. by Th. Pangl, University of Chicago Press, Chicago 1983.
63. See R. Dworkin, *Law's Empire*, II ed., pp. 114-117. A good example of Dworkin's "conventionalism" is offered by Charles Eisenmann's, a Kelsenian French jurisprudent's view of adjudication: see for instance his article <<El jurista y el derecho natural>>, in *Critica del derecho natural*, transl. by E. Diaz, Taurus, Madrid 1966, in particular pp. 262 ff. Eisenmann first shapes the judicial decision as a purely deductive operation, to later admit that in front of the rules' indeterminacy the judge should act as a legislator and continue and fulfil the law-making process.
64. R. Dworkin, *Law's Empire*, 2nd ed., p. 152.
65. *Ibid.*, p. 227.
66. See *ibid.*, p. 243.
67. See *ibid.*, pp. 164-165.

68. R. Dworkin, *Taking Rights Seriously*, 2nd ed., Duckworth, London 1978, p. 107.
69. Cf. J. Mackie, <<The Third Theory of Law>>, in *Ronald Dworkin and American Jurisprudence*, ed. by M. Cohen, Duckworth, London 1984, p. 161.
70. See R. Dworkin, *Law's Empire*, 2nd ed., pp. 65-67.
71. See *ibid.*, pp. 255-256.
72. R. Dworkin, <<A Reply>> , in *Ronald Dworkin and Contemporary Jurisprudence*, ed. by M. Cohen, p. 254.
73. See R. Dworkin, *Law's Empire*, pp. 348 ff.
74. See R. Dworkin, *A Matter of Principle*, Oxford University Press, Oxford 1986, pp. 134 ff.
75. *Ibid.*, p. 143.
76. *Ibid.* Italics mine.
77. See J. Habermas, *Between Facts and Norms*, Polity Press, Cambridge 1997, chapter 3.
78. It is only this function, the methodological or gnoseological one, that a non-ideologizing legal positivism is left with (that is, one that does not assert that the law always deserves obedience as such, and does not simply identify State and law). On legal positivism as "theory", "ideology" or "methodology", I refer to the classic contribution by N. Bobbio, *Giusnaturalismo e positivismo giuridico*, Comunità, Milan 1965, pp. 101 ff.
79. Cf. e.g., F. J. Laporta, <<Etica y derecho en el pensamiento contemporaneo>>, in *Historia de la ética*, Vol. 3, *La ética contemporánea*, ed. by V. Camps, Alianza, Barcelona 1989, pp. 253-254.
80. See N. MacCormick, <<Dworkin as Pre-Benthamite>>, in *The Philosophical Review*, Vol. 87, 1978, pp. 585 ff., and Id., <<Wie ernst soll man Rechte nehmen?>>, in *Rechtstheorie*, Vol. 11, 1980, pp. 1 ff.
81. Cf. H. L. A. Hart, *The Concept of Law*, Clarendon, Oxford 1961, pp. 121 ff., 138 ff. and see N. MacCormick, *H.L.A. Hart*, Edward Arnold, London 1981, chap. 10.
82. Read R. Dworkin, *Taking Rights Seriously*, 2nd ed., pp. 14 ff., 46 ff.
83. See N. MacCormick, <<Discretion and Rights>>, in *Law and Philosophy*, Vol. 8, 1989, pp. 23 ff.
84. R. Dworkin, *Taking Rights Seriously*, p. 185.
85. *Ibid.*, p. 280.
86. *Ibid.*, p. 279. Italics mine.
87. In this connection note what Klaus Günther has written: <<The principle of integrity however must not necessarily find its limits in the given context of a political morality. The right to equal respect and concern, which is introduced by Dworkin as an instantiation of integrity, reveals namely a universalistic content [*Das Prinzip der integrity muß jedoch nicht zwangsläufig am gegebenen Kontext einer politischen Moral seine Grenze finden. Das Recht auf equal respect and concern, als dessen Verkörperung Dworkin integrity einführt, weist nämlich einen universalistichen Gehalt auf*]>>(K. Günther, *Der Sinn für Angemessenheit. Anwendungsdiskurse in Moral und Recht*, Suhrkamp, Frankfurt am Main 1988, p. 351). "Integrity" (meaning coherence with past decisions and with the whole of the legal order) as a supreme principle of adjudication and judicial reasoning is also vindicated by Michael Oakeshott (see his book *On Human Conduct*, p. 136: <<The adjudicator is always the custodian of the *integrity* of the system>>(italics mine)) and by John Finnis (see his article <<On 'The Critical Legal Studies Movement'>>, in *Oxford Essays in Jurisprudence*, Third Series, ed. by J. Eekelaar and J. Bell, Oxford

University Press, Oxford 1987, p. 161: <<It is this requirement of coherence – of the *integrity* of the system [...] – that distinguishes legal thought from 'open-ended' practical reasoning>> (italics mine)).

88. Those who take the normative viewpoint, asserting the validity of a particular statement, whether "thoreretical" or "practical", ipso facto imply that, rebus sic stantibus, that is, given the state of available knowledge, it is the best possible, and therefore represents the "one right answer". (Subject, obviously, to revisions due to increases in knowledge relevant to the case under consideration, and to the assessment of arguments thitherto unknown to anyone, nor adopted by anyone). This is proved very well and emphatically by Immanuel Kant, in extending the normative viewpoint to the whole of philosophy: <<When someone announces a system of philosophy as his own product, this is equivalent to his saying: 'before this philosophy there was as yet no other one'. Had he to concede that there was however an other (true) one, then there would be on the same subject two true philosophies, which is contradictory [*Wenn also jemand ein System der Philosophie als sein eigenes Fabrikat ankündigt, so ist es eben so viel, als ob er sagte: 'vor dieser Philosophie sei gar keine andere noch gewesen'. Denn wollte er einräumen, es wäre eine andere (und wahre) gewesen, so würde es über dieselben Gegenstände zweierlei wahre Philosophie gegeben haben, welches sich widerspricht*]>> (I. Kant, *Metaphysiche Anfangsgründe der Rechtslehre*, *Metaphysik der Sitten*, Erster Teil, ed. by B. Ludwig, p. 7). Accordingly the target is missed by all those criticisms that either take the "one right answer" thesis as a sociologizing descriptive hypothesis (meaning that this right solution actually exists), or else reduce the idea to a "regulatory ideal", in the sense of one of the various possible "ideologies of judges" (for this attitude towards the American scholar's work, cf. e.g. L. Prieto Sanchís, <<Cuatro preguntas a propósito de Dworkin>>, in *Revista de ciencias sociales*, Universidad de Valparaiso (Chile), Vol. 38 (1993), pp. 69 ff.). Nor should it be forgotten that the thesis of the "one right answer" as regulatory ideal is, as Habermas shows, the basis of the legitimacy of the democratic political order: <<Deliberative politics would lose its point – and the democratic rule of law its legitimation ground –, if we as participants to political discussion could not convince and learn from others. Political controversies would forfeit their deliberative character and degenerate in mere strategic power struggles, if the people concerned would not assume – of course, moving from the fallibilistic assumption to be subject at any time to errors – that the controversial political and legal problems might find a "right" solution. Without an orientation to the aim of problem solving to be proved through reasons participants would not even know what to look for [*Die deliberative Politik würde ihren Sinn – und der demokratische Rechtsstaat seine Legitimationsgrundlage – verlieren, wenn wir als Teilnehmer an politische Diskussionen nicht andere überzeugen und von anderen lernen könnten. Der politische Streit würde seinen deliberativen Charakter einbüßen und zum ausschließlich strategischen Machtkampf degenerieren, wenn die beteiligten nicht auch – gewiß in dem fallibilistischen Bewußtsein, sich jederzeit irren zu können ß davon ausgehen würden, das – die strittigen politischen und rechtlichen Probleme eine 'richtige' Lösung finden könnten. Ohne die Orientierung am Ziel einer durch Gründe auszuweisenden Problemlösung wüßten die Teilnehmer gar nicht, wonach sie suchen sollten*]>> (J. Habermas, <<Replik auf Beiträge zu einem Symposion der Cardozo Law School>>, in Id., *Die Einbeziehung des Anderen. Schriften zur politischen Theorie*, Suhrkamp, Frankfurt am Main 1996, pp. 325-326).

89. N. MacCormick, <<Legal Reasoning and Practical Reason>>, in *Midwest Studies in Philosophy*, 1982, p. 282. See also N. MacCormick, <<*The Concept of Law* and the

Concept of Law>>, in *The Autonomy of Law. Essays in Legal Positivism*, ed. by R. P. George, Clarendon, Oxford 1996, p. 189: <<There is an implicit 'claim to correctness' behind every act of determining the law, and this is especially salient in the case of judicial decision-making>>.

90. For an anticipation of this thesis cf. Th. Viehweg, *Topik und Jurisprudenz*, V ed., p. 118: <<Whoever enters in a speech situation takes on obligations, which on the other hand are obvious to the practising lawyer's understanding [*Wer sich auf eine Redesituation einläßt, übernimmt Pflichten, die wiederum dem Verständnis des praktizierenden Juristen sehr naheliegen*]>>, and in Italian legal-philosophical culture E. di Robilant, *Sui princìpi di giustizia*, Giuffrè, Milano 1961: <<That a criterion is capable of being 'founded' means that arguments can be adduced in its justification; but these are aimed at proving to anyone, especially the unconvinced, that the criterion itself deserves approval. Adducing arguments to justify a criterion, that is, implies the at least implicit claim to its universal validity>>.
91. Jerome Frank's: he condemns the principle of "certainty of law" to the role of a rhetorical ornament on the permanent irrationality of legal decision, the real motivations of which are sometimes instead to be sought even in the more-or-less troubled digestive processes of the judging subject (cf. J. Frank, *Law and the Modern Mind*, 6th reprint, Anchor Books, New York 1963, chap. 12). However, Jerome Frank's decisionism is attenuated by the consideration that decision is an event that escapes the subject's free disposal, and is instead largely determined by processes over which human will has very little grip. In this connection see the critical considerations by N. Bobbio, <<La certezza del diritto è un mito?>>, in *Rivista internazionale di filosofia del diritto*, Vol. 29, 1952, pp. 146 ff., and B. Ackerman, <<Law and the Modern Mind by Jerome Frank>>, in *Daedalus*, 1974, pp. 119 ff.
92. Th. Viehweg, *Topik und Jurisprudenz*, V ed. p. 119.
93. R. Dworkin, *Law's Empire*, p. 82.
94. See R. Alexy, *Theorie der juristischen Argumentation*, pp. 263 ff. Note that this is also the opinion of Neil MacCormick (see N. MacCormick, *Legal Theory and Legal Reasoning*, pp. 263 ff.) and of Jürgen Habermas (see J. Habermas, <<Replik auf Beiträge zu einem Symposion der Cardozo Law School>>), who has however declared his opposition to the thesis of the special case (see J. Habermas, *Faktizität und Geltung. Beiträge zur Diskurstheorie des Rechts und des demokratischen Rechtsstaats*, Suhrkamp, Frankfurt am Main 1992, pp. 283 ff.), to that extent accepting the theses of Klaus Günther (see K. Günther, *Der Sinn für Angemessenheit*, pp. 309 ff., and especially K. Günther, <<Critical Remarks on Robert Alexy's "Special Case Thesis>>, in *Ratio Juris*, Vol 6., 1993, pp. 143 ff., in relation to which read Alexy's prompt reply, <<Justification and Application of Norms>>, in *Ratio Juris*, Vol. 6, 1993, pp. 157 ff.).
95. <<The decisive point in distinguishing rules from principles is that *principles* are norms which require that something be realized to the greatest extent possible given the legal and factual possibilities. Principles are *optimization requirements*, characterized by the fact that they can be satisfied to varying degrees [...]. By contrast, rules are norms which are always either fulfilled or not>>(R. Alexy, *A Theory of Constitutional Rights*, English transl. by J. Rivers, Oxford University Press, Oxford 2002, pp. 47-49, italics in the text).
96. J. Habermas, *Between Facts and Norms*, p. 220.
97. *Ibid.*

98. *Ibid.*
99. K. Günther, <<Critical Remarks on Robert Alexy's "Special Case" Thesis>>, p. 156.
100. J. Habermas, *Between Facts and Norms*, p. 229.
101. *Ibid.*, p. 232.
102. N. MacCormick, *Rhetoric and the Rule of Law. A Theory of Legal Reasoning*, Oxford University Press, Oxford 2005, p. 23.
103. See the "conclusion" of G. Calabresi, *Ideals, Beliefs, Attitudes, and the Law. Private Law Perspectives on a Public Law Problem*, Syracuse University Press, Syracuse, N. Y. 1985.
104. See e.g. R. Alexy, <<Rechtssystem und praktische Vernunft>>, in Id., *Recht, Vernunft, Diskurs. Studien zur Rechtsphilosophie*, Suhrkamp, Frankfurt am Main 1995, pp. 23 ff. Cf. R. Dreier, *Konstitutionalismus versus Legalismus – Zwei Arten juristischen Denkens im demokratischen Verfassungsstaat*, now in *Konstitutionalismus versus Legalismus? Geltungsgrundlagen des Rechts im demokratischen Verfassungsstaat*, ed. by E. E. Dais et al., Franz Steiner, Stuttgart 1991 (Archiv für Rechts-und Sozialphilosophie, Beiheft No. 40), p. 95.
105. See R. Alexy, *Theorie der Grundrechte*, Suhrkamp, Frankfurt am Main 1986, pp. 71 ff. It is interesting to recall that Habermas, on whom too Alexy's thought largely draws, is obstinately hostile to this reconstruction of the notion of principle, since he feels it opens the door to an economistic instrumentalization of the institution of law and is too generous with the need to coordinate rights (expressed by norms of principle), with the consequence of making every fundamental right able to be compensated for or derogated from by considerations of another sort (for instance, assessments of the public good). See J. Habermas, *Faktizität und Geltung*, p. 255.
106. Cf. T. Campbell, <<Legal Studies>>, in *A Companion to Contemporary Political Philosophy*, ed. R. E. Goodin and Ph. Pettit, 2nd ed., Blackwell, Oxford 1996, p. 184: <<The most distinctive concern of legal philosophers is the nature of legal process itself, and in particular the analysis and criticism of legal argumentation as it is manifest in the selection, interpretation and application of laws, principally in the setting of the court room. This central aspect of legal philosophy has important implications for political philosophy in that it raises issues about the institutional and philosophical presuppositions of the idea of the rule of law, one of the principal ideological foundations of liberal politics and the theory of democracy. For this reason competing philosophies of legal argumentation feature centrally in this exposition of those aspects of the discipline of law which are of evident relevance to political philosophy>>.
107. See R. Dworkin, *A Matter of Principle*, chap. 1.
108. See H. L. A. Hart, *The Concept of Law*, pp. 70 ff.
109. This is for instance, Gregorio Peces-Barba's thesis on Article 1 (I) of the 1978 Spanish Constitution, despite intransigently legal positivist positions elsewhere taken by the same author. Cf. G. Peces-Barba, *Los valores superiores*, Teanos, Madrid 1986, and G. Peces-Barba, <<Los valores superiores>>, in *Archivo de filosofia del derecho*, 1987.
110. Cf. C. L. Ten, <<Constitutionalism and the Rule of Law>>, in *A Companion to Contemporary Political Philosophy*, ed. by R. E. Goodin and Ph. Pettit, Blackwell, London 1996, pp. 401-402.

111. His critique of legal positivism and the "constructivism" it is allegedly an expression of is certainly not far from similar formulations of Dworkin's: see F. A. Hayek, *The Constitution of Liberty*, Routledge & Kegan, London 1960, pp. 205 ff.
112. See J. Raz, <<The Politics of the Rule of Law>>, in *Ratio Juris*, Vol. 3, 1990, pp. 331 ff.
113. For a similar position cf. J. Waldron, <<Rights>>, in *A Companion to Contemporary Political Philosophy*, ed. by R. E. Goodin and Ph. Pettit, pp. 537 ff.
114. See R. Alexy, *Theorie der Grundrechte*, pp. 395 ff.
115. See J. Habermas, *Faktizität und Geltung*, C. S. Nino, *Derecho, moral y política*, Ariel, Barcelona 1993, and C. S. Nino, *The Constitution of Deliberative Democracy*, Yale University Press, New Haven, Conn. 1996.
116. See R. Alexy, *Theorie der juristischen Argumentation*, pp. 234-235.
117. N. Chiaromonte, *Che cosa rimane - Taccuini 1955-1971*, Il Mulino, Bologna 1996, p. 186. Cf. also J. Habermas, *Faktizität und Geltung*, p. 274, and especially K. Günther, <<Communicative Freedom, Communicative Power, and Jurisgenesis>>, in *Cardozo Law Review*, Vol. 17, 1996, pp. 1035 ff.
118. R. Alexy, *The Argument from Injustice. A Reply to Legal Positivism*, transl. by S. L. Paulson and B. Litschewski Paulson, Oxford University Press, Oxford 2002, p. 127, and cf. the original German work: R. Alexy, *Begriff und Geltung des Rechts*, Alber, Freiburg 1992, p. 201.
119. D. de Saavedra Fajardo, *República literaria*, ed. by J. C. De Torres, Gedisa, Barcelona 1985, p. 125.
120. Which is more or less equivalent to the non-violent constitutional order, that Ulrich Klug suggestively calls "anarchy", and that I have outlined *supra* at the end of first chapter.

CHAPTER 3

THE PRACTICE OF LAW AND LEGAL ETHICS

I. "JURISTS, BAD CHRISTIANS"

I. 1. Lawyers according to the Tradition

"Juristen, böse Christen" (Jurists, bad Christians) – this judgment was handed down by Martin Luther and is final.[1] In *Tischreden*, or *Table Talks*, the text it comes from, Luther so much as says that he should rather wish his son dead than see him by any mischance decide to become a jurist. In this condemnation without appeal, Luther echoes and drives to extremes some Augustinian and Pauline themes.

It is the law as such that is under suspicion here, for the law is what paradoxically, as Saint Paul says, makes it possible for us to sin: <<Cursed is every one that continueth not in all things which are written in the book of the law to do them>>(*Epistle to the Galatians* 3:10). What also come under suspicion are all the activities and functions bound up with the law; first among these, judging: <<Judge not, that ye be not judged>> is a precept of the Gospel (Matthew 7:1). Now, these flings taken at the person of the judge do not spare the lawyer, either. Lawyer and judge are both jurists, or *nomikói*, experts in the law: they saddle others with too heavy a burden and yet won't do anything to help them (Luke 11:46); worse, these people, the lawyers, detain the key to knowledge and prevent the layperson from having any access (Luke 11:52).

Lawyers will not make so bold as to appoint themselves judges and pass sentence on their own peers, to be sure. But their activity often consists in seeking judgment, or recurring to a judge, and exacerbating conflict rather than looking to smooth out existing differences. Thus, the Gospel urges any two parties in conflict to make an earnest attempt at finding some common ground and conciliating before going to law. Matthew (5:23) and Luke (12:58) make the point that trying to work out an amicable solution with an adversary is much better than invoking the stern, implacable proceedings of a legal action and turning oneself over to the officers of the law: <<Agree with thine adversary quickly, whiles thou art in the way with him; lest at any time the adversary deliver thee

to the judge, and the judge deliver thee to the officer, and thou be cast into prison>> (Matthew 5:25). Yet in the Christian tradition, the lawyer is not equated through and through with the judge. The office of the judge is at best a necessary evil; lawyering, on the other hand, is construed as being in essence a work of mercy, an endeavour to aid the weak and the needy. "Advocate" is the appellation that in Catholic liturgy, in the rosary for instance, is given to the Virgin Mary – for she intercedes with her son so that humankind may be redeemed from its life of sin.

There is therefore a deep ambiguity in the Christian depiction of the man of law. This ambiguity carries over into the classic tradition, cuts across the radical Enlightenment critique, and reaches our day. It is remarkable in this regard that the French Revolution suppresses the profession of the lawyer and shuts down schools of law, writing into the 1791 constitution a mandatory conciliation procedure – prior to litigation – couched in language that echoes the Gospel's recommendations just mentioned.

Judge and lawyer are therefore ambiguous types, but they are so in different ways. The judge is at once *pater et filius iustitiae*. Just like the prince and the king, the judge (*basileus* in Hesiod's *Works and Days*) is at the same time *imago equitatis* and *servus equitatis*, says John of Salisbury (*Policraticus*, IV, c. 2). We have here the tension present in a subject who is thought of as both *legibus solutus* and *legibus alligatus: legibus alligatus*, or bound by the law, because the judge's role is to carry into force laws the judge does not create, but only applies, and *legibus solutus* – above the law – because the judge creates a norm (the individual norm framed by the ruling) that was previously not there. It is the judge's competence to pass sentence on concrete cases, and in this capacity the judge brings into effect specific rules. Every such decision will enter into the system of laws, where it previously did not exist, and so necessitates an act (the ruling) that is ultimately an expression of sovereignty and superiority.

This ambiguity in the office of the judge spans the entire course of legal philosophy, up to the present day, becoming sharper with the crisis of legal positivism. In its classic form, this doctrine is minded to put a check on judicial power, if not to annul it altogether. Legal positivism emerges out of the convergence of two great historical movements: absolute monarchy on the one hand, which paves the way for the modern state, and Enlightenment and democratic political philosophy on the other, which gives the modern state its fragile liberal casing. The absolutist looks on the judge's power as a hindrance to the "monopoly of violence," which expression encapsulates in rather a brutish manner the idea of state sovereignty, one and indivisible. We can see this attitude exemplified in the admonition that Francis Bacon addresses to Edward Coke, saying of judges, <<Let them be lions, but yet lions under the throne: being circumspect that they do not check or oppose any points of sovereignty>>.[2] The independence of the magistracy championed by Coke sits poorly with the absoluteness of monarchic power, looming behind which is this new, formidable historical manifestation: the State.

This conflict was even starker in France under the *ancien régime* on account the feudal organization of the Parlements, the law courts competent to register royal edicts. The king's ministers were all focused against the Parlements, as was Enlightenment and democratic critique, which, too, cannot accept a separation between *iurisdictio* (judicature) and *gubernaculum* (state or political will). But with this fundamental difference: that the absolutist understands this will to be unshared – it belongs to one person only – whereas democrats understand it to pertain to many, to the people or the nation. In a polity now mainly conceived as a "machine" there is little room for more than just administration or management. Indeed, Germany's Cameralism – very much driven by the idea of the State as "machine" – was not all friendy towards the legal profession either. <<Judicial offices occupied an incospicuous place in this scheme, and (like the *philosophes*) Cameralists had little use for *parlementaires*>>.[3]

I. 2. The Legal Positivist Myth

Legal positivism brings back into operation Cicero's idea of the judge as the "law's mouth," but frames it in a mechanistic way. Thus, on the legal positivist conception, the judge is the law's mouth, not as the oracle from which the law's content is deduced, or through which it is revealed – for this is properly the task entrusted to legal codes and to the statutes issued by the lawmaker – but rather in the sense that the judge simply *reiterates* what has already been said elsewhere, in the selfsame articles and sections of the State's laws and codes. Legal positivism in essence equates law with enacted statutes, so the judge exits the scene, or rather gets upstaged, joining the ranks of judicial bodies deputed to administrative functions.

The leading character in this play staged by the legal positivist is the lawmaker, not the judge, and much less the lawyer or the advocate. Judicial reasoning does nothing but apply the law mechanically. A legal education will consist mostly in notional content, an artless knowledge of laws and decrees. No reference is made to the jurist's argumentative skills or to the moral responsibilities that may be incurred in this capacity. Rhetoric, previously taught at law schools, is banished from the realm of legal knowledge and from jurisprudence curricula, and all the more so are all kinds of deontology and philosophy (sometimes a subject of learning). *Oratio* is now replaced by *ratio*, and reasoning by arguments is reconceptualised as reckoning by given inputs. The model for the jurist to follow is no longer the orator or the humanist, but the mathematician or the scientist – Rudolf von Jhering tellingly speaks of the chemist. Jurisprudence morphs into a kind of philology, taking two main forms: the French school of exegesis (the interpretation school known as the *école de l'exégèse*) and German conceptual jurisprudence (*Begriffsjurisprudenz*), which advances a pretence of "system".

But this mechanistic conception and the image consequent upon it of the judge as a "robot-like processor of laws," – which actually is the central myth of legal positivism, fails to account for fact and for concrete judicial experience. <<The dominant ideal picture of lawyers is the following, that of a higher State officer endowed with academic education, sitting in his cell and armed only with a thinking machine, surely one of the finest kind>>[4] – so says Hermann Kantorowicz in the opening section of his *Der Kampf um die Rechtswissenschaft* (Heidelberg 1906). Experience shows this ideal to be grossly amiss: the judge *interprets* the law before applying it. This operation (interpreting) precedes syllogistic deduction and is a complex process, not merely a cognitive one. The judge must deal with gaps and "general clauses," and with hard cases: here the letter of the law will not suffice to give us the rule we need to reach a decision (nor will it give us the major premise in the legal syllogism). Fact finding and ruling are the outcome of a mutual adjustment.

The judge must phenomenologically produce a rule rather than simply ascertain its existence. But here the legal-positivist conception short-circuits, so to speak: its underlying voluntarism (by which a rule expresses the sovereign's will) applies also to the figure of the judge, so we end up saying that the judge, too, decides: the judge wills openly and unqualifiedly. Kantorowicz – influenced by the Romantic movement, which found a strong following in nineteenth-century Germany, and which, mind you, makes up the very core of legal positivism – accounts for the judge's decision-making capacity on the basis of a generic thesis (reminiscent of Fichte) by which the will always precedes the intellect: <<It is always a will that keeps reason by the nose>>.[5] Hans Kelsen and H. L. A. Hart take this one step further. For Kelsen, the judge produces, but does not know, the law: what makes the difference between a ruling and a law (between an "individual norm" and a "general norm," in Kelsen's lexicon) is only the extent of their semantic and denotative ranges.[6]

The judge, in Kelsen's view, does not extract a ruling from the law by deduction. What the law does is to vest the judge with a competence to hear cases and decide them, but it does not also dictate how a decision is to be reached: the "general norm" (the law), while it indicates who is to rule on concrete cases (the judge), does not also go into the substance of the ruling, whose content is therefore not determined in advance by law. Hart, too, is influenced by logical neopositivism – by its practical irrationalism, so attuned to the Romanticism of legal positivism – and observes, in this same vein, that only when deciding an easy case does the judge apply a rule. When the situation at hand falls under the "shady" area of a rule's semantic content, the judge simply *decides*, or better yet acts in the manner of a <<conscientious legislator>>.[7] And this view, as is known, would later draw upon Hart the acute critique of Ronald Dworkin.[8] The figure of the judge therefore wavers between that of an impartial ascertainer of laws (a kind of notary public) and that of an active maker of norms:[9] between a conservative reproducer of the legal system and a reformer, if not a subverter, of that system; between one who abides by the law and one who enforces or imposes a law. So we have here again the question of *legibus alligatus* versus *legibus solutus*.

The lawyer by no means escapes being portrayed in a twofold manner, either. The powerful paradigm of legal positivism obscures our understanding of the lawyer, too, just as much as it obscures that of the judge, and sometimes even more so. It will be said to start with that the ambiguity that the judge falls subject to becomes strikingly conspicuous in the lawyer. Here, we are not looking at the tension manifest in making law by the very process of submitting to it, but rather at the conflict between the impartiality built into the proceedings that one is a party to and the partiality of the outcome the same person seeks through those very proceedings. The lawyer contributes to the fairness of a legal proceeding, and possibly to the justice of its outcome, to be sure, but is often moved in doing this, not by a desire to effect the triumph of justice or of the law, but by personal gain and by the gain of the clients represented: it is these particular interests, rather than the general interest of the community, that guide the lawyer's actions. Hence the abiding disdain that, with few exceptions, lawyers meet with in Western culture.

I. 3. Plato, Kant and Modern Jurisprudence

Plato, it is known, abhors the sight of them, and in his *Laws* sets out a rigid system designed to regulate legal practice and drastically curtail lawyers' ability to promote their clients' interest, especially when this activity goes against the collective good of justice. The Enlightenment philosophers – with perhaps the single exception of Voltaire, who would complacently style himself a "provincial lawyer" – directed a great deal of invective against lawyers. So much so that Frederick the Great of Prussia, as well as the French revolutionaries, would later opt to strike the advocate's function out of the trial. Kant, too, does not exactly smile on lawyers, and this despite conceiving of his critique of pure reason as a kind of judicial process. Like Plato, he denounces their sophistry, their inclination to persuade rather than to convince. Kant's criticism that law ultimately relates to coercion does not have anything against the concept of a rule or against things juridical. But one can recognize in the lawyer the tension between justice and power. The lawyer (*der Jurist*) – he says –, <<who has made not only the scales of right but also the sword of justice his symbol, generally uses the latter not merely to keep back all foreign influences from the former, but, if the scale does not sink the way he wishes, he also throws the sword into it (*vae victis*)>>. This is a practice <<to which the lawyer, when he is not also a philosopher, even in morality, often has the greatest temptation, since his office is only to apply positive laws [*vorhandene Gesetze*], not to inquire whether they might not need improvement. Such a function, which is the lower one in his faculty, he counts as the higher because it is invested with power>>.[10]

Here Kant anticipates what survives as the position of the legal positivist jurist even today: he anticipates the "neutral" stance, and the justification for it is the pretext of practicability and the widely trumpeted realism of those who, in contrast, do nothing but celebrate a *fait accompli*, and do so unremittingly. It is not the principles of reason that the lawyer is fain to invoke, but *authority*.[11] Hobbes says, <<*Auctoritas, non veritas, facit legem.*>>. But Kant, in the excerpt quoted, exposes and criticises as well the lawyer's ambiguity, by noting how lawyers declare themselves committed to rendering justice, but then do not hesitate to tip the scales of judgment with the weight of the sword, or of power. Now, this description is more in character for the judge, so the lawyer would seem to be clear of danger – were it not that, on Kant's view, the lawyer, too, uses power and hence, does not escape the ambiguity referred to.

In the *Critique of Pure Reason* Kant speaks with some hostility, and with thinly veiled contempt, of the "special pleader's proof," designed not to convince, but to <<take advantage of an opponent's carelessness – freely allowing the appeal to a misunderstood law, in order that he [the special pleader] may be in a position to establish his own unrighteous claims>> (*Observation on the First Antinomy*, *On the Thesis*, A 430).[12] The lawyer's power, then, is not the sword proper, which Matthew the Publican is often represented as holding, and which the judge uses to enforce a ruling. The power in question is rather the orator's manipulated and manipulative discourse by which interests are disguised as rights; it is the rhetorical and procedural devices by which personal gain acquires the veneer and dignity of a collective good. The lawyer's power sometimes resides in a client's wealth, power and clout, and these things the lawyer will not expunge from the trial but will use as shields.

Legal positivism, I was saying earlier, is unsympathetic to lawyers and in fact regards them as nonentities. In some ways this attitude comes by way of political liberalism, with which legal positivism has been historically connected. As is known, liberalism has generally been adverse to trade associations and societies because of their similarity and even their equivalence to craft and merchant guilds under the old establishment. This hostility has of course been targeted at bar associations as well, which in fact were abolished in the course of the French Revolution and were reestablished only in the Restoration period. Membership of an association regulating the profession of law was seen as an impediment to the full exercise of citizenship, which on a radical democratic stance requires that citizens know the law and be competent as to its use.

It shouldn't be that citizens have to seek the counsel of an expert to be informed on what the law says and to be able to use the law to their advantage. Citizens need to be self-sufficient in this sense. The idea is that we should be bound by the law only if we have the ability to produce laws and so only if we can know and use them. What is more, a democratic polity should have an institutional framework within which citizens acquire a sense of self-worth – they will be encouraged to acquire a political, and so a legal, competency – and to this end an arena should be in place within which citizens can exercise and develop their sense of justice.[13] We should therefore see figuring among the powers of citizenship the power to defend oneself at law, without, that is, having to go through a legal counsel.

This is roughly the position espoused by the 1789 revolutionaries who would later make up the constituent assembly. A different vision is put forth in *The Limits of State Action*, a famous essay in which Wilhelm von

Humboldt conceptualizes and largely celebrates the ideas behind the 1789 revolution. In chapter 10 of this essay, Humboldt looks favourably on the idea of having some kind of public control on the legal profession.[14] The argument is laid out as follows. Because the lawyer (like the medical doctor) is an expert in the field and as such is qualified to render a certain service, and because citizens can find themselves in need of this service and expert knowledge for any number of reasons, it follows that proficiency in the same knowledge and skills should fall subject to certification by an body set up to answer the needs of the public and guarantee that these are met. If we are to make sure that private citizens do not fall prey to incompetent impostors, it will be necessary that the State set up a public register of individuals who have passed a given examination and so are certified as having attained the know-how and moral code required to practice law. It is not pretended that only those people enrolled in the register as members of the association in question can legitimately offer and provide legal services. But the State will not certify the competence and integrity of anyone who is not so enrolled. Here Humboldt seems to be advancing a view that liberal lawyers would later uphold once the ostracism against lawyers was finally lifted. It was reserved for one Francesco Carrara to be the staunchest proponent of this view in Italy, which is that the lawyer discharges a public function, even if we are still loath today to consider this function a power of government properly so called, on a par with judicial power, or to make it constitutionally equivalent to such a power.[15]

The liberal focus on the lawyer finds nothing of the kind in the legal positivist theory of law, despite the affinity that to some extent obtains between liberalism and legal positivism. If the judge, in this theory, is a robot-like operator – a machine that takes laws as input and issues rulings as output – the lawyer is not even discussed. There is nothing on the lawyer's role and activity in Austin, Savigny (clearly hostile to lawyers), Kelsen or Hart. Legal realism, for its part, puts up a wholesome reaction to the formalist tenor of legal positivism and in so doing, brings to the fore and in fact makes central to the legal domain, the figure of the judge. Here, too, there is no talk of the lawyer. This is probably due to two features of this current of thought that we find in most modern conceptions of law, namely: the identification of lawmaking with the making of a decision and the clear-cut distinction between law and morals. If law is essentially connected with decision-making – with a more or less sovereign power – then, plainly, advocacy gets pushed to the periphery of the legal system, for the advocate, it is known, does not decide. The lawyer is marginalized because not possessed of any sovereignty, power, or authority, especially none that can be likened to the power or authority to make decisions that are binding upon others or to wield a monopoly of violence.

By the same token, if we find that law is entirely independent of morality, then ethical and deontological questions will likewise be cast outside the legal system. But the lawyer's ambiguity previously outlined is, unlike the judge's, a preeminently moral ambiguity: recall, it concerns what goes on between the partiality of the interests defended and the impartiality, integral to the idea of justice, which those interests invoke in order that they may be answered. If morality falls outside the purview of law, the problems and dilemmas afflicting the legal profession vanish too. In other words, if everything that is not interdicted (because not subject to punishment by law) is therefore legal and so legitimate, then the lawyer will no longer be facing any deontological questions, but only legal questions as to what can be done without incurring any penal consequences. This thought pushes us further into an amoral vision of the practice of law.[16]

A view of this kind finds support in legal realism, especially in the American variety of it. Its foremost exponent, Oliver Wendell Holmes, states with some cynicism that the legal point of view is, strictly speaking, the bad man's point of view, meaning by this that the law must look at things from the perspective of a self-centred person who is prone to a relentless pursuit of personal interest, but who finds in doing this a roadblock in the shape of the law, which sets out punishments for civil and penal offences and so attaches a cost or a bad consequence to all misconduct.[17] So the legal point of view is that by which we seek to reinforce this barrier designed to thwart efforts by citizens – essentially viewed as bad people – to break or circumvent the law. The theatre of law therefore stages a struggle between those who seek to break or elude the law and those who work to impede such actions: the former role is played by private citizens and, mind you, by their attorneys and legal counsels; the latter, and nobler, role is the judge's (and the lawmaker's). Another American legal realist, Karl Lewellyn, models this contraposition by splitting up the legal rule into two constituents: one of these he calls the prediction-rule, which the lawyer uses and the other is the ought-rule, which is what the judge needs; the one is predictive and only the other is normative, or deontological.[18] The lawyer, in this reconstruction of the experience of law, becomes one with the bad man (irremediably so) and even with the criminal. There is hardly any way, in conclusion, that we can ascribe a truly moral role, and so a deontological code, to someone who, almost by definition, sides with the bad man.[19]

II. AMBIGUITY OF DEONTOLOGICAL RULES

II. 1. Deontological Codes

Not incidentally, the tension and polarity that unsettles the legal profession from within, making its function ambiguous, is reflected in the deontological norms by which it is governed. It is in fact only recently that the bulk of these norms have been written down or made explicit. In Italy, for example, no code of legal practice was in place on a national scale until 1997, and until an even more recent past most of the governing boards of our national bar association had published no best practices or canons of professional conduct. The code of legal practice in Italy had until then largely developed out of customary law, and it found a written (and so a more settled) form only with the body of regulatory rulings issued by the boards of our bar association and by the Consiglio Nazionale Forense, as well as by the Court of Cassation, competent to hear on appeal the rulings of this latter body. Even the American Bar Association Rules date back no further than the 1960s, and the subsequent Model Rules of Professional Conduct date to the early 1980s. Similarly, the Spanish code of legal practice was approved on 30 June 1995, and the European code went into effect in 1987.

Now, what becomes immediately apparent as we take a look at these documents is the diversity of the duties that the lawyer is said to be bound by, and sometimes even the conflicting claims these duties impose on the lawyer. Thus, for example, article 6 of the Italian code sets out the duties of fidelity and correctness, to be understood essentially and in the first instance as duties to the administration of justice (to the judge) and to the adverse party. But the articles immediately following establish the duties of fidelity, due diligence, and confidentiality to the party represented (articles 7, 8, and 9 respectively). So, on the one hand, there is an obligation for the lawyer to seek after the sound administration of justice and after a fair and speedy trial understood as proceeding by the application of rules and as framed to effect the common good; on the other hand, there is the suggestion that the lawyer's fidelity, diligence, and confidentiality are all aimed at advancing the client's interests. English and Welsh barristers are called upon to stay away from any and all conduct <<likely to diminish public confidence in the legal profession>> (*Code of Conduct of the Bar of England and Wales*, § 301); their duty of confidentiality to the client is strict, and yet judicial decision has set forth that a barrister <<has the power to act without asking his client what he can do. He has no master, but he is regulator and conductor of the whole thing>>.[20] Similarly, *The Guide to the*

Professional Conduct of Solicitors sets out as requisites <<the solicitor's independence or integrity>>, under point (a) of Practice Rule 1, and <<the solicitor's duty to act in the best interests of the client>>, under point (c) of the same rule. Witness, too, the *Code of Conduct for Lawyers in the European Union*, which under article 2.7 requires that the lawyer do everything within the bounds of the law to advance the client's interest (<<Subject to due observance of all rules of law and professional conduct, a lawyer must always act in the best interests of his client and must put those interests before his own interests or those of fellow members of the legal profession>>), in contrast to article 2.1, on the lawyer's independence, which sets down a duty to act independently of any and all pressures and special interests. This last value or principle is emblematic of the ambiguity that marks out and afflicts the lawyer's role.

So what kind of independence is it that we are looking at here? The traditional understanding of this notion, parallel to its use with regard to the judicial function, is that of independence from the public powers – from the government and the judge. This independence is expressly set out in article 2.1 of the European code and in article 1.1 of the Spanish code; the Italian code makes reference to it under article 1.1. Independence from the State powers is what all these provisions underscore with special emphasis. But then article 45 of the Italian code disallows contingent-fee arrangements (under which the attorney is due a percentage of the settlement or trial award, and nothing if the client obtains no compensation for damages),[21] and this disallowance argues an altogether different notion of independence, namely, the lawyer's independence from the client and from the personal gain there is to be had with the lawsuit. The Spanish code is explicit in this regard. Article 7.5 makes it a prohibition to have personal interests in the lawsuit: <<En ningún caso el Abogado adquirirá intereses personales en el pleito o asunto>>. And article 6.1 of the same code sets out the lawyer's freedom to accept or reject a suit, and this <<without having to explain the reasons behind the decision>>. According to the Prologue (*Vorspruch*) of the German *Grundsätze des anwaltlichen Standrechts* a lawyer <<übt einen freien Beruf aus>>, exercises a "free profession". And her work is not a business: <<Seine Tätigkeit ist kein Gewerbe>>. Finally, ABA model rule 1.2 (b) states that <<a lawyer's representation of a client [...] does not constitute an endorsement of the client's political, economic, social or moral views or activities>>.

So the lawyer is portrayed as independent from the State as well as from the client. But, as we learn from article 1.4 of the Spanish code, independence from the State is not to say that the lawyer does not

<<take part in the public function of administering justice>>. The Prologue of the German *Grundsätze* reads that <<der Rechtsanwalt ist ein unabhängiges Organ der Rechtspflege>>. Said in the words of a great Italian criminal law scholar, Francesco Carrara, <<even the defence counsel is a public official>>.[22] The prime duty which the defence is bound by is, in this view, the duty of <<fidelity in all legal work>>.[23] This fidelity will have to be qualified, however. And we do this by bringing back into play the elements that vivify the conflict or tension which the lawyer's function seems unable to shake off. <<The duty of fidelity does not place the defence counsel under an obligation in the *positive*, but only in the *negative*. It binds the lawyer to *not do* something, that is, to *not make* statements contrary to due process, and to *not effect*, by contrivances and false evidence, the triumph of falsity>>.[24] It will be noted here in passing that fidelity understood as an obligation to not contravene due process is almost tautological in a sense, in that the process of law is determined in part by the very action of the lawyer at trial. Thus, from this angle, the duty of fidelity can be construed as a duty to be loyal to one's own strategy of litigation, and so as no more than a duty of coherence with respect to the claims advanced at law.

II. 2. Civil Law and Common Law

These tensions and this wavering of the duties prescribed for the lawyer obviously stem in large part from the institutional makeup of practice at law and from the legal system in which they are embedded. In this regard, we cannot fail to take into consideration the difference between the legal systems of continental Europe and the systems of common law.

The traditional contraposition or difference between common law and civil law can be rendered with reference to the figure of the judge. As is known, common law is case law: it is judge-made, based on precedent, on bodies of judicial decision. In contrast, the understanding (and self-understanding) of continental European law passes through legislation, which is central to this kind of law, and for this reason the French have called it a system of *legicentrisme*. These systems of law centre around the figure (and myth) of an all-powerful, all-knowing legislator. The Anglo-Saxon systems of law – for all the differences that set them apart, and for all that they pride themselves on the sovereignty of the parliament (especially in Great Britain) – confer on the judge a role and powers that the jurist in continental Europe finds inconceivable. Consider that the principle of binding precedent is a doctrine growing up at the end of Nineteenth century through several cases dealt with by the House of Lords, the United Kingdom's supreme court of appeal: this principle did not come by way of legislation or a constitutional norm, and it was abrogated by the same court in 1966 by way of a simple statement, which is not a mere declaration, a ruling or a decision.

We can say in rough approximation that the difference between the two systems turns chiefly on their differing conceptions of the legislative function, which in the common law, though supreme, makes no pretence to legislate on every matter or in any exhaustive and general fashion. This conception of the legislator is bound up with a conception of the judicial function, such that before us is an alternative between the "judge as lord of the law" (in the system of common law) and the "judge as functionary" (in the Continental system of law). Moreover, this alternative can be said to be a recurrent theme in the history of law, and not only in the West. On the one hand we have judges detaining a power that in a sense is their own, and they are sources of legitimacy in themselves; on the other hand we have judges vested with the power of another, a power that they administer by proxy, as it were, and so without detaining any independent legitimacy. The first kind of magistrate we can call the law-lord judge; the second, the law-clerk judge.

In turn, each of these two ideal-type judge figures takes in a number of more-specific characters. Thus, the law-lord judge typically occurs in the guise of the judge king – who originally merged or tends to merge the powers of *iurisdictio* and *gubernaculum* – or again in the more modest guise of the judge as arbiter, who lacks *gubernaculum*, or sovereign power, but whose legitimacy is self-authenticating. This last feature comes by way of the unassuming position and prerogatives detained (this judge presides over the proceedings, but does not also institute or dominate them) as well as by way of the values embodied: impartiality, fairness, and procedural justice. The law-clerk judge likewise takes different forms, generally (a) the judge as notary public, (b) the judge as censor, or (c) the judge as an organ of state power. This last form is that which has been preeminent in modern States since the Napoleonic codification.

These two judge types have their analogues in two understandings of the lawyer. It bears pointing out to start with that the lawyer has acted historically in three rather distinct roles: (i) as attorney (the person appointed to act for another in legal matters), which we have in the old French *avoué;* (ii) as legal counsel, the expert legist acting to advise one of the parties on pertinent points of law; and (iii) as defender at trial, which figure we see exemplified in the orator, in the English barrister and in the French *avocat* prior to the 1971 reform. Now, the law-lord judge generally finds a counterpart in the lawyer as counsel and adviser, or even, in a twisted kind of way, as an advocate in the sense of one who sides squarely with one party and works zealously to advance and assert this party's cause and position. When a trial is set up as merely the clashing of contrary parties, as it tends to be in the adversary system, the lawyer will be compelled to further as much as possible the interests and rights of the party defended. But by so doing the lawyer risks becoming less of a legal counsel and more of a zealous advocate. The judge as notary finds a counterpart in the lawyer as politician, the statesman celebrated by Anthony Kronman.[25] The trial in this case is set up to reproduce deliberative procedure, and its closure to create new law. The procedure is not designed to assert the parties' rights and interests, but to promote the public good. Here, the judge ensures the correctness of procedure and affixes a seal of approval, thus acting as a kind of keeper of the seals.

The censor judge finds a counterpart in the lawyer as censor. The entire procedure is here one of censorship, for it is designed to assert morality in behaviour and so to police and curb behaviour on the basis of a moral standard. It is not the rights of the parties that the trial procedure is meant to secure, but their righteousness. Historically, this kind of trial precipitated the reform of judicial procedure launched by Frederick the Great in Prussia in the mid-eighteenth century. The roles of judge and lawyer are interchangeable, in that judge and lawyer are equally in charge of *Rechtspflege*, of protecting the legal order and its substantive morality.[26] Lastly, the judge as an organ of State corresponds to a lawyer who is likewise an organ of State, but whose powers are different and of lesser weight than those vested in the judge. The lawyer is, in this conception, one of three subjects (the other two being the judge and the public prosecutor) making up the trinity of the trial (lawyer, judge, and public prosecutor) and is now metaphysically joined to the party into a single entity.

In a brilliant and erudite essay, Mirjan Damaška[27] conceptualizes legal and processual systems in an account that comes into particular use here. He conducts a comparative study in which he classes legal systems as either hierarchical or coordinated: the former type tends to describe more accurately the civil-law systems of continental Europe; the latter captures many of the features distinctive to systems of common law. In coordinated systems, judges are laypersons, in the sense that they may act as jury and that they often become judges after practising another profession, or as members representative of the community at large, or by popular election. In a hierarchical system, judges are rather more like functionaries and professionals, and are generally appointed on a meritocratic basis. The trial system here is likewise hierarchical, such that the ruling pronounced by one judge can, on appeal, be made subject to a subsequent ruling issued by a judge serving in a higher court. The appeal is therefore geared not so much toward guaranteeing the rights of the parties as toward empowering a higher court to review the judicial work of the lower court. Appeals are uncommon in a coordinated system, and there is no clearly set-out hierarchical structure by which different judgeships are related.

Further, there is no marked distinction in hierarchical systems between judge and prosecutor, this because the judge, too, can institute a prosecution and indict someone, and because judge and prosecuting attorney belong to the same branch of government. But in a coordinated system, judge and prosecutor have two clearly distinct roles, and the prosecutor has no powers in addition to those of a non-prosecuting attorney. Lastly, coordinated systems are more focused on bringing out a substantive justice from each ruling, in contrast to hierarchical systems, whose ambition is almost to present a pure procedural justice, by which the formality of procedure – if followed closely – suffices to ensure the justice of its outcome.

Damaška believes that the two forms of legal system just presented can be connected with two ideal-type manifestations of the State, namely, what he calls (a) the reactive State and (b) the activist State. These two State-types, in turn, connect up with two types of end which the courtroom trial seeks to achieve. In a reactive State, the trial is chiefly framed to end a dispute; in the activist State, to implement this or that public-policy line. All these differences and connections cannot but structure the lawyer's role in various ways. In the conflict-solving trial, the parties in dispute play the role of *dominus* (or master) of the trial: so the lawyers might well not appear in principle, and if they do appear they will be rigidly subordinated to the interests and wishes of the party represented. <<Counsel must zealously advance his client's interests only as the latter defines them [...], even if he himself is not convinced that these arguments constitute the best interpretation of the law>>.[28] Here the lawyer is not involved in the administration of justice and so does not work as an organ of justice. This lawyer's manner of working is rather aggressive – the client's defence is paramount.

Things look quite different in a policy-implementing trial. Here the lawyer acts less as a party's legal representative and more as an organ of state, a functionary – along with the judge – in the administration of justice. Playing the *domini* in a procedure of this kind are not the parties to a suit, but the organs of State, first among which is the judge. The lawyer's role in this context is to increase the likelihood that the outcome yielded by the trial procedure will be correct from the standpoint of the administration of justice: <<In a legal system characterized by the tendency to favour smooth implementation of State policy, there is no place for lawyers who serve the self-interest of clients and create obstacles to the realization of State programmes>>.[29] The lawyer pledges fidelity in the first instance to the legal system and then to the client: fidelity to a client can be maintained only to the extent the client's rights and interests do not collide with those pertaining to the administration of justice.

Plainly, the picture outlined by Damaška simplifies and in a way radicalizes reality. This is because it presents an ideal-type: institutional reality is much more variegated, and the framework of a trial procedure, far from being simple, is actually quite fragmented.

But if we take this variegation and fragmentation and work from it by abstraction until the most condensed forms are achieved, what we come down to is two basic conceptions of the lawyer vying for recognition. One is roughly liberal and views the counsel as a zealous but neutral upholder of the party represented: the counsel acts on the party's ends as the chief basis of the legal work to be undertaken. The other is roughly communitarian – ethical, perfectionist – and views the counsel as an administrator of justice, and hence, as engaged (like the judge) in effecting the justice of the concrete case. This alternative takes different forms, to be sure, but it cuts across divisions: we find it in the legal systems of continental Europe (closer to the hierarchical model briefly described) as well as in systems of common law (closer to the coordinated model). This is so even as the latter are so framed that they foster the doctrine of "neutral partisanship" while the former share greater affinity with the communitarian and ethically freighted visions.

Regrettably – with the single exception of the research on legal ethics conducted in the United States[30] – philosophy of law has not gone into this topic in any depth. The prime focus of legal philosophy has long been the person of the sovereign and the lawgiver, and more recently that of the judge. And yet we do find suggestions and considerations here and there that are worth taking up, some of these from outside the United States, even if in this case the lawyer's function is looked at by and large from a deontological standpoint rather than from a conceptual one. In Italy, two scholars of different expertise and intellectual backgrounds have written insightfully, however briefly, on the subject: they are Professors Giovanni Tarello and Luigi Lombardi Vallauri. They stand on opposite sides of the question that theoretical reflection is taking on with regard to the lawyer's role and duties. Professor Tarello puts forward a vision of the lawyer as a neutral partisan, so to speak; Professor Lombardi Vallauri looks ahead to a lawyer as quasi-judge. Let us take up these two ideas in turn.

III. TWO OPPOSED PARADIGMS

III. 1. The Legalistic Approach

Professor Tarello brings to us in the first place a legal-positivist and vaguely sociological understanding of law. We can deduce deontological rules, he says, "<<by analyzing the makeup of the legal framework in question>>," and then by analyzing culture, <<which in a historically situated society the legal practitioners share with fellow citizens>>.[31] This way, it bears pointing out, deontology becomes severed from ethics and moral philosophy and finds its place next to the study of positive law and sociology. This methodology falls in line with legal realism and with the radical metaethical non-cognitivism of Giovanni Tarello's own legal philosophy.

Thus, in working to provide the legal profession with a code of conduct, Tarello proceeds from what is stated in the Constitution of the Italian Republic. We find in this text the principles that are to govern directly the activity of a legal counsel. Article 24, paragraph 2, of the constitution reads: <<The right of defence is inviolable at every stage and level of the proceedings>>. And article 27, paragraph 2, states that <<the defendant is not considered guilty until the final judgment is passed>>. Now, from these two articles – from the fact of there being a fundamental and inalienable right to counsel – we have to deduce, says Tarello, that in the Italian legal system <<criminal defence attorneys must understand defence to be, not their *first*, but their *only* commitment, and this understanding they must act on. In particular, they must never understand themselves to be a judge's aide or collaborator, and so must never act in this capacity>>.[32]

From this general conception of legal practice, Tarello extracts three deontological rules that he views as central to the client/attorney relationship: (a) a lawyer selected to defend someone cannot decline such legal representation except when factors exist that can impair the lawyer's ability to adequately safeguard the prospective client's interests; (b) <<the defence provided shall be fully proficient – in what concerns the technical quality of the legal services rendered and in what concerns questions of fact – without allowing personal feelings, opinions, or

convictions to obtrude on the legal work undertaken>>;[33] and (c) a lawyer must abstain from any and all action that may come in conflict with the duties of fidelity to the client framing the lawyer's role.

On this deontological approach – proper to what was earlier called the stance of neutral partisanship – there are no ethical limitations which the lawyer is bound by save those set forth in the law: <<The defence must be conducted in the most effective way possible and must keep account only of the boundaries of the law (whose word on this matter is to be interpreted in the most restrictive way), and this with a view to fully effecting a client's basic rights and freedoms>>.[34] A paradoxical conclusion is to be drawn from a position of this kind, which is that deontological codes, as against codes of law, come to no use: they have no specific function if it is assumed that the only strictures put on a defender's activity are those set by law.

When it comes to the relationship between lawyer and judge, Tarello recommends a deontological principle that seems quite frankly disquieting. The lawyer is allowed – and in fact compelled, because bound by duty – to turn to advantage all of the judge's human frailties in the effort to provide the best defence for a client. When pushed to the limit, this attitude (a strategic if not cynical and Machiavellian attitude) reaches the point of corruption or of law-breaking. The judge cannot be corrupted but can be overreached and deceived in a way. A case can, and in fact must, be brought to judgment in the tribunal that is friendliest and most sympathetic to the claim advanced; therefore, dilatory tactics (in violation of speedy-trial provisions) and judge shopping (soliciting a change of venue in violation of constitutional rights to an impartial trial under due process of law) do not seem to Tarello to be in any way reproachable: <<The lawyer's professional code requires the lawyer – in working at a successful defence – to make the most of the prejudices the judge indulges in. The defence must therefore be gauged to the judge: an attempt must be made to bring the proceeding, or part of it, before the judge or judges with whom a given line of argument is expected to be most likely to find favour; the defence counsel can (and in fact is under an obligation to) evolve the most insidious tactics short of corrupting the judge>>.[35]

But even Tarello, this steadfast supporter of the lawyer's partiality, cannot eschew the tension or the ambiguity incident to the legal profession. The judge's prejudices must be turned to account, it is true, but this manner of proceeding will in a sense elicit partiality in the judge, too. So the lawyer's deontological partiality collides with the impartiality that Tarello himself understands as defining the judge's role. <<The lawyer>>, he states, <<collaborates best with the judge by being a good defence lawyer – by being partial to the client>>.[36] But how can one stand for a situation in which the lawyer's partiality finds no counterweight in the judge's impartiality and is in fact *bound* to spill onto the judges themselves? It may be that if Tarello could witness firsthand what goes on today in certain courtrooms in Italy – where dilatory defences, intimidation and judge shopping have long been common practice among lawyers at the service of the powerful – then he may just come round on the question of the counsel's right to seize on the judge's prejudices and weaknesses of character and <<evolve the most insidious tactics>>.

Also a question, when we look at the arguments advanced by one in whom partiality has become deeply ingrained and extreme, How well will such arguments play with an audience set on seeking the correctness of reasons (as a tribunal is presumed to be)? The deadening request to get to the point, which many a judge has made to a lawyer engaging in profuse oratory, can find its justification in the very partiality (and so the untrustworthiness) that the lawyer so proudly wields. If the lawyer were truly a "partisan," the performative contradiction, <<My client is right but I don't believe those words (or, in a different version, I don't care)>>, would be lurking around every bend, always ready to steal up on the argument brought forward and disprove it.

If, on Tarello's view, the lawyer is under an obligation to accept any kind of legal representation whatsoever, and must not be squeamish in this, or wallow in moral judgments extraneous to questions of law (and dangerous, too, because they are contrary to the principle of <<presumed innocent until proven guilty>>, a principle that Tarello leaves us to understand as having great moral valence) – if, in other words, the lawyer cannot shy away from the duty to provide an indictee with a competent defence – the way to go about handling the cause, says Tarello, can only depend on the lawyer, and not on any of the client's wishes or instructions. It is the lawyer, and only the lawyer, who interprets and handles at trial the party's rights and interests, and does so in full independence. It will be noted here in passing that this thesis does not entirely cohere with the doctrine of neutral partisanship, by which the defender proceeds upon the party's instructions and largely depends on these when it comes to setting up a defence. Damaška views this dependence of the lawyer on the client as a distinguishing feature of coordinated and conflict-solving systems, as against hierarchical and policy-implementing systems. In this latter case, lawyers are not a party's representative but act on their own account and on their own initiative as organs of the administration of justice.

<<The client>>, says Tarello, <<has no right to impose this or that line of defence, this or that trial strategy, this or that argument. From a juridical as well as from an ethical standpoint, legal representation is no doubt geared towards protecting the client's interests. But the protection afforded does not proceed on the subjective understanding the client has of these interests; rather, it proceeds upon the objective configuration that they take under the law, and only on this understanding does the law make such protection a basic right>>.[37] The lawyer, then, can be said to defend, not the private, particular and subjective interests of a party, but a basic freedom that finds its specification in the right to counsel, in keeping with an *objective* understanding of this right and not with the party's perception of it (or with any representation based on this perception).

What Tarello is doing here, is letting in through the back door what he had kicked out through the front, namely, the lawyer's leaning towards objective values (presumably the values of justice). So the lawyer's partisanship will have to be construed as partial, not so much to the interests of the party defended, as to the basic rights of the person in the objective configuration that these rights take within the legal system. <<The professional code sets out clearly for the lawyer>>, Tarello concludes, <<a duty not to yield to any pressure exerted by the client for or against a certain line of defence or manner of proceeding at trial: the lawyer has the final say here and must dismiss any direction of this kind that he or she judges to be detrimental to the defence>>.[38] There is still a strong accent on the strategic approach instrumental to success, but this element links up more or less explicitly with the effort to secure a *basic right*, a right that forms the bedrock of any justification of the legal profession.

On final consideration, the thesis of neutral partisanship returns a positive image of the lawyer and of the history of lawyering. Or rather it returns a sense of pragmatic optimism, plumping for the *status quo* of the legal profession in actual practice or for the ideology by which lawyers like to present themselves. Quite different is the moralistic perspective, which in a sense charges itself with interpreting the permanent veil of suspicion that Western culture and literature have cast on the figure of the lawyer.

III. 2. The Moralistic Approach

I have spoken already of Luther and his verbal excesses. Others have followed suit. We cannot forget, in Alessandro Manzoni's novel *The Betrothed*, the Azzeccagarbugli – the pettifogger, or quibbling lawyer – a character we can easily recognise today, and who, like Don Abbondio, is strong with the weak and weak with the strong. The Azzeccagarbugli refuses to defend Renzo: he fears and truckles to the strongarm man of the moment, Don Rodrigo, a timeless personification of political costume in Italy. Still, for all that Manzoni scorns pettifoggers, he does not loathe them. It is William Shakespeare who in *Henry VI* has one character say, <<let's kill all the lawyers>> (part 2, act 4, scene 2). His *Measure for Measure* is no less critical towards judges. To speak nothing of the venal and corrupt *letrados* that Spanish Baroque literature bristles with. Antonio Perez says of lawyers in his *Norte de Principes* that they suck our blood and flourish thanks to our vices: <<Viven de nuestra sangre>> and <<Se autorizan de nuestras indignidades>>.[39] So, too, some of the lowliest characters in Fyodor Dostoyevsky's novels practice the noble art of law: witness Lebedev, in *The Idiot*, and Lužin, in *Crime and Punishment*. "Homme de chicane", "quibbling man": this is Victor Hugo's definition of the lawyer, and Marius, the young hero of his *Les Miserables* is strongly advised not to "avocasser", not to obtain a living as attorney.[40]

Now, this very suspicion and disdain is what the moralistic approach can be said to interpret. And we have an example of this attitude in Italy with Professor Lombardi Vallauri. <<There is – he says – something of an intellectual opaqueness and moral shadiness in the lawyer's role as legal representative at trial – as the author of pleas and harangues, of demurrers and appeals. The quest for truth and the battle for right against wrong jar with the ready disposition to sell one's own logic to the first passerby>>.[41]

Luigi Lombardi Vallauri proceeds upon the assumption that the lawyer <<usually intervenes in cases of pathology of action, and in particular where such pathology affects human relationships>>.[42] When divisive conflict begins, when communicative action between human beings has broken down, there the lawyer has crept in. And in such cases, Lombardi Vallauri is keen to point out, the lawyer does not seek to resolve the question, by helping the disputants work out their differences, but seeks to embitter feelings even further and aggravate the situation in the extreme, that is, to the point where the case is brought to trial. The trial is therefore looked on as a pathological process of law, an event that comes to violence in a way, an exchange that is anything but communicative. And the lawyer's intercession is likewise anything but communicative or reconciliatory. For what the lawyer does is to speak, not to the counter party and counsel, but to a third party – the judge, the lawyer's only interlocutor. Further, the lawyer speaks words <<interwoven with presumptions, all of them malicious to the adversary and favourable to the client. These words make no appeal to their addressee and no attempt to convince this person>>.[43] <<The lawyer supports a party, not a relationship between parties [...]. And if we speak to each other through lawyers, that means that we are no longer speaking to each other at all>>.[44]

These considerations prompt Lombardi Vallauri to put forward a revision of the legal profession, or rather a sweeping reform of it. The lawyer – presently a "therapist at law" – should transform into a "preventer at law," in much the same way as the judge, now a "legal pathologist", should be reconceptualized as a social worker, so to speak. The lawyer ought to intervene, not *after* a fraying relationship has developed into a face-off, but *before* this development, when a line of communication can still be reestablished between the parties. The judge and the lawyer should in a sense undertake to perform a pedagogic and therapeutic function. The lawyer should serve as a kind of family doctor, checking up on patients regularly throughout their lives, even when they are not under any particular conditions, and especially in these cases. <<In this role, the lawyer becomes a kind of "goodwill promoter (*consigliere di pace*)>>.[45] It is the lawyer's task, in this conception, to get the disputants to focus their attention on the basis of their choice (to enter into a dispute) and on the values that join them rather than on the interests that divide them and lead to conflict. So what happens here, says Lombardi Vallauri, is that <<the roles of judge and lawyer move closer together, since the lawyer is viewed more as a legal counsel and expert pacificator than as a dialectical representative at trial>>.[46]

It is at this point that Lombardi Vallauri ventures to make his proposal for a reform of trial procedure. Once the parties to a lawsuit have each selected a legal counsel, the two lawyers appoint a third lawyer they both trust. This group of three will make up a judging panel charged with issuing a preliminary decision on the merits of the case. Before reaching a decision (by majority vote) the three lawyers must <<make their best effort to settle the lawsuit amicably>>.[47] Each of the two parties can challenge the decision and bring the case before a regular judge. But by making this motion the panel and the parties will incur a hefty penalty for failure to reach a final settlement: <<A litigation cannot be brought before a regular judge without previously going through a settlement procedure (with lawyers acting as quasi-judges) and paying a penalty>>.[48] Once a regular judge is called in to try the case, the trial proceedings take their regular course. If no appeal follows the decision reached by the quasi-judge lawyers, this decision will stand and will close the matter definitely. If the lawyers fail to settle the case and decide to go forward to a final court judgment, no additional costs will be payable to them.

What seems to prompt this model put forward by Lombardi Vallauri is, not only a mistrust of lawyers, but also, and more importantly, a concern with the realities of legal action. There is at base a consummately negative vision of the trial, such that the very initiation of one amounts to checkmating the right and dooming the law to failure. Still, Lombardi Vallauri sees in the judge the alpha and omega of the legal practitioner. Legal reasoning, he argues, is in essence judicial reasoning: <<Only with the judge do we have authentic and complete reasoning>>.[49]

But even the idea of justice is viewed with suspicion in this perspective. Justice is valued subordinately to goodness and fellowship. Human relationships ought to be guided by friendship more so than by justice. Thus, conflict, contention, and the "brawl for rights" correspond to as many failings and imperfections. The lawyer must in a way be at one with the judge: it is recommended that <<the judge and the lawyer converge in their modes, finding a common ground in the effort to achieve impartiality of decision and taking on the responsibility that comes with this agency>>.[50] Even the judge often withdraws from the role of arbiter in a conflict between parties, becoming less of a "lord" who dispenses justice and more of a "functionary" who applies a rule, an "expert in structures," in the words of Giovanni Cosi, a student of Lombardi Vallauri.[51] An expert in structures is one who can maintain the fabric of physiological jural relations, injecting them with all the morality they can soak up. The judge here resembles the "goodwill promoter" previously referred to, a righteous and moralising figure that Cosi relates to that of a good father and family man: <<This person is one who may be called upon to take up any matter of law and so must possess the entire 'morality' the law can express>>.[52]

In this convergence of roles, the lawyer, too, becomes a judge, or a "pre-judge," says Lombardi Vallauri – an "expert in structures," a "goodwill promoter," and even a "good father and family man." The lawyer, no longer an agent of conflict, becomes a paternal subject and, more importantly, a paternalistic one.

IV. LEGAL ETHICS AND THE CONCEPT OF LAW

IV. 1. The "Moral Amorality" Thesis

Can a lawyer working in defence of a client pursue a course that will cast aspersions on a third party, and this without having any proof of this person's guilt or any conviction about it? Can a lawyer lead, degrade and throw as much discredit on a witness as possible, so as to prevent this person from producing probatory elements damaging to the client? Is it legitimate for a lawyer, in looking to set straight a situation that is shaping up to be clearly hurtful to a client, to discredit the judges who have incriminated or have been designated to pass sentence on this person?

Can a lawyer repeatedly and pertinaciously raise procedural objections designed to obstruct the regular course of a trial that is producing mounting evidence against the client? Is it permitted for a lawyer, bound by the principle of independence from the public powers, to argue a case and at the same time serve in the executive? Is it legitimate to bring into operation during trial provisions on judicial procedure which one is debating and enacting as a member of parliament, and which therefore can affect the outcome of the trial being conducted by this very person serving double duty as lawyer and as member of parliament? Is it legitimate to manoeuvre a situation in the attempt to divert an investigation or trial from the venue previously ascertained by law, thus putting the proceedings in the hands of a judge known or assumed to be prone to look at the case from a point of view favourable to the client? None of these questions can be answered unless we have previously worked out the difficult points pertaining to the deontological code of the legal profession.

Now this code, it was previously observed, finds itself in a tight spot, cornered between two opposite and antagonistic conceptions. On the one hand we have the doctrine of neutral partiality, which also goes by the name of "moral amorality." In this view, the answer to all the questions just asked should properly be yes, even if this way we risk offending public sentiment and people's normal sense of justice. On the other hand, we have the ethical and paternalistic vision of a moralist lawyer whose action anticipates that of the judge. This lawyer would view every cause as being "right," every client as being "good," and every party as being entitled to the assistance of appointed counsel. Were it not that sometimes, if not often, there is no way of knowing for certain where right and wrong lie in litigation. Especially so before examining and debating the claims, pleas, allegations, and arguments advanced by the parties. But then again, even the worst murderer is entitled to a defence at law, for otherwise it would not be a judgment (however severe) that this person will be made subject to, but simply an act of vengeance. The worst murderer, too, will have a chance to put forth any attenuating circumstance and may even appeal to the court's mercy. To deny these things is to resort newly to the lawlessness (and irrationality) of revenge and lynching.

The justification for the lawyer's "moral amorality" finds its ground, in a way, in a kind of objective logic that by spontaneous generation yields – at least in the long run, out of the sum total of the tiny amoralities of conduct at law – the morality of the administration of justice. This in roughly the same way as a market economy is said to operate, where the tiny (or great) sufferings of today will yield the happiness of tomorrow, or so we are told: the happiness of a time which cannot be pinned down with any precision, but which definitely projects into the future. But in this long run, as John Maynard Keynes commented caustically, we will all be dead and gone. Something along these lines can be said of the legal system as well: the legal system thrives on a myriad immoral acts that yield as such, not only an immediate and in no way future unhappiness, but also a concrete and permanent injustice.

There is a heavy holistic assumption involved in this argument of the spontaneous generation of morality out of a base of "immoralities." What is taken into consideration is the happiness or justice of the whole, the complete thing, or, as the Nazi Karl Larenz would complacently say, *des Ganzen*. <<Die Gemeinschaft ist alles, du bist nichts>> – one could read up on the walls of German cities from 1933 to 1945: The community is everything, you are nothing. But now, can a dictate of this kind be actually subscribed to? Can an everyman accept to be inflicted with a wrong in view of a future overall justice of "the whole"? And does not "the whole" lie also and especially in its constituent parts? The problem at issue here can be likened to that discussed by Ivan Karamazov: How can a child's suffering be justified teleologically? For instance, how can the torture that Josef Mengele inflicts upon a hapless Jewish child be justified by invoking the future safety of the human race? Nothing, says Karamazov, can compensate for that suffering, and no one is entitled to attempt any such compensation. It grates on our most deep-rooted moral intuitions to justify convicting an innocent, say, by invoking the future or even the present result of maximizing convictions of guilty people and acquittals of innocent ones. Recent justifications of torture adopt a similar teleological strategy, but fall foul of the unbearable pain inflicted.

There is another argument for the "moral amorality" thesis, this time based on the special status of professional ethics. Acting in a role and embodying the morality that comes with it, it is said, can cause one to deflect from common morality. And this is so because built into that role as such, in its objective and systemic operation, is a function designed to achieve an end of great moral import. The argument develops in four phases as follows.

In the first of these, a morally controversial or questionable practice, or even a clearly unacceptable one, is justified by reference to a certain role or profession. The practice at issue – and this is phase two of the argument – is then found to be necessary or appropriate for the role or profession referred to. In phase three, this role or profession is justified as internal to a given system: as functional to the adversary process in the Anglo-American legal system, or to the republican constitutional order in the strategy of Tarello. Lastly (phase four), the enveloping system is justified by making appeal to further functional necessities or to the normative purport of the whole system.

Now, this line of argument appears to fall back onto the holistic method just criticised, and is flawed so much the more that it sets up a wholesale, full-out contraposition between professional ethics and ordinary universal morality: there can be no skewing of any kind of a professional ethic from the background morality of all – much less any irremediable or intolerable contrast between the two – without the ethic ultimately having to lose its universalizability. A doctrine of rules of conduct that fails irremediably of universalizability cannot be considered a morality. Morality is possible by way of an ideal exchange of roles: we need to be able to exchange one role with another. But this is exactly what one tries to avoid at all costs with a morality of roles, for its point is precisely to make each role case-hardened and difficult to overcome.

There is also out there the idea by which professional ethics – because they lean on written codes and disciplinary bodies, and so become highly institutionalised – cannot be said to make up an autonomous normative system, or a critical morality, but can only be heteronomous and hence close to positive law. It was Professor MacCormick who advanced this thesis: <<Heteronomy is also a feature of professional ethics where that is delegated to professional corporations or their disciplinary tribunals or ethics committees for decisions in problem cases. Professional ethics so understood is also institutional, authoritative, and heteronomous>>.[53] A thesis of this kind will strip legal ethics of its moral status and suggest treating them according to the classic canons of legal positivism: a rigid distinction is effected between what these ethics "are" and what they "ought to be," such that this last question gets committed to moral philosophy and to the "politics of law" and denied any *vis directiva* (or directive force) on lawyerly conduct. In short, legal ethics are what they "are" because, like positive law, they are institutionalized and heteronomous; the ethical question is pushed outside this space – outside the compass of the ethics of profession – and into the critical morality that we all hold with independently of our social functions and of the duties we incur institutionally or in a given capacity. But the upshot of this view is not that the principles of professional ethics are made universalizable, hence highly normative, and hence open to moral discussion; on the contrary, as we see happen when positive law is viewed in the same way, legal ethics become isolated and made autonomous from morality. Of course what will be said here is not that lawyers cannot act morally, but only that if they wish to act in a professionally correct way they will have to comport themselves in accordance with the point of view of (universal) morality.

This way of accounting for professional ethics is, however, less than satisfactory. It is so at least insofar as lawyers, in this view, if on the one hand they must follow the professional code in force, they cannot, on the other, do so without interpreting this code in light of what is morally considered a good lawyer. And in fact, absent a written or accurate professional code (such was largely the case in Italy and other countries until only a few years ago), or given a gap in this "positive" code of professional conduct (the dramatic situation we are now facing in Italy, in a way), lawyers cannot be said to be in a position where they can fight shy of making any "non-positive" considerations on their professional conduct. Institutionalization may well be of support to lawyers deliberating on and seeking the guidance of their code of conduct, but it cannot replace any such code. In this sense, the function served by lawyers' codes of conduct cannot be said to be equal to that served by the legal positivist's positive law, and this is so even when such codes are institutionalized and to some extent brought under the judicial apparatus (as is the case in Italy, where all matters pertaining to the professional conduct of lawyers are decided on final hearing in the Court of Cassation, which takes on appeal the decisions made by the Consiglio Nazionale Forense).

The specific function served by professional codes comes through in the explicit connection they maintain with critical or normative morality: these codes are by their very nature interstitial, so to speak, in that they effect a liaison between the rules of positive law on the one hand (witness the penal norms setting out punishments for illicit conduct in the legal profession, such as infidelity to the client) and commonsense morality on the other. The meaning and use of professional codes lies in this very borderline territory, in those pockets of ambiguity where norms are silent or fail to apply, in such a way as to bring to light issues that the sense of justice or of morality relative to the function in question cannot ignore, for doing so would amount to welcoming effects incongruent with the same function or with the meaning (Wittgenstein would say the "Witz") of the institution serving that function. In the words of Roberto Mangabeira Unger, <<every thoughtful law student or lawyer has had the disquieting sense of being able to argue too well or too easily for too many conflicting solutions>>.[54] These feelings of uneasiness cannot go unanswered and it is here that that the deontology of professional codes becomes of service.

IV. 2. The "Full Morality" Thesis

The alternative to the "moral amorality" thesis is the thesis of the lawyer's "moral activism." We have a good example of it in the neo-natural law theory advanced by the so-called Sheffield school, whose leading exponents are Deryck Beyleveld and Roger Brownsword. Their natural law is not religiously inspired – it is rather laic from the ground up. This is not to say, however, that their doctrine is not exacting: it is more so in many ways than the Thomistic neo-natural law theory defended by John Finnis.[55] Thus, for example, while Finnis's seven higher values, the seven basic goods he singles out, are not susceptible to any ranking (all are equally basic), the Sheffield school views practical reason and moral judgment as subject to the operationalism of formal logic.

What is more, Beyleveld and Brownsword believe there is a logical foundation to the supreme moral principle, the Principle of Generic Consistency (PGC), under which every agent is a holder of generic rights, or rights to the satisfaction of needs necessary to individual human agency. I cannot expatiate now on this point or on the legal philosophy of Beyleveld and Brownsword.[56] Suffice it to say here that they argue the concept of right to issue from a real definition deducible from the PGC, the supreme principle of morality. The same holds for judicature – which therefore becomes instanter a moral notion and institution – as well as for the legal profession.

Thus, at this point we will need to look at the way these two British authors understand the trial. What makes up the essence of the trial, they argue, is the fact that the parties to a process for settling controversies are sincerely and earnestly intent on bringing forth a morally and legally correct decision for the case being heard.[57] It follows from this that the parties to a suit (and the lawyers representing them) are bound by the same professional code of intent the judge is bound by, which consists in aiming for a correct decision: <<Both Litigants and Legal Advocates must attempt to have the facts brought to light and to have the PGC correctly applied to the facts>>.[58] We can gain a better understanding of what these two authors mean here by looking at the examples they discuss of the shortcomings of trial procedure.

The trial comes short, for instance, if a party with access to certain pieces of evidence fails to produce such evidence in court, lest it should work against the case being made. So, too, the parties can lie by putting forward legal arguments whose invalidity they are intimately convinced of. Again, it may happen that the judge should make a ruling without being convinced of its moral justifiability. In all these cases the trial will prove flawed or inadequate, falling short of its goal. The trial, in this conception, is framed to bring out the common good, satisfying the collective interest in having a decision that is legally as well as morally correct. The single parties fade out of focus, as does the individual interest that each has in seeing the controversy find a certain solution.

The parties must therefore collaborate actively with the judge in finding the evidence necessary to establish the facts of the case truthfully as well as in working out the legal arguments most likely to lead to a correct decision. What is important is that this collaboration must not be adversarial, or such that it comes through by way of the parties' struggle to put out the most compelling evidence and arguments, each side advancing claims incompatible with the other. The lawyer is rather understood to be a kind of *amicus curiae*, a consultant to the judge rather than to a party: <<We conceive of a legal Advocate (an Advocate at Law) as one who through his advocacy and general involvement in the handling of the dispute attempts sincerely and seriously to promote a correct legal-moral determination of the matter>>.[59]

The gist of this argument is that the lawyer's code of conduct is basically the same as the judge's. But this is feeble help at best, for the argument collapses the lawyer's role into that of the judge – a conclusion that fails to take into account the phenomenological situation of the trial. The error incurred here is similar to that involved in the legal-positivist account of judicature, understood in this conception as proceeding essentially by the application of rules. So much so that Kelsen, for example, brings down to a minimum or even extinguishes the difference between the executive function (administration) and the judiciary. Beyleveld and Brownsword encounter a similar error: they, too, understand adjudication to consist in the application of a rule, only in this case the rule in question is the supreme moral principle, the PGC.

In this philosophical context – largely a Platonist one, with the notion of "essence" and the tool of the "real definition" plied almost obsessively – there is even the argument by which no true trial or adjudication can be said to have taken place in a controversy between A and B heard by a judge C if neither party (A or B) undertook to pursue the end of a legally (and morally) correct decision. Thus, if B is the defendant and lies in the course of the trial, or is guilty and yet pleads innocent, then we would have before us a perversion of the trial and hence something that "in essence" is not a trial.[60]

Now, this is patently contrary to the accused person's basic right to a defence – a right that takes in the right (famously stated in the Fifth Amendment to the United States Constitution) not to testify against oneself – and in addition makes it impossible to pass any judgment involving a "good guy" against a "bad guy," or someone "in the wrong" against someone "in the right," for what is asked of the "bad guy," or of the one who is in the wrong but does not admit to it, is to substantially adhere to a set of strict moral principles, such as requiring a commitment to the moral justness of the judge's decision. More than that, the thesis being defended clashes violently, I should say, with the subject's right to autonomy (which traditionally takes in the right of self-defence in case of danger or necessity). Yet this very right to autonomy is foundational to the extolled supreme moral principle, the PGC, a principle made to derive from the phenomenological situation of individual agency.

The problem here, often besetting the moral Platonist or objectivist, is an inability to think out ways to operationalize moral principles. The Platonist and the objectivist basically understand the application of these principles to flow of itself in some automatic fashion, bypassing the phase of subjective and intersubjective deliberation, certainly a critical and risky phase, but one that is necessary to the exercise of the moral point of view. The formalist legal positivist commits the same error by holding that legal norms find their own application and that the judge is merely a robot-like processor of norms, or at best is the law's mouthpiece (*bouche de la loi*). Natural-law theorists and legal positivists alike misconceive the nature of the trial's phenomenological situation. A trial is in the first instance a controversy (a conflict or dispute), whose resolution makes it necessary to resort to a third party – not a self-appointed intervener, but rather one whose intervention the litigants request. This investment of power comes by virtue of the nonpartisanship this person embodies, being extraneous to the conflict, a circumstance that makes it possible to be impartial, the first virtue required of the judge.[61] Here we can immediately perceive the reason why it is unacceptable that the lawyer be fashioned into a judge: lawyers are parties to the suits they argue. It is therefore a good thing that they are not also judges, lest they should judge their own causes: *nemo judex in re sua*. Any other arrangement would inevitably end up violating the principle of impartiality by which the judge's activity is to proceed.

We therefore find ourselves in a cleft stick, forced to choose between two alternatives. One is the deontological-code vision that hinges on the notion of a "moral amorality," by which the lawyer must identify with the party's interests unswervingly, even if these interests are illegitimate or lack moral justification. The other is a vision of the lawyer as a "moral activist" in the manner of the judge. Neither alternative is acceptable, or so I argue, because each presents us with a warped view of the judge's function: on the one hand the lawyer is made out to be a counsellor and unwavering partisan; on the other, a judge's auxiliary, a kind of official consultant. The lawyer, however, is neither a mere defender of private interests nor simply a law clerk. What now?

IV. 3. A Pragmatist Alternative and the Radbruch Formula

There is a different strategy that I believe can help us to arrive at a satisfactory account of the lawyer's deontological position. Namely, we can undertake to reconstruct analytically the history and practice of the legal profession. And we will immediately notice something very much worth going into. In common law and continental European law alike, the lawyer traditionally takes up either of two roles: on the one hand we have the attorney, in the sense of a legal agent representing the interests of a party, and on the other the trial lawyer. This duplicity is present in the English system, where the barrister pleads cases in open courts of law and the solicitor is more of an agent acting in someone's behalf and following their instructions; likewise in French law, where – up until 1971 at least – the *avocat*, on the one hand, and the *avoué*, on the other, discharged functions similar to the barrister's and the solicitor's respectively.[62]

This duplicity of roles is highly instructive, especially considerating that the barrister and the *avocat* generally have no direct contact with their clients, and that their service has never been juridically framed as a performance (a *prestazione d'opera* in Italian law) and hence, as the object of a contractual relationship. In a word, the lawyer is, in this capacity, independent above all from the client. And the principle underlying this independence is set out in almost every code of professional conduct presently in force: the ideal trial lawyer, far from looking to advance the client's particular interests, is rather concerned (and entrusted) with defending the rights the client has under the law. This principle importantly affects the lawyer's deontological code, in that the lawyer is asked to keep a certain distance from the client's interests and wishes, exercising as well a measure of neutrality or impartiality in this regard. Indeed, professional codes in Europe underscore that contingency fees are prohibited and that the lawyer must not act, in pleading a case, at the direction of the client. In other words, in Europe at least the lawyer is not a derivative person, whose duties fully flow from the clients.[63] The lawyer – as is said in article 7.5. of the Spanish Code – should never have a personal interest in the case.

So the way the lawyer acts in the client's best interest is indeed as a "friend," as Charles Fried argues.[64] But this friendship is the noble kind so excellently illustrated by Aristotle – a friendship that does not commit us to approve of our friends' behaviour indiscriminately, nor does it require us to second their every initiative.

> We are not able to see what we are from ourselves (and that we cannot do so is plain from the way in which we blame others without being aware that we do the same things ourselves) [...]; as then when we wish to see our own face, we do so by looking into the mirror, in the same way when we wish to know ourselves we can obtain that knowledge by looking at our friend. For the friend is, as we assert, a second self (*Magna Moralia*, 1213a 15–23).[65]

The lawyer-as-friend here acts as a mirror held up to the party so that this person may ponder over the preferences initially expressed and reconsider them.

"Lawyer – *conscience for rent*," says Dostoyevsky.[66] This statement, plainly framed to be an insult, can actually be reinterpreted as having some truth to it and as making at its core a deontological point, without being spiteful. The lawyer can be said to be a conscience for rent, not in the sense of a readiness – given any misdeed – to take that side and lay out a defence for it, but in the sense that the lawyer's function is to get each client to do some soul-searching and so reflect on the egocentric conscience on account of which the litigation was initiated in the first place. The lawyer's is a conscience that sides with the client's and helps it to grow sensitive to the claim to justice implicit in every legal action. For otherwise, the lawyer would be not so much a friend as a "broker", at least on the understanding of this figure that we get from Gerolamo Cardano: the broker as a purveyor of advice, as an intermediary and a business agent, as the kind of friend whose only connection with us is one of prudential calculus. Whether the ends we seek are right or wrong, this does not concern the broker. What matters is only the instrumental adequacy and efficacy of the means chosen to achieve purposes and life plans with which this person – unlike a true friend – is completely unconcerned. Cardano's broker will not hesitate to recommend corruption or intimidation to fix a trial or slink away from it: <<*In litibus, ab initio (si potes) conare excindere testes, corrumpendo et iudicem adversariumque leniendo vel deterrendo*>> (*Proxeneta*, CXII). But not everyone agrees that to fashion the lawyer into a broker is to smear the lawyer's name.[67] In his Brescia lectures on lawyering – a celebration proper of the legal profession – Giuseppe Zanardelli says of lawyers that they <<must never lose sight of the fact that their lodestar is justice, not utility and that this idea of justice will have to dominate without cease over the interests entrusted to them>>.[68]

And yet, if we ask a professional today what the lawyer's first virtue is, we will quite likely get in answer something along the lines of what would fill the lawyer so well depicted in Tolstoy's *Resurrection* with pride. The lawyer's virtue consists here in an ability to argue successfully an impossible case – a manifestly unfounded and unjust cause – against an adversary whose action, in contrast, is grounded on every good reason. A "good lawyer," in this sense, is one who can turn wrong into right and right into wrong, or rather can make it look so by effect of the ledgermain employed during trial. But if this were truly the lawyer's virtue, then a question would come naturally to mind: how can anyone hope to retain any integrity while making a living out of practices so repugnant?

We must not forget here that many professional codes require the lawyer to argue in good faith. Contrary to what the morally concerned theorists believe, this is not necessarily a requirement to apply a supreme moral rule, such as the PGC, but it does prohibit the lawyer – while defending someone's rights – from giving in to a temptation to "abuse the right".[69]

The lawyer-as-friend is a kind of personalization and activation of the classical idea of prudence and good judgment, generally depicted in iconography as a woman looking contentedly at herself in the mirror. In this sense the lawyer can arguably be said to be, not a party in litigation, but rather a mirror held up to this party, a "cooling-room" where each claim can find a sense of perspective, or a "legal sieve" in Lord Lawton's words,[70] indeed a *speculum rei.*[71] The lawyer is there to make it possible for the sober individual to make an appeal to the inebriated individual.

This deontological conception of the lawyer as a <<mirror held up to a litigant>> is not resistant to an operationalist analysis. We can understand this conception as an application to the legal profession of the "extreme injustice" thesis advanced by Gustav Radbruch.[72] As is known, Radbruch, after abandoning his initial legal positivism and ethical relativism, arrived at the view that a morally unjust law is a legally invalid one, too.[73] But then again, he never ceased to value the certainty of the law and therefore, was not saying that *every* unjust law is thereby invalid. For otherwise, a good measure of uncertainty would seep into the law. So what also comes to bear in this connection is the principle of inertia by which a State – here a positive law – is assumed to be legitimate until proven to the contrary. Only when a law is intolerably unjust is it, in this view, considered invalid.

Radbruch's formula can be applied to the lawyer's activity, too, if this activity is regarded as consisting in the application of rules, or as subject to compliance with such rules. In particular, this will be possible if we accept that legal discourse in general is subject to a transcendental claim to correctness. This is true of both the judge' and of the advocate's discourse, in so far as they adopt the participant's perspective before the law. Though – as Professor Alexy points out – <<at the centre of the participant's perspective stands the judge>>,[74] nevertheless participants refer to the judge as a kind of regulative ideal of their discursive strategy As a matter of fact their arguments should be able to be replicated in a judicial ruling. This is a point very much stressed by Alexy: <<When other participants – say, legal scholars, attorneys, or interested citizens – adduce arguments for or against certain contents of the legal system, they refer in the end to how a judge would have to decide if he wanted to decide correctly>>.[75] Dworkin's stress on the "one right answer" expresses a similar point in a slightly different way: the judicial process is oriented to "discover" parties' rights, not to "invent" them, whereby truth or correctness are a condition of its validity.

Once we acknowledge the fundamental unity of aim (or regulative ideal) of legal discourse in its variety of forms, Radbruch's formula will then be plausible even for zealous advocacy. Applied to the lawyer's conduct it will read as follows. *The lawyer is morally and legally legitimated, within the bounds of the law, to deploy in favour of a client arguments and tactics unconnected with justice (understood as a moral value), or even contrary to it, provided that the lawyer's actions do not eventuate in any injustice so gross as to prove intolerable.* Lawyers are restricted even inside the law in what they can legitimately do to further their clients' interests and satisfy their wishes. Otherwise, and with good reason, we would have to reiterate, "*Juristen, böse Christen.*"

Radbruch's formula however – it should be noted – can apply only if we discard a strict positivist concept of law according to which criteria of justice and strong normative criteria are not operative in the application of the law. Law is accessible to a descriptive attitute even in its internal operations – this is in the end the dogma and the defining feature of legal positivism. Here there will be no difference between the so-called inclusive and exclusive sorts of positivism. If they can differ about the admission of strong normative "entities" in the definition of the law, both should accept that the law is in principle applicable without recourse to those very normative elements. Now, this would contradict the Radbruch formula. It can therefore be integrated into an operative concept of law only through reference to a preliminary and foundational practice, which produces and re-produces the law. Such is the reference to the notion of a constitution.

Modern constitutionalism according to which the law is in essence a non-violent discursive practice, does indeed favour the advocates' strong inclusion within the practice leading to judicial decision making. Suppose the law is a fully autocratic enterprise, a set of commands backed by violence: adjudication in such a picture either is equivalent to the phenomenology of sheer power or is instrumental to it. In both cases advocacy would not expedite the commands' implementation; it would represent at least a halt in the process and might also introduce a counterweight however small. It is not just due to a question of taste that absolutist powers do not like advocates: <<ce tas de bavards, artisans of revolutions>>, <<this bunch of chatterboxes, craftsmen of revolution>> – as Napoléon famously called them. <<Je veux qu'on puisse couper la langue à un avocat qui s'en servirait contre le gouvernement>> – he added.[76] In any case, though without employing Napoleon's extreme measures, an autocratic system of law would resist giving lawyers a proper role in adjudicative procedures.

If, on the contrary, the law is argumentative in that it bases on the mutual recognition of citizens' rights, parties' dignity in the judicial process is the starting point of normative reasoning. But the defendant's dignity would diminished if this were to be levelled with the prudential, cost and benefits-oriented amoral position of Holmes' "bad man". A party in the judicial process claims to have (universalizable) rights, not just to promote her own (particular) interests. This is partly what Dworkin means by his "rights thesis", whereby the American jurisprudent defeats the positivist pretension of neutrality within the participant's perspective. From the internal point of view, from the standpoint of a participant, legal argumentation is a question of rights, which can immediately be translated into a claim to be right. <<A claim of right>> – says Dworkin – is <<a special [...] sort of judgment

about what is right or wrong>>.[77] A strong normative assumption of rightness here is inevitable. This is also connected to the fact that a rule of law régime and in particular the constitutional State, is a "community of principles". The "bad man" of the moral amorality perspective can hardly be acknowledged as a member of a principled scheme of cooperation.

Now, the advocate is the actor who makes it possible for that strong claim of rightness to be operative. Advocacy would guarantee the reflexivity of such a claim, its plausibility, which is constitutive for the adjudication's legitimacy. The claim to correctness or rightness, rendered explicit by the reference to having a right, should be able to be endorsed by other citizens through some reference to universalizability. A particular interest, however strong, could not serve this purpose. This is then the advocate's proper task: to act as *speculum rei*, to hold a mirror before the rights claimed in order to see reflected and endorsed the client's interests from an independent but nevertheless sympathetic, point of view. In this way the lawyer would aquire the status of a *constitutional* actor, on the same footing as the judge, in so far as she helps the judicial controversy to be considered a "principled" and thus a civic domain and not just an instrumentalist, parasitic procedure in a dark corner of the public sphere.

NOTES

1. M. Luther, *Tischreden*, ed. by K. Aland, Reclam, Stuttgart 1981, p. 205.
2. F. Bacon, *Essays*, Grant Richards, London 1904, p. 153.
3. M. Oakeshott, *On Human Conduct*, Clarendon, Oxford 1975, p. 300.
4. <<Die herrschende Idealvorstellung von Juristen ist die: Ein höher Staatsbeamter mit akademischer Ausbildung, sitzt er, bewaffnet bloß mit einer Denkmaschine, freilich einer der feinsten Art, in seiner Zelle>> (H. Kantorowicz, *Der Kampf um die Rechtswissenschaft*, Carl Winter, Heidelberg 1906, p. 1).
5. <<Immer ist es der Wille, der den Verstand am Gängelbande führt>> (H. Kantorowicz, *Der Kampf um die Rechtswissenschaft*, p. 22).
6. Kelsen therefore understands the difference between legislation and judicature to be one of quantity rather than of quality, of intensity or degree rather than of substance, for they simply mark two stages in the process by which law is produced (<<zwei Stufen des Rechtserzeugungsprozesses>>). What result from these processes are "general norms" in the case of legislation and "individual norms" in the case of judicature. See in this regard H. Kelsen, *Allgemeine Staatslehre*, Springer, Berlin 1925, pp. 231 ff.
7. See H. L. A. Hart, *Essays in Jurisprudence and Philosophy*, Clarendon, Oxford 1983, p. 7: <<Though the search for and use of principles underlying the law defers the moment, it cannot eliminate the need for judicial law-making, since in any hard case different principles supporting competing analogies may present themselves and the

judge will have to choose them, relying *like a conscientious legislator* on his sense of what is best and not on any already established order of priorities among principles already prescribed for him by the law>> (italics in original). See also H. L. A. Hart, *The Concept of Law*, Clarendon, Oxford 1961, p. 138 ff., and H. L. A. Hart, <<Positivism and the Separation of Law and Morals>>, in *Harvard Law Review*, Vol. 71, 1958, pp. 607 ff.

8. See R. Dworkin, *The Model of Rules*, now in R. Dworkin, *Taking Rights Seriously*, revised edition, Duckworth, London 1978, pp. 14 ff. For a critique of Hart's theory of judicial decision, see also R. Sartorius, <<The Justification of the Legal Decision>>, in *Ethics*, Vol. 78, 1968, pp. 171 ff.
9. This second view finds a radical exposition in the words of a legal positivist of the standing of Michel Troper. See his <<Constitutional Justice and Democracy>>, in *Cardozo Law Review*, Vol. 17, 1995, p. 284.
10. I. Kant, *Perpetual Peace: A Philosophical Sketch* (1795), Second Supplement, <<Secret Article for Perpetual Peace>>. I quote from I. Kant, *Zum Ewigen Frieden. Ein philosophischer Entwurf*, ed. by Th. Valentiner, Reclam, Suttgart1983, p. 51.
11. One might object to this point by quoting Dante: <<Videant nunc iuriste presumptuosi quantum infra sint ab illa specula rationis unde humana mens hec principia speculatur, et sileant secundum sensum legis consilium et iudicium exhibere contenti>> (*De Monarchia*, II, ix, 20).
12. Immanuel Kant, *Critique of Pure Reason*, a translation by Norman Kemp Smith.
13. See J. Cohen, <<Deliberation and Political Legitimacy>>, in *Deliberative Democracy: Essays on Reason and Politics*, edited by J. Bohman and W. Rehg, Harvard University Press, Cambridge, Mass. 1997, p. 69.
14. W. von Humboldt, *Ideen zu einem Versuch, die Grenzen der Wirksamkeit des Staats zu bestimmen*, Reclam, Stuttgart 1987, pp. 123–24.
15. See, for example, pronouncement no. 359, dated 22 July 1999, of the Italian Constitutional Court (in *Giurisprudenza costituzionale*, 1999, pp. 2770 ff.)
16. Tom Campbell, a scholar who defends an ethical interpretation of legal positivism, says that because it is a deontology of litigation we are looking at, <<we are concerned with professional standards which go beyond the legal minimum>> sanctioned by positive law (T. D. Campbell, *The Legal Theory of Ethical Positivism*, Dartmouth, Aldershot 1996, p. 103).
17. O. W. Holmes, <<The Path of Law>>, in *Harvard Law Review*, Vol. 10, 1897, p. 459.
18. <<The discrimination between when it will and when it ought to, is the discrimination between rules for counselors and rules for judges. The counselor's basic need is accurate prediction; the judge's is clear guidance as how to decide.>> (K. Llewellyn, *My Philosophy of Law*, now also published in part in *Lloyd's Introduction to Jurisprudence*, ed. by M. D. A. Freeman, 7th ed., London 2001, p. 837).
19. See D. Luban, <<The Bad Man and the Good Lawyer>>, in *The Path of Law and its Influence. The Legacy of Oliver Wendell Holmes, Jr.*, ed. by St. Burton, Cambridge University Press, Cambridge 2001.
20. Rex vs. Registrar of Greenwood County Court [1885], 15 QBD 54, 58 (Lord Brett).
21. The same proscription is found, tellingly enough, in treatises of moral theology: <<The lawyer will sin who should defend, or continue to defend, a cause that is unjust as to its propriety [...]. And so much the more if the lawyer negotiates a contingency fee (*quota parte litis*)>> (A. de Liguori, *Degli obblighi de' giudici, avvocati, accusatori e rei*, ed. by N. Fasullo, Sellerio, Palermo 1999, pp. 46–47).

22. F. Carrara, *Programma del corso di diritto criminale, Parte generale*, vol. 2, 11th ed., Cammelli, Florence 1924, p. 493.
23. *Ibid.*, p. 499.
24. *Ibid.*, italics in original.
25. This in A. T. Kronman, *The Lost Lawyer*, Harvard University Press, Cambridge, Mass. 1993. For a critique, cf. C. Silva Marques, <<Anthony Kronman on the Virtue of Practical Wisdom>>, in *Ratio Juris*, Vol. 15, 2002, pp. 328 ff.
26. On this, see E. Döhring, *Geschichte der deutschen Rechtspflege seit 1500*, Duncker & Humblot, Berlin 1953, and A. Weißler, *Geschichte der Rechtsanwaltschaft*, Frankfurt am Main 1967.
27. See M. R. Damaška, *The Faces of Justice and State Authority*, Yale University Press, New Haven, Conn. 1986.
28. *Ibid.*, p. 142.
29. *Ibid.*, p. 175.
30. For an introduction and overview of these studies and the theses they defend, see *The Good Lawyer: Lawyers' Roles and Lawyers' Ethics*, ed. by D. Luban, Rowman & Allanheld, Totowa, N.J. 1983; *Ethics in Practice: Lawyers' Roles, Responsibility, and Regulation*, ed. by D. Rhodes, Oxford University Press, Oxford 2000; and R. O'Dair, *Legal Ethics: Text and Materials*, Butterworths, London 2001.
31. G. Tarello, <<Due interventi in tema di deontologia>>, in *Materiali per una storia della cultura giuridica*, Vol. 12, 1982, pp. 215–216.
32. *Ibid.*, p. 209.
33. *Ibid.*, p. 210.
34. *Ibid.*, p. 213.
35. *Ibid.*, p. 214.
36. *Ibid.*, pp. 216–217.
37. *Ibid.*, p. 214.
38. *Ibid.*
39. A. Perez, *Norte de Principles*, Editorial Americalee, Buenos Aires 1945, p. 153.
40. V. Hugo, *Les miserables*, ed. by Y. Gohin, Vol. 2, Gallimard, Paris 1995, p. 32 and p. 754.
41. L. Lombardi Vallauri, *Corso di filosofia del diritto*, CEDAM, Padua 1981, p. 625.
42. *Ibid.*, p. 624.
43. *Ibid.*, p. 622.
44. *Ibid.*, p. 631.
45. Cf. G. Cosi, *Il giurista perduto*, Quaderni del "Notiziario Forense", Florence 1987, p. 136. See also Id., *La responsabilità del giurista. Etica e professione legale*, Giappichelli, Turin 1998.
46. L. Lombardi Vallauri, *Op. cit.*, p. 625.
47. *Ibid.*, p. 626.
48. *Ibid.*, italics added.
49. *Ibid.*
50. *Ibid.*, p. 627.
51. G. Cosi, *Il giurista perduto*, pp. 144 ff.
52. *Ibid.*, p. 151, underlining in original.
53. N. MacCormick, <<The Concept of Law and The Concept of Law>>, in *The Autonomy of Law. Essays on Legal Positivism*, ed. by R. P. George, Oxford University Press, Oxford 1996, pp. 170–171.

54. R. M. Unger, *The Critical Legal Studies Movement*, Harvard University Press, Cambridge, Mass. 1986, p. 8.
55. See his main work, *Natural Law and Natural Rights*, Oxford University Press, Oxford 1980.
56. More is said *infra*, in Appendix A.
57. See D. Beyleveld and R. Brownsword, *Law as Moral Judgment*, 2nd ed., Sheffield Academic Press, Sheffield 1996, p. 390.
58. *Ibid.*, p. 389.
59. *Ibid.*, p. 406.
60. *Ibid.*, p. 397.
61. Cf. W. Lucy, <<Adjudication>>, in *The Oxford Handbook of Jurisprudence and Philosophy of Law*, ed. by J. Coleman and S. Shapiro, Oxford University Press, Oxford 2002, pp. 206 ff.
62. Cf. K. Zweigert and H. Kotz, *An Introduction to Comparative Law*, 3rd rev. ed., English translation by T. Weir, Clarendon, Oxford 1998, pp. 124 ff., 191 ff.
63. For a possible difference with respect to the lawyer's duties in Europe and in the U.S.A., cf. L. S. Teny, <<An Introduction to the European Community's Legal Ethics Code. Part I: An Analysis of the CCBE Code of Conduct>>, in *Georgetown Journal of Legal Ethics*, Vol. 7, 1993, especially pp. 51 ff.
64. See C. Fried, *Right and Wrong*, Harvard University Press, Cambridge, Mass. 1978, chap. 7.
65. English translation by St. George Stock, in *The Works of Aristotle*, Vol. 9, ed. by W. D. Ross, Clarendon, Oxford 1925.
66. F. Dostoyevsky, *The Brothers Karamazov*, Book 5, Chap. 4.
67. See D. Pannick, *Advocates*, Oxford University Press, Oxford 1992, p. 8: <<Lord Esher declared in a judgment in 1889, counsel is not 'bound to degrade himself for the purpose of winning his client's case'>>.
68. G. Zanardelli, *L'avvocatura: Discorsi*, 9th reprint, Società editrice "Unitas", Milan 1920, p. 189.
69. On "abuse of a right", see M. La Torre and G. Zanetti, *Seminari di filosofia del diritto*, Rubbettino, Soveria Mannelli 2000, chap. 6.
70. Sajf Ali v. Sydney Mitchell & Co. [1978] QB 95, 105.
71. I treat this point in greater detail in *Il giudice, l'avvocato e il concetto di diritto*, Rubbettino, Soveria Mannelli 2002, chap. 2.
72. This idea was suggested to me in the course of a discussion with Professor Robert Alexy, to whom I am thankful.
73. G. Radbruch, <<Gesetzliches Unrecht und übergesetzliches Recht>>, in G. Radbruch, *Rechtsphilosophie*, ed. by R. Dreier and S. Paulson, Müller, Heidelberg 1999, p. 216; cf. R. Alexy, <<A Defense of Radbruch's Formula>>, in *Recrafting the Rule of Law: The Limits of Legal Order*, ed. by D. Dyzenhaus, Hart, Oxford 1999.
74. R. Alexy, *The Argument from Injustice. A Reply to Legal Positivism*, Transl. by S. L. Paulson and B. Litschewski Paulson, Clarendon, Oxford 2002, p. 25.
75. *Ibid.*
76. Cf. Y Ozanam, <<Histoire et avenir des avocats>>, in *Droit et déontologie de la profession d'avocat*, Presses universitaires de France, Paris 2002, p. 22.
77. R. Dworkin, *Taking Rights Seriously*, 2nd ed., Duckworth, London 1978, p. 139.

EPILOGUE

Advocacy as a central part of legal reasoning as well as adjudication and the resistence of legal ethics to any attempt to conceive the application of law as just a matter of enforcement of rules, show the inadequacy of the traditional positivistic concept of law. This is strongly linked with notions such as coercion, sanction, command and prescription. Now, the practice of legal argumentation reveals that there is much more in the law than those crude phenomena, and that behind the enforcement of rules we find as necessary conditions principles and ideal criteria of rightness and justice.

In particular, legal reasoning cannot do without referring to a highly idealized form of discourse where what counts and prevails is not the sheer force, or brute power, but *arguments*, or – if you like – the force and power of the best argument. Thus, unexpectedly the law, which is usually conceived and practiced in the crude form of command, discretion and sanction to be operative, should refer to a phenomenological situation, or to a normative condition, whose main trait is the absence of coercion and violence. It is now the *zwangloser Zwang*, the "uncoercive coercion"– to use Habermas' wording – of the last and best argument that replaces the physical or psychological compulsion produced by an imperative or a prescription. This surprising development is confirmed and strengthened by the contemporary evolution of constitutionalism. This is not so much a practice of self-limitation, a gag rule, of an intrinsically violent and somewhat intractable entity, the State, or political power, which graciously accepts being restrained by its own laws and commands. Nor is it a thumb rule for policy-oriented, or costs and benefits, instrumental and manipulative considerations.

Contemporary constitutionalism – as has been shown in the first chapter – is much more and much better than that. It is the idea that a political and legal order is a matter of societal self-production and that such a special productive moment is not an existential, romantic *fiat*, but rather a process of practical deliberation and mutual recognition and learning among citizens. This is why a distinguished German constitutional lawyer, Professor Häberle defines the constitution a "public process" (*öffentlicher Prozess*), and adds that a constitution <<lives on interpretation>>.[1] It is a concept and a practice based on the practice of citizens' participation.[2] A constitutional polity is an open community of interpreters, whose main virtue is the congruence, or co-originality, between law-giver and addressee of the law. This virtuous circle between production of the rule and its compliance implies however, a rejection of any form of hierarchical vision of the legal phenomenon as such. This should be conceived instead as an ongoing practice where discourses prevail over threats, and hope and projectuality takes the upper hand over fear. Legal positivism in this sense is indeed the legal philosophy of fear. But the ideal discourse to which, in particular within a constitutional setting, legal reasoning finally should refer, could not take place under a regime of fear. Trust and hope, trust in the sincerity of the addresser and hope in the good faith of the addressee, are among its foundational assumptions. This is why, before any further moral consideration, there is no place for torture in the law.

Legal ethics points out a similar conclusion – as I have tried to show in the third chapter. Legal reasoning likewise – this was the main point dealt with in the second chapter – could not escape the necessity of discourse and morality. So that law without some reference to the moral point of view becomes blind and in the end uninformative and therefore inapplicable. If the lawyer, as the advocate, is a central figure in the judicial process, a fact that legal positivism tends to obscure or neglect, and if advocacy cannot do without some legal ethics, there is at least a practical if not a conceptual connection between law and morality. We would not be able to practice law without taking into account some moral criteria, and consequently without entering into some kind of ethical consideration of the merits of the case at hand.

There is however a further implication of the centrality of advocacy and legal ethics within legal reasoning. This makes us a full circle and brings back to the issue of constitutionalism. The lawyer and advocate is a central figure in the legal process; this is hardly to be denied. The lawyer accordingly will be subject to many of the restrictions that are usually seen to invest judges' work in so far this is an actor in the procedure leading to an impartial ruling for the concrete case. In this context the virtue of independence, which we have seen is considered to be the core of several deontological codes, takes a special institutional relevance. If the advocate is an important part of the adjudicative process, she should then be accountable and subject to the constraints appropriate to that process. In particular, there is no reason not to apply to the advocate the principle of separation of powers, which guarantees, together with other devices, that adjudication will be impartial. The independence of the judge from both legislative and executive powers is a well established standard of modern constitutional States. Now, coherence and prudence would suggest to extend such a standard to advocates as well. These will be accordingly considered as a sort of constitutional "agencies" to whom hence, constitutional constraints fully apply. Advocates might even held – as has sometimes been proposed in the Italian jurisprudential debate – as a kind of "constitutional power": they will thus be addressed not only by constitutional restaints but also and equally by constitutional "empowerments".

In this way advocacy will no longer be subject to the disparaging strategies that not seldom governments (and judges) try to adopt to render the legal process smoother and functional to their purposes and policies. Advocates defend rights, not policies: this is their constitutional role. They are more than just "tools" or "instruments", or "auxiliaries" of the judicial decision. More dignity and further powers, however, will bring more accountability, and therefore explicit ethical responsibility. Constitutionalism and an explicit constitutionalization of the lawyers' role and status will thus involve that they give up the "bad man's" manipulative attitude and re-orient their activity from mere success to rightness, or in other words, from compulsion to discourse. Which is the road that I have recommended to the theories of the concept of law in this book.

NOTES

1. P. Häberle, V*erfassung as öffentlicher Prozess*, Duncker & Humblot, Berlin 1978, p. 83. Cf. J. A. Estévez Araujo, *La constitución como proceso y la desobediencia civil*, Trotta, Madrid 1994, pp. 80 ff.
2. See P. Häberle, V*erfassung as öffentlicher Prozess*, p. 156.

APPENDIX A

NATURAL LAW: "EXCLUSIVE" VERSUS "INCLUSIVE"

I. "EXCLUSIVENESS" AND "INCLUSIVENESS" IN LEGAL POSITIVISM AND NATURAL LAW

In this first appendix I would like to clarify the constitutional implications of discourse theory by comparing this approach to other non-positivistic concepts of law. This I will do by attempting an exercise in analogy. That is, I will try to use the recent distinction between an "exclusive" and an "inclusive" positivism to discuss the merits of natural law. I believe that we could usefully classify natural law doctrines as "exclusive" and "inclusive" too, and that such classification could shed some light on our discussion and, more generally, on the merits of natural law or non-positivistic, approaches.

"Exclusive" and "inclusive" positivism differentiate according to the respective attitude to the issue of relating law and morality. Both forms of positivism defend a separationist thesis and contrast the view of a necessary connection between law and morality. They however diverge in the way they conceptualize that relationship. "Exclusive" positivism believes that the law can be defined and assessed without ever referring to moral criteria. The "nature" of law as such rejects any connection with moral principles. This view is supported by two main arguments. One is the so-called "Social Thesis". Law is a product of special "sources"; these are social facts. To know the law, therefore, it is sufficient to refer to its "sources", to those social facts and to describe or to report about them. No strong normativity is involved in such an enterprise. Legal positivism is said to be "normatively inert".[1] A second argument is that legal interpretation or application is already given by the rule.[2] The rule determines its own meaning and its own instance of application. Legal interpretation is a grammatical exercise which – it is contended – does not require an explicit or implicit reflective attitude.

A further argument is that legal philosophy is detached from legal practice and from ordinary legal reasoning. While such reasoning can be imbued with moral principles and actually is a special kind of moral reasoning, this is not the case of legal theory or philosophy. The latter being a detached exercise, it cannot indulge in being too much involved or interested in practitioners' diatribes. These can very well be moral disputes, without however implying that they can be relevant for the nature of law. This is mainly given by the fact of its being enacted, or its being given validity. Reasoning about the law is only a subordinate and somehow parasitic exercise with respect to the assessment of the nature of law.

"Inclusive" positivism allows for the possibility of moral principles to be covered or included by the sources of law and especially by the ground rule of a legal system, the rule of recognition. This rule will no longer be only a set of "secondary rules", or rules ascribing powers, enabling rules, according to H. L. A. Hart's original understanding. Conceding to Ronald Dworkin's criticism, rules are no longer considered to exhaust legal ontology. Principles – as distinct from rules – could also be the content of a rule of recognition: they could but they should not.[3] This means that there might be indeed a relationship between morality and law. But since principles might also be lacking within a positive rule of recognition, the relationship between law and morality is far from being a conceptual or a necessary one. In any case for the "inclusive" positivist the law is ascertained through a rule of recognition, which is a social fact and such a social fact does not always comprise moral requirements and is not, as such, an instance of strong normativity. (The obligations stemming from the rule are not moral duties).

The difference between "exclusive" and "inclusive" positivism therefore is the following: the former excludes that positive law should refer for its determination to moral principles; the latter does not exclude such a possibility, so that to assess the contents of positive law, morality might be taken into account. For both views legal validity is a matter of "pedigree", of genealogy, of being derived from given "sources", not of justice. For "inclusive" positivism however, justice as a distinct feature might sometimes be embedded in the "pedigree" itself. In such cases a rule's legal validity could be somehow an outcome of the rules' moral merits.[4] For "exclusive" positivism on the contrary morality, being contingently absorbed by positive law sources, is not especially significant or visible. The validity criterion here will remain "pedigree" and moral merit will not transcend as a qualifying test.

II. "EXCLUSIVE" NATURAL LAW

II. 1. John Finnis' Neo-Natural Law

I believe we could apply the dichotomy "exclusive" vs. "inclusive" to natural law too. It is useful and instructive to distinguish two kinds of natural law theories. On the one hand, we have doctrines which defend that the validity of positive law can be ascertained through substantive moral criteria. A positive rule will thus be valid, law in the proper sense, only if its contents satisfy special material requirements set by natural law. The act of volition, the fact of deliberation, the social fact of legal positivity, are not considered a normative requirement for the existence and validity of law. On the other hand, there is a different view of natural law, according to which positive law has to play a special role in permitting moral principles to be articulated and validated through a collective and public enterprise.

This does not mean that "exclusive" natural law believes or asserts that it can do without positive law. Natural law usually is said to "precipitate" into positive law, which often has to add some determination to the very general principles embedded in natural law. The "position" of rules, their positive enactment, by a concrete legislator or law-maker is not ignored or excluded by natural law theories. What is excluded – at least in one of the two versions to which I would like to draw your attention – is the normative relevance of positive enactment. This may play the role of a condition of application of a natural law rule, but cannot enjoy the status of a condition of justification or validity of that rule. Rules, to be applicable in the imperfect and contingent world of human affairs, have to be made public and enforced by an authority endowed with the power to make the rule effective. This is why in some cases of natural law doctrines political authority is not thematized and is assumed uncritically as that instance which successfully holds sovereign powers. Consent by those subject to the power is not required. Authority does not need a special legitimacy beyond its being effective, that is, capable of enforcing its rulings and thus obtaining co-ordination of conduct. This is what John Finnis, who takes such an approach, suggestively calls a <<perhaps scandalously stark principle>>.[5] A similar stance – we might remember – is adopted by a philosopher who is, so to say, light years away from Finnis: Friedrich Jacob Fries, Hegel's opponent and a post-Kantian German scholar living at the beginning of the XIX century.[6]

For Fries too, as for Finnis, it is not particularly relevant whether political power is a matter of one person, of a few or of many. <<As the classics said – claims Finnis – the ruler may be one, or few, or many ('the multitude', 'the masses'). There are social circumstances where the rule of a very narrow, or a very wide, class will be best>>.[7] What really does matter is whether political power, whatever shape it might take, follows, or fails to follow, or violates, the supreme moral principle, Finnis' natural law, or Fries' "Rechtsgesetz", which can be ascertained and validated independently from any positive or public process of deliberation. This is what I would here propose to label *"exclusive natural law"*.

Now, my contention is that both the natural law heralded by John Finnis and the one defended by Deryck Beyleveld and Roger Brownsword are of this first kind. That is, they are both "exclusive".

"Exclusiveness" or "inclusiveness" here has much to do with the way that basic principles of morality are said to be known and with what degree of certainty these principles claim to attain. If we take the case of John Finnis's natural law, we are confronted with two main strategies. On the one side, while the assessment of law is accepted to be a matter of the internal point of view, that is, of those individuals using and applying legal rules, this point of view is screened through the reference to a central case, which already has an explicit moral content, the one taken by Aristotle's wise man, <<by the *spoudaios* (the mature man of practical reasonableness)>>.[8]

Moreover, Finnis makes an idiosyncratic use of Max Weber's notion of "ideal type". As is well known, according to Weber knowledge of social phenomena and institutions implies a prior conceptualization of those phenomena and institutions. According to the German sociologist, however, "ideal types" do not contain moral implications, nor are they comparable with Aristotelian or Platonic "essences", since they are fully conventional and claim only to be an epistemological device. The paradigmatic use of a central meaning, when dealing with a social phenomenon, does not refer to its moral merits. All social phenomena or institutions could be studied through a corresponding "ideal type". We may, thus, have an "ideal type" even for social phenomena or institutions, or situations, instantiating a case of gross injustice or perversion or corruption. For instance, in a Weberian perspective, when studying prostitution as a social phenomenon it would not be inappropriate, nor would it be sound indecent, to consider and speak of the "ideal type" of prostitution.[9] Or take the case of capitalism, or imperialism, or totalitarianism: in each of these contexts a Weberian political scientist might sensibly pose the question of the "ideal-typical" constellation of such power forms. Finnis, on the contrary, takes the Weberian "ideal type" out of its constructivist epistemology and its non-cognitivistic metaethics and gives it the status of a "focal case" as a model driven by an inner teleology that would aspire to some kind of flourishing or perfection. This approach – I am afraid – is a misunderstanding of Weber's neutral sociological method, making (social) knowledge suddenly dependent not only on epistemological assumptions and hermeneutical pre-understanding, but also and mainly on normative, moral requirements.[10]

According to Finnis – we have seen – the central case of law is the one where people with the internal point of view take a moral (or a "practically reasonable") stance. But here – I would like to stress – the claim of taking this stance will not suffice. Finnis indeed seeks to obtain a stricter requirement. <<The central case viewpoint itself – he says – is the viewpoint of those who not only appeal to practical reasonableness, but also *are* practically reasonable>>.[11] The central case of the internal point of view by which we only reach and see the real nature of law is not the one of people *just claiming* to be practically reasonable or wise but only of those who *are indeed* reasonable and wise.

On the other side, Finnis' natural law is rooted in the idea that we can intuitively, through practical reasonableness, identify as evident (seven) basic goods. Among these we found religion, but not freedom. These goods will then offer the normative foundation for further and specific moral requirements. Processing such requirements is a monological exercise and requires <<intensely active contemplation>>. <<Discourse is in the reason and the will of individual>>,[12] and leads to far from emaciated outcomes, such as, for instance, a woman (or a man) having sex outside marriage is equivalent to prostitution,[13] or that the death penalty might be morally admissible,[14] while abortion is abominable murder and contraception is evil.[15] Nonetheless, in spite of his "normative virility"[16] Finnis does recognize the necessity of a positive determination of natural law and his views on legal reasoning are much more positivistic than, say, those defended by Ronald Dworkin. <<Human law – he says – is artefact and artifice, and not a conclusion from moral premises>>[17]. It should not therefore be too surprising that according to Finnis' most faithful pupil, Robert P. George, the validity or legal binding force of natural law is fully exhausted through constitutional legislation. <<The natural law itself – says George – confers no authority on judges to go beyond the text, logic, structure or original understanding of the Constitution>>.[18] Finnis himself, indeed rejects the hermeneutical equivalence between esthetic and legal interpretation and insists on the conversational, intersubjective structure of legal understanding, such that the author's intention remains pivotal in the application of the rule. He thus stresses that juridical interpretation, differently from the historical one, will be much less inclined to label a concrete meaning as "unjust". In a sense he states a kind of presumption of justice for legislative acts.[19]

For Finnis there is no right answer in hard cases, since basic goods and fundamental moral principles are incommensurable. These could be weighed through arguments but not submitted to computation.

Incommensurability, however, is said to lead to the superiority of "reasons against" over "reasons for" and to negative "moral absolutes" (duties not to...), which would pass a universalizability test.

Incommensurability – Finnis believes – allows for a good amount of discretion as far as judicial decision is concerned. His criticism to Dworkin's coherentist strategy for legal reasoning (centering around the two criteria of "fit" and "justification") rests on the averment of incommensurabilty among values, that is, on the <<absence of any metric which could commensurate the different criteria>>. Dworkin's "integrity" accordingly is reshaped and played down as a moralizing recommendation in the context of a decisionist practice: <<bear in mind, conscientiously, all the relevant factors and *choose*>>.[20] Since for both the post-Thomist Finnis as for the post-Kantian Fries positive law and rules have no moral purport in their own right and are seen as a technique, simply as a tool to implement moral criteria, legal reasoning accordingly is a matter of technical expertise, a kind of engineering, a domain of "making" – says Finnis –, not of "doing".[21] Hence, he does not minimize the need for authoritative sources in lawyers' arguments.[22] Something as a relation of reciprocity between discretion and black-letter law is stated Legal reasoning thus for Finnis is quite different from moral reasoning, in so far as it does not need to indulge in moral considerations and especially in so far as it relies on a final act of decision. It is only after the decision has been taken and because it has been taken – he says – that that decision could now be presented and justified as the right answer. Nonetheless, both for the legislator and for the judge there are a few domains where discretion seems to be excluded. One of these domains eminently is sexual morality. Here natural law does not allow for too much *determinatio*. <<Unjust laws are not laws>>.[23]

Finnis' ideal political form thus is "limited government". This here should not be read as equivalent to liberal constitutionalism. It is rather a government whose range of action is not allowed to infringe upon (a few) moral absolutes. Such "absolutes" do not shape the institutional structure of government but only set limits to the agenda and issues that the government can freely legislate upon. Finnis' sovereign is not "absolute", at least in so far as this has to pay respect to some moral requirements. Such respect however, does not need to be operationalized through specific constitutional arrangements; and in principle it has not to be guaranteed through democratic accountability either. Here, at the end of the day, there would be nothing to protect constitutional rights but the *character* of those who hold supreme power.[24]

Suggestively, public reason in such a view, is not in principle hostile to "civil strife". When discussing John Rawls' notion of political liberalism and his criticism of fundamentalist "rational believers" who contend that their beliefs are <<so fundamental that to insure their being rightly settled justifies civil strife>>, Finnis finds such criticism "curious". He actually vindicates that some appeal to "civil strife" is endorsed by the "central tradition in philosophy".[25] Civil strife hence seems to be rehabilitated and considered an open option for a reasonable stance in the public domain. Finnis moreover argues that <<the use of reasonable force to rescue the unborn from their killers>>, which under present conditions would mean – he adds – launching a "civil war", might indeed be justified, if there were some prospect of winning the fight. He however estimates that <<that condition is not, in present circumstances, satisfied>>.[26] In this way the most we get is a "liberalism of fear", that is, a *modus vivendi* regime where one party refrains from coercively or violently enforcing a substantive moral view not because of endorsing toleration as a value, but just <<for fear of provoking a war>>.[27] Political liberalism or constitutionalism here might mean only a compromise *rebus sic stantibus*, the outcome of a contingent balance of ideological and societal forces.

II. 2. The Sheffield School and the Principle of Generic Consistency

My contention – as I have already indicated – is that Beyleveld's and Brownsword's natural law is "exclusive" too. This very much depends on the highly ambitious claims that their general approach raises about the possibility of deriving positive law more or less directly from strong substantive moral principles.

Beyleveld's and Brownsword's approach – as is well known – bases on a supreme normative requirement, the PGC, the so-called Principle of Generic Consistency, actually a notion proposed by Alan Gewirth in his seminal book *Reason and Morality*. According to the PGC one would be bound, whenever acting, to respect the generic rights of others, that is, their right to freedom or autonomy and their right to well-being. Now, following Gewirth, Beyleveld and Brownsword hold the PGC to be an *absolute* principle, in the sense of being supported by objective logical evidence. An agent, whatever agent, would contradict herself, if she tried to oppose the PGC – this is very briefly their thesis. The claim is not that the PGC is argumentatively plausible but that there is a logical proof for its truth. I cannot enter into a detailed discussion of the arguments used to assess the absolute logical foundation of such principle. Here, I will only refer to two main reasons for perplexity.

(i) First, a logical inference is still not a strong normative argument to uphold a substantive moral attitude. A logically sound argument might still be a grossly false one. A practice, and qualifications which are essentially contested (as is the case of morality), cannot be settled simply through logical operations. <<Logical reason and practical truth are *disparates*>> – remarked Hazlitt once.[28] A logical proof in this domain has indeed a limited impact.

It is in any case difficult to see how one could logically contradict oneself by not assuming certain moral criteria if one has not previously made any moral statement, or at least if one has not assumed a normative standpoint. Gewirth, Brownsword and Beyleveld found their "proof", the cornerstone of their entire system, not on a pragmatical contradiction – I would like to stress this point –, but on the purely *logical* contradiction, which they say would afflict any agent not endorsing the PGC. According to Gewirth <<the PGC and its entailed moral judgments are analytically true>>.[29] There could not be a stronger statement.

(ii) Second, the PGC is the outcome of a strictly monological reasoning, moving from an instrumental, prudential, that is amoral, if not immoral, approach to action, that one would like to reach an aim, whatever this might be. The hope is that <<prudential reason implies a deep structure of morality>>.[30] Indeed, there is not too much dialectics in the so-called "dialectically necessary method" vindicated by Gewirth, Beyleveld and Brownsword. This method is "dialectical" in so far as it is supposed to begin with statements made not by themselves (by the theorists), but by various interlocutors.[31] However, their method does not allow any special room or moment for opponents to be heard. The statements by which the "dialectically necessary method" starts are those of agents as represented by the theorist, not those which might be issued against agents by third parties or other people concerned. The monological strategy adopted by PGC defenders is quite patent in the following acknowledgment by Gewirth: <<My own argument proceeds not from what *other persons* may *demand* but rather from the *agent*'s having to accept, through universalization, that all other prospective agents *have* the generic rights>>.[32] The argument here is a fully *private* one. It is embedded in a "first person" standpoint, which to be overcome, to reach the "second person" perspective, has no better resource than again taking a "first person" stance.

The others, that is, any person beyond the agent in question, have no voice in the logical proof of the PGC. This exclusion – I believe – has fatal consequences. In particular, it contributes to making the logical proof a pragmatic failure, since it does not offer a compelling reason to give others the same normative position as the one taken by the agent for herself.[33] In such monological perspective there is no step where the agent might find a limitation to her own speculations and calculations originating from the outside world and especially from other selves. In short, in such an approach there is no need for the agent *to listen* to others. One might also add that a mere monological reason is not far from remaining a mystery to third parties.[34]

On the other side, since the construction of the basic principle of law bases on a purely monological exercise, this leads to a view of positive law as a more or less deductive operation or practice where public controversy and deliberation do not play a central role. Institutions are thus seen as either a piece of nature – which is then to be considered as a condition for the application of supreme principles – or just as a precipitation – as it were – of those principles. Their ontology is either that of brute facts, simple empiricity or that of higher normativity, of supreme principles. Society, here, has eventually disappeared. A downgrading of society we also encounter in Finnis' doctrine. Praxis ("doing") for him is only "existential" or "moral" but not cultural or societal. Culture and technique are classified under the label of "making", a lower sphere with regard to "doing". Language (words, poems) as well as ballistic missiles belong – he stresses – to the same domain: "making".[35]

It is quite telling that Beyleveld and Brownsword, whenever they try to define or conceptualize institutional settings or collective arrangements, constantly refer to individual virtues and morality. Adjudication thus is seen as the proper activity of the (good) judge. A judgment is nothing less than <<a ruling/decision handed down by someone who acts as a Judge>>.[36] Adjudication coincides with judicial morality and deontology much in the same vein as the rule of law equates with the supreme moral principle: <<Judgments can only be yielded when judicial role-morality is observed>>;[37] <<the Rule of Law quite simply *is* the Rule of the PGC>>.[38] Likewise, within Finnis' doctrine, if there is a rationale in positive law beyond coordination, this is not that a citizen should be obliged only by rules which she would have been herself able to discuss and agree to; it is to make it possible for judges to be impartial.

We will have law, constitution, legislation, adjudication, advocacy, etc., only if all these institutions can be assessed as an instantiation of the supreme moral principle. <<Only if the material constitution is actually morally legitimate under the PGC – we read in *Law as Moral Judgment* by Beyleveld and Brownsword – is there a legal constitution>>.[39] The fact of constitution, the fact of people gathering together and deciding about their social destiny and the sense of their communal life, their discussions and deliberations, all this does not have here an independent normative or moral relevance. <<The PGC – say Beyleveld and Brownsword – is the constitutional norm of any legal order>>.[40] Here law – to use a phrase by Finnis – <<purports to occupy the same place in the world as morality>>.[41]

As it happened within Finnis' doctrine, the fact that citizens give themselves their own rules is not a situation as such endowed with moral significance. Indeed, for Finnis that people rule themselves is an "ideological myth".[42] Authority is what matters. What is needed is only <<to recognize some persons as having the responsibility and thus the authority to change the answer to the question What truly should I do?>>.[43] Social regulation is mainly seen as <<patterning of behaviour contrary to particular-occurrent wishes>>.[44]

What is really significant is that the PGC be followed and applied, or in the case of Finnis' "classical" theory that the seven basic goods (which sometimes become eight by including Roman Catholic marriage[45]) be all realized. <<The PGC – say Beyleveld and Brownsword – can, in principle, resolve directly the problem of which behaviours are optional/obligatory/prohibited>>.[46] Therefore, in such a view the practice of law as a communal enterprise, as a special friendship, is instrumentalized to the main purpose of implementing the basic moral standard fixed outside that communal enterprise by an act of normative wisdom. Legal authority becomes "transparent" with regard to pre-legal morality.[47]

<<A legal order – say Beyleveld and Brownsword – is to be distinguished from an *attempted* legal order>>.[48] However, for practical purposes an "attempted" legal order can be treated – they concede – as a proper legal order, if it is able to gain moral legitimacy in terms of "agent moral rights". Since the law is defined as a rule that there is a moral right to give for attempted enforcement, it is fundamental to be clear when such moral right can be considered to hold. Beyleveld and Brownsword here distinguish between an "act" moral right and an "agent" moral right, while the former is defined in terms of achievement (the PGC being realized) and the latter signifies an attempt to realize the PGC. Although the PGC is primarily concerned with "act morality", that is, with its own achievements and Beyleveld and Brownsword<<define law in terms of act moral rights>>,[49] nevertheless, because of the controversiality of PGC interpretations and the many limitations of the human condition, practical authority (the exercise of agent moral rights) may suffice to give validity to legal rules. Now, the distinction between "act moral rights" and "agent moral rights", and

especially that other distinction between a "legal order" and an "attempted legal order" may somehow remind us of the tension between a claim to justice and a full statement of justice (tension which is – I assume – the very core of "inclusive" natural law). In a sense, we could thus say that Beyleveld and Brownsword at the end of the day take a perspective which is not too distant from the one assumed by Habermas and Alexy. Hence, we might conclude that the difference between the two views is simply a matter of stress or of methodology, the outcomes being more or less the same.

The problem, however, is that Beyleveld and Brownsword strongly moralize the distinction between "attempt" and "achievement", so that an "agent moral right" is said to hold only if there is a sincere, *good-faith effort* to apply the PGC on the part of the person positing the legal rule. The "attempt" in question is thus immediately and directly referred to a particular comprehensive moral doctrine. Alexy's and Habermas' reference to the claim of justice on the contrary operates without requiring an endorsement of specific moral criteria and without even a specific awareness of those criteria by the agent. The "claim to justice" here is the result of a "claim to correctness" embedded in the language itself, that is, in the pragmatic conditions of felicity of the social act carried on. Since the claim to correctness to be satisfied should apply for reasons and these have to be accepted by a universal audience, correctness here will lead to universalizability and this will bridge the gap with the notion of justice. <<With the assertoric sense of her statement – says Habermas – a speaker raises a criticizable claim to the validity of the asserted proposition [...] A justified truth claim should allow its proponent to defend it with reasons against the objections of possible opponents [...] With each truth claim, speakers and hearers transcend the provincial standards of a particular collectivity>>.[50]

A judge, even if in good faith, would fall in a performative contradiction if he happened to say "I condemn X to prison and this is unjust". And for someone to be able to communicate, he should be considered as claiming to be truthful, even he is in bad faith in that particular case. The attempt or "claim", *Anspruch* in German, here is not just an individual performance but a pragmatic and therefore *collective* assumption. Moreover, the "claim to justice" thesis does not immediately base on a particular moral theory, leaving open the way by which its own satisfaction should be assessed. Discourse theory does not need to explicitly moralize agents' behaviour in order to state a connection between social action and normative requirements. The discourse pragmatic conditions will suffice for the job.

III. "INCLUSIVE" NATURAL LAW. DISCOURSE THEORY

Opposed to "exclusive" natural law we find what I would propose to call its "inclusive" version. Its main feature is that the supreme moral principle justifying the legal enterprise is not found through a monological operation, but instead requires a common practice, interaction, *discourse*. Such a version of natural law is "inclusive" first of all because the "other", third persons, are immediately included in the process by which natural law, i.e., morality principles and more generally, criteria of correctness, are established and assessed. <<Because no one has direct access to uninterpreted conditions of validity, "validity" (*Gültigkeit*) – says Habermas – must be understood in epistemic terms as "validity (*Geltung*) proven for us">>,[51] proven, that is, in the debate between proponents and opponents. It is not enough to take on the others' point of view by an exercise of sympathy; one has to go a step further: not only have others' interests to be taken into account, but also and above all, their *voice*. This second version of natural law is then "inclusive" in an additional and perhaps even more important sense, that is, that for the validity of law to be assessed, positive law should be included as a source of validity itself. For the law is not only a device to give stability and effectiveness to the public debate about morality, but it is also in a sense, coextensive with that debate.

In this second kind of natural law the definition of law does not comprise a statement of the law being just but much more modestly and simply the claim that the law be just. Such a claim could be then proved to be unjustified without however, except for extreme cases, making the rule in question no longer valid. <<Below the threshold of extreme injustice – says Robert Alexy, whose theory I would propose as an exemplary version of "inclusive" natural law – the claim alone and not its satisfaction can establish a necessary connection between law and correct morality. To focus on the satisfaction of the claim is to say too much>>.[52]

What makes it possible to establish a necessary connection between law and morality is the claim to rightness and justice, which is said to be intrinsic in whatever legal practice is considered from the participant's perspective and only that claim. It is just this claim which shows that a law cannot conceive of itself as being flatly unjust. Said differently, every legal operation is done by raising a claim to correctness or justice. But it is one thing for a claim to be just, which refers to a later assessment and quite another for the positive statement of being just because of following or satisfying a material requirement or because of being supported by logical or intuitive evidence.

A law is a law only by virtue of a claim to justice and not because of stating it as positively being just. This is the main thesis of "inclusive" natural law. This is "inclusive" especially because it assumes positive law as a definitional condition for valid law. This is due to the fact that in order to satisfy the claim to justice we cannot do without positive law, without public deliberation as it is instantiated in constitutional and legal practice. As a consequence <<a violation of morality means not that the norm or decision in question forfeits legal character, in other words, is not law (a classifying connection) but rather, that the norm or decision in question is legally defective (a qualifying connection)>>.[53] This conclusion indeed is at variance with Roger Brownsword and Deryck Beyleveld's bold statement that <<no immoral rule should be regarded as a rule of law>>,[54] while on the contrary it is supported by Ronald Dworkin's use of the concept/conception distinction. As is well known, principles according to Dworkin are "concepts", general normative standards, which are still to be filled in by substantive doctrines and requirements ("conceptions"). Legal reasoning is hence seen by him as an argumentative search for the "conception"that best fits and justifies that particular "concept".

Now, my contention is – as I have already indicated – that a good example of "inclusive" natural law is offered by Robert Alexy's and Jürgen Habermas' discourse theory. Here first moral principles have a procedural gist, so that for them to become substantive there is the need to refer to a concrete practice of deliberation. In the public domain this will be the democratic production of rules through participation and representation. Positive law will here play a central role in so far as it is not thought of as just a device for applying moral rules but is raised rather to the status of a constitutive moment for the recognition and meaningfulness of those very rules.

Habermas develops his view of legal theory moving from the conjunction of two basic elements: (i) the principle of discourse referring to an ideal situation of communication and participation; (ii) what Habermas calls *Rechtsform*, "the form of law", which according to him implies individual rights. Habermas' concept of positive law thus is the outcome on the one side of a discoursive situation where people give themselves their rules, and on the other side of basic rights functionally given by the "legal form". Human rights and constitutional moment therefore are ascribed an equal normative dignity: they are "co-original".[55] In such a view the "form of law" is not to be "deduced" from the ideal discourse structure;[56] the "form of law's" contents could be made concrete only through a public and real exercise of the ideal discourse requirements. Moreover, the "form of law" here heavily relies on individual rights (*subjektiven Rechte*) which are not moralized: they are rights to do wrong too.[57]

According to discourse theory, democracy and constitutionalism are the way by which one reaches a conclusive public agreement on the first principles of correct morality and the basic common goods. These are not fully identifiable prior to the public deliberation of the people concerned. Moreover, their conclusiveness is not "absolute", though they are not relative to subjective moods or whims. They are open-ended and considered elements of justice until new, better arguments are possibly brought to the public fore. Their connection to the argumentative *status quo* make of such conclusions more claims to justice than absolutely just and true statements.

The notion of claim to justice here plays a twofold role. (i) It is a definitional character of law and legal practice, which opens up legal reasoning to moral reasoning and accordingly makes it possible to establish a necessary connection between law and morality. (ii) It is the epistemic status reached by substantive conclusions within public moral deliberation. This remains pivotal also for *private* moral deliberation, since this latter to proceed and avoid the trap of subjectivism and self-indulgence is called first to simulate, even *in foro interno*, a public discussion, and second, to bring its own outcomes to concrete intersubjective and public confrontation as soon as possible. Even for a Cartesian philosophy, morality cannot be authenticated solely through the inner operations of the self: a public moment is required from the outset. This has not necessarily to do with a communitarian celebration of positive or predominant social morality or with some kind of Devlinian rejection of critical morality as subversion of law and order.

From the perspective of discourse theory, public institutions acquire an independent ontological and normative dimension. They are no longer – as happens within "exclusive" natural law – derivations of basic normative requirements, nor could they be seen as merely brute facts. They are an independent, existential domain, characterized by two fundamental features and notions: communicative rationality and constitutive rules.

Moral requirements here have their sense only in a framework of social actions which is not an outcome of them. Categorical imperatives are mainly regulative rules, that is, rules prescribing a mode of conduct which is not logically dependent on the rules themselves. But a form of life, or a life in society, or, if you like, a flourishing human life could not develop following only regulative rules. These cannot give a special sense or ascribe meaning to fact, objects, or actions. A prohibition or a command could make sense only if you are already acting in a meaningful context of social conducts. This is possible, moreover, only through a rationality (and an anthropology) according to which the agent is not just a subject driven by her private needs, but a fellow, a partner, a lover, a citizen, in short a complete human being for whom sense prevails over pleasure.

The meaningfulness of commands and prescriptions is further possible only if there are rules by which new modes of conduct, i.e., *change*, may be brought about. This is why H. L. A. Hart introduces for developed legal systems further secondary rules, beyond the primary rules, which only impose obligations. In short, "disabling rules" are meaningful, only if there are "enabling rules" and not just categorical moral prescriptions, rules, that is, which "project" and "invent" kinds of communal life, or types of actions within a communal life. All this can never be drawn or inferred by whatever basic normative or moral principle. As a matter of fact, basic moral principles will take different shapes and colours, without however, being degraded to relative criteria, according to the concrete institutional setting in which fellows, partners, lovers, citizens, etc., will discuss, deliberate and act. From this perspective law thus will be a permanent, open-ended enterprise, without absolute certainties but also without too much risk of self-indulgence and radical subjectivism.

I am not sure whether the ontological implications I am speaking about are fully shared by Robert Alexy. I am not sure either that I am offering a faithful picture of Habermas' theory of society and anthropology. I am, however, quite convinced that discourse theory does indeed lead to the view of the social dimension I have just sketched.

IV. CRITICISM OF POSITIVE LAW AND COLLECTIVE LAW-MAKING

Which version of natural law, if any, do we prefer? The "exclusive" or the "inclusive"? A further contention of mine here is that we should favour the "inclusive" version. This is so – I believe – for two main reasons. (i) The first is that "inclusive" natural law can actually eschew one important objection usually raised against natural law in general. This objection is raised for instance by H. L. A. Hart. Commenting on John Finnis's defence of classical natural law, Hart stresses that <<it has to be elaborately explained how it is that famous phrases such as Aquinas's statement that "law is nothing else than an ordinance of reason for the

common good" is quite compatible with his statement that "laws framed by men are either just or unjust">>.[58]

Natural law theories – says Hart – are not able to articulate a criticism of positive law in a sensible way. Since those theories assume that valid law is equivalent to just law, their only possible attitude when they are confronted with unjust law, will be to deny it the very title or quality of "law". By this strategy however – argues Hart – it will be a flat contradiction to speak of an unjust law, so that any law will be automatically acknowledged the quality of justice. In this way criticism of law will become an impossible or paradoxical enterprise.[59] As a consequence, natural law will disrupt the critical attitude towards the law – which actually plays such an important role in the reform and the improvement of positive law. Natural law will work in the end as an ideology by which either the *status quo* of positive law is on the whole legitimated and even sometimes celebrated, or a "revolutionary", somewhat anarchist manifesto, by which positive law is doomed to be permanently unjust.

Now, "inclusive" natural law – as I said – eschews Hart's objection. Since it does not equate positive law with just law but only with a law raising some claim to justice, it will be possible on the one side to identify positive law without recurring to substantive moral criteria and even ascribe validity to rules whose justice might be controversial or disputable, while nevertheless subjecting the law and its rules to a strong normative judgment. Basing simply on the claim to justice standard, one will be able to address the question of the justice of positive law without however falling into a *petitio principii* or in a flat contradiction as it seems instead to be "exclusive" natural law's destiny. Alexy's and Habermas' discourse theory allows for such solution in so far as law's strong normativity, its own material principles, become evident and take substantive shape only in the process of public deliberation, that is, in the process of positive law production. Here the constitutional moment acquires a definitional and a strongly normative character.

(ii) This takes us to the second reason why "inclusive" natural law is to be preferred. "Exclusive" natural law does not grant special dignity to a positive constitution and legislation. The most it does is to re-conceptualize the constitution as a depository of the supreme moral principles, ignoring however the constitutional or foundational *moment*, that is, the fact that a constitution is a special process of self-definition and self-legislation of a community – which in this way constitutes itself. By "exclusive" natural law the constitution is reshaped in terms of mere "constitutionalism", and this is reinterpreted as a substantive rule of law, the rule of specific moral principles over communal life. In this way it is also sometimes related to a strong idea of judicial review, when courts or the judiciary are made to play the role of guardians of supreme moral principles. Judges – claim Beyleveld and Brownsword – are not bound <<to the *de facto* ground rules of the polity (whatever those ground rules)>>,[60] so that a constitutional court would be competent to review the very positive constitution.[61]

A kind of normative Platonism might be the final outcome of such an approach, a rule by "wise men", or by philosophers who have a privileged access to moral truth.[62] At other times this truth is even seen as so difficult to understand and to endure that it is recommended that it should not be extended. Philosophers will have to engage in gentle deception and rely on robust and handsome "gentlemen" for the implementation of their principles on a mass of people whom the philosophical wisdom could only spoil.[63]

"Inclusive" natural law – according to which moral truth is not a matter of philosophical knowledge but of public debate and deliberation – will not have any of such disquieting implications. Constitutionalism for "inclusive" natural law is much more than the rule of law and is strictly connected with the constitutional moment, seen as a special legislating process of a community in search of its own political identity. "Exclusive" natural law is tendentially "monarchical", if what is said to count about political regimes is that their laws should be just and not that they should be approved by those called upon to abide by them,[64] or else it is anarchical, when all citizens are given the status of philosopher kings who can ultimately act without consulting their fellows. On the contrary "inclusive" natural law is deeply "republican", in the sense that it bases on democracy as the regime most appropriate to the public deliberation and interaction, which are the gist of law.

Even if agents in a political community were all committed to the PGC or any other supreme moral principle, as citizens they would need a public situation to express their commitment. An institutional moment would be required, in which and by which they were able to meet, exchange their views, discuss the supreme moral principle, its interpretation and its range, reach an agreement, and commit themselves reciprocally and collectively to follow that agreement. Without such a public moment they simply *would not know* that they universally follow the same principle and that they commit themselves to do so. Even where all citizens are individually and personally committed to the supreme moral principle, the "external problem of authority" – to adopt a terminology used by Beyleveld and Brownsword – is yet to be solved. For this purpose the "dialectical necessity" of the PGC will not suffice, since, as we have seen, such necessity can only hold for the subject who states it. In fact, it is rooted in a first-person perspective, which does not ask for endorsement from the interlocutors' standpoint. Reciprocity and universalizability, as the possible agreement by all concerned, cannot be simply logically inferred from a monological and prudential attitude. By such an attitude one can hardly expect to justify authority or power to exercise over *others*, who are stuck for ever in a second-person standpoint. When the "external problem of authority" arises, and it inevitably arises when asking about the law to be followed, it cannot be dealt with simply by reference to the intrinsic, logical or "dialectical" necessity of any supreme moral principle. People concerned should in principle be able to pose questions and be answered, to raise claims and be satisfied, to agree but also and most basically, to disagree.

It is as if for this version of natural law there were only *the* man and the fact of the *plurality* of human beings were irrelevant. Indeed, "exclusive" natural law would claim to be valid even if there were only *one* man. It does not take seriously that – to say it with Hannah Arendt – while *the man* is God's creation, *men*, human beings in the plural, are a product of human beings themselves; men's (and women's) plurality is men's (and women's) business: that is, a matter of *politics*.[65] This is why politics is fully misunderstood by "exclusivist" natural lawyers, for it is conceived by them as a matter of technique and implementation or else of deductive reasoning. If the relevant category is *the man*, and not *men* in the plural, we might have rules directing the man's conduct without any discourse whatsoever and without any institutional deliberation. Should we however assume the plurality of human beings as a fundamental feature of the human condition and accordingly, of morality and law, we are no longer able to by-pass the question of human beings' participation in the enactment of common binding rules.

Following once more Hannah Arendt's view, we might also say that politics is a domain where judgments are not possibly given through a stringent deductive scheme. It is rather an area whose affairs are to be judged through "Utrteilskraft", the "faculty of judgment", which takes hold once one cannot dispose of pre-established or previously given premisses.[66] Now, if this is true or plausible, "exclusive" natural law, which mostly relies on and moves from strong evidences and intuitions, shows again to be inadequate to deal with public affairs and issues of politics.

V. RECONCILING "INCLUSIVE" AND "EXCLUSIVE" LEGAL POSITIVISM

I would now like to conclude with a small coda. Allow me, please, to indulge again in "exclusive" and "inclusive" legal positivism. I believe that the shortcomings shown by both approaches will bring a new and somewhat paradoxical argument to support "inclusive" natural law.

"Inclusive" positivism – we have seen – accepts that a law can include moral principles in its sources. This, however, is considered a matter of choice or contingency. There is no necessity for morality – "inclusive" positivists say – to be covered or incorporated by positive sources of law. In any case, since morality is introduced into the system of law only by a social fact, this will not alter the descriptive or neutral approach proper to positivism. The assessment of law remains strictly a matter of description, of theoretical statements.

The problem with the "inclusive" positivist strategy – one may object – is that it does not take principles seriously. Once principles are accepted to be part of the rule of recognition, of the source of law, since they are general standards and thus to be operative need to be stated precisely and to be balanced, citizens and lawyers will have to enter into a process of moral reasoning, if they want to give such principles a more determinate content. Legal reasoning, in the sense of assessment of a valid legal rule, will not suffice here. The assessment that such and such principles are contained in the rule of recognition will be only a preliminary step. At this stage we do not still know what precise contents these principles will take in relation to that specific case. To give a content to principles, however, we need to combine them, to weigh the one against the other, thus an exercise in moral argumentation. We will have to reconstruct the said principles within the theory that best justifies them. We will have to reproduce the arguments supporting them, trace back other relevant principles and build a more or less coherent scheme for the ruling. But if this is so, there will no longer be room for the thesis that law in general is a practice unrelated to morality and that its assessment is a purely theoretical account.

The "inclusive" positivist will then reply that even if the law is in general related to morality, this is a matter of contingency, depending on what the given "sources" of law say and allow. However, once moral principles are "received" among the sources of law, the account of law cannot be simply "theoretical": positivism as a neutral and descriptive methodology will cease to work. Moral principles as "concepts" to be assessed will need and refer to "conceptions", which are strong normative (moral) accounts. "Inclusive" positivism then will probably discover that it cannot afford to be positivist any longer.

If legal reasoning needs moral reasoning to be operative, there is indeed a necessary connection between law and morality. Now, "exclusive" legal positivism (in the version offered by Joseph Raz) acknowledges all that. Legal reasoning and moral reasoning are related the one to the other – Raz is quite positive on this point. One would then expect that he was going to develop a non-positivistic concept of law. Quite surprisingly, what happens is just the opposite. Raz maintains a stark positivistic approach. His contention is the following: legal reasoning is somehow necessarily intertwined with moral reasoning: <<Legal reasoning is an instance of moral reasoning>>.[67] But legal reasoning – he then adds – has nothing or very little to do with the law and its "nature"; which is mirrored not by legal reasoning as a whole but only from a special type of reasons used by lawyers and judges: <<authoritative positivist considerations>>. Accordingly, a theory of adjudication should be carefully distinguished from a theory of the nature of law. The former <<is a moral theory>>,[68] while the latter can be purely descriptive.[69] Raz believes that the "nature of law" is independent from legal practice, hence also from the internal point of view, that is, the point of view of judges, lawyers, other officials or citizens who use and apply the law. Or, said in a slightly different way, <<not all the norms of legal practice – the norms that apply to legal practitioners because they are legal practitioners – are legal norms>>.[70] In this way it is possible to defend once again that law (the "nature of law") and morality are two unconnected domains.

To justify his thesis Raz, however, has to pay a very high price: he has to repudiate Hart's methodological approach according to which law can only be understood from the internal point of view, the participant's stance, the one taken by legal practitioners and that the study of law has a hermeneutical foundation. <<There is something inherently implausible – he claims – in adopting the lawyer's perspective as our fundamental methodological stance>>.[71] The "exclusive" positivist, to persist on being positivist, has to assume a pre-Hartian programme, that is, at the end of the day, an external point of view likewise applicable to artifacts, brute facts, empirical regularities and inanimate objects.

But to identify a legal system as such and eventually to distinguish between different legal systems, and between a legal system and other normative systems, we need to refer to the legal reasoning of those actors who do use the rule of recognition. Viewed from the outside, from the external point of view, we could only observe regularities of conduct. Raz's "nature of law" would not permit an observer to assess what is valid law and what is not. Or else it might authorize the assessment of a system of law which, though corresponding to external regularities, would actually be non-existent, because it is unknown from the participant's viewpoint.[72]

Now, an "inclusive" natural lawyer would be able to fruitfully combine the most promising and plausible insights of both "inclusive" and "exclusive" positivism. From the "inclusive" positivist he would accept the insight that moral principles can play a role in the rule of recognition and in the definition of what a concrete positive law requires. From the "exclusive" positivist he would receive the view that legal reasoning necessarily refers to moral reasoning, its autonomy being limited.[73] Taken together, these two fundamental theses will amount to something very close to the approach that I have just proposed to label "inclusive" natural law. Institutionally, the two theses will be embodied in a constitutionalist order, where legal principles are explicitly drawn from public moral discourse and citizens' interpretation. We might thus conclude somewhat ironically that it is only through natural law (in its "inclusive" version) and *constitutionalism* (as an open community of interpreters) that we can perhaps succeed in reconciling "exclusive" and "inclusive" positivism.

NOTES

1. J. Gardner, <<Legal Positivism: 5 1/2 Myths>>, in *The American Journal of Jurisprudence*, Vol. 46, 2001, p. 202.
2. See for instance A. Marmor, *Interpretation and Legal Theory*, Oxford University Press, Oxford 1992, p. 153.
3. This is the main point made by Hart's *Postscript* attached to the second edition of *The Concept of Law* (Clarendon, Oxford 1994).
4. See for instance W. J. Waluchow, <<Charter Challenges: A Test Case for Theories of Law>>, in *Osgoode Hall Law Journal*, Vol. 29, 1991, pp. 183 ff.
5. J. Finnis, *Natural Law and Natural Rights*, Oxford University Press, Oxford 1980, p. 250.
6. Cf. for instance J. F. Fries, *Philosophische Rechtslehre* (1803), now in Id., *Sämtliche Schriften*, Vol. 9, ed. by G. König and L. Geldsetzer, Scientia Verlag, Aalen 1971, p. 105: <<Before the law it is indifferent who is the regulator, whether one or hundred, provided the law is in force thanks to him [*Vor Recht ist es gleich, wer der Regent sey, ob einer oder hunderte, genug, wenn durch ihn das Gesetz gilt*].
7. J. Finnis, *Natural Law and Natural Rights*, p. 252.
8. *Ibid.*, p. 15, and cf. D. Beyleveld and R. Brownsword, <<The Implications of Natural-Law Theory for the Sociology of Law>>, in *Post-Modern Law–Enlightenment, Revolution and the Death of Man*, ed. by A. Carthy, Edinburgh University Press, Edinburgh 1990, p. 144, where we find a parallel claim.

9. <<Es gibt Idealtypen von Bordellen so gut wie von Religionen>> (M. Weber, <<Die "Objektivität" sozialwissenschaftlicher und sozialpolitischer Erkenntnis>>, now in Id., *Gesammelte Aufsätze zur Wissenschaftlehre*, ed. by J. Winckelmann, Mohr, Tübingen 1988, p. 200).
10. Finnis' fallacious step from a causalist or functionalist explanation to a moral (or moralist) attitude is very well instantiated in the following statement: <<So the enquiry we are hypothesising, the enquiry about law, starts humbly enough as: Why *have* the sort of thing or things that get called the law and legal system, legal institutions, and processes and arrangements that we call the law of our time and town? "Why have it?" is of course elliptical for "Why, if at all, should we have it?" The enquiry is nakedly about whether and if so why I, the reflecting person doing the inquiring, should want there to be this sort of thing, and be willing to do what I can and should to support and comply with it (if I should)>>(J. Finnis, <<Law and What I Truly Should Decide>>, in *The American Journal of Jurisprudence*, Vol. 48, 2003, p. 108, italics in the text). Accordingly for Finnis the enquiry about the causal origins or the functions of a social institution like law could be, more or less immediately and without loss or alteration of meaning, translated into the question whether one, as a moral agent, has an obligation to obey the law. The interrogation "Why do we have law?", indeed a humble empirical or factual or sociological enquiry, would thus be equivalent to the question "Ought I to abide by the law", undoubtedly a supreme moral dilemma. If this equivalence were not an infringement of the is-ought methodological separation, there would hardly be occasions for a violation of the kind.
11. J. Finnis, *Natural Law and Natural Rights*, p. 15. Italics in the text.
12. J. Finnis, <<Natural Law and Ethics of Discourse>>, in *Ratio Juris*, Vol. 12, 1999, p. 364.
13. <<There is no important distinction in essential moral worthlessneess betweeen solitary masturbation, being sodomized as a prostitute, and being sodomized for the pleasure of it. Sexual acts cannot *in reality* be self-giving unless they are acts by which a man and a woman actualize and experience sexually the real giving of themselves to each other – in biological, affective and volitional union in mutual commitment, both open-ended and exclusive – which like Plato and Aristotle and most people we call marriage>>(J. Finnis, <<Law, Morality, and Sexual Orientation>>, in *Notre Dame Journal of Law, Ethics & Public Policy*, Vol. 9, 1995, pp. 29-30. Italics in the text).
14. <<The choice to kill someone as capital punishment can perhaps be made justifiably, because the action chosen immediately and in itself instantiates the good of justice and so the death of the one punished is not being used as a means to an ulterior end>>(J. Finnis, J. Boyle, and G. Grisez, *Nuclear Deterrence, Morality and Realism*, Oxford University Press, Oxford 1989, p. 317). See also J. Finnis, *Moral Absolutes. Tradition, Revision, and Truth*, The Catholic University of America Press, Washington D. C. 1991, p. 80: <<It seems possible to hold that, just insofar as the action chosen immediately and of itself instantiates the good of retributive justice, the death of the one punished is not being chosen either as an end in itself or as a means to an ulterior end>>.
15. See, for instance, G. Grisez, J. Boyle, J. Finnis, and W. E. May, <<"Every Marital Act Ought to Be Open to New Life": Toward a Clearer Understanding>>, in *The Thomist*, Vol. 52, 1988, pp. 365 ff.

16. Cf. J. Finnis, <<Law and What I Truly Should Decide>>, p. 121, and p. 125.
17. J. Finnis, <<The Truth in Legal Positivism>>, in *The Autonomy of Law. Essays on Legal Positivism*, ed. by R. P. George, Oxford University Press, Oxford 1996, p. 205.
18. R. P. George, *The Clash of Orthodoxies. Law, Religion, and Morality in Crisis*, ISI Books, Delaware 2001, p. 198.
19. See J. Finnis, <<The Priority of Persons>>, in *Oxford Essays in Jurisprudence*, 4th Series, ed. by J. Horder, Oxford University Press, Oxford 2002, pp. 12-13.
20. J. Finnis, <<On Reason and Autority in *Law's Empire*>>, in *Law and Philosophy*, Vol. 6, 1987, p. 344. Italics mine.
21. See J. Finnis, <<Natural Law and Legal Reasoning>>, in *Natural Law Theory. Contemporary Essays*, ed. by R. P. George, Oxford University Press, Oxford 1994, pp. 134 ff.
22. <<Such sources, so far as they are clear and respect the few absolute moral rights and duties, are to be respected as the only reasonable basis for judicial decision, in relation to those countless issues which do not directly involve those absolute rights and duties>>(*ibid.*, p. 151).
23. J. Finnis, <<Law and What I Truly Should Decide>>, p. 114.
24. For an interesting comment on such point, cf. H. Beecher Stowe, *Uncle Tom's Cabin or, Life Among the Lowly*, Penguin, London 1986, p. 619.
25. J. Finnis, <<Abortion, Natural Law, and Public Reason>>, in *Natural Law and Public Reason*, ed. by R. P. George and Ch. Wolfe, Georgetown University, Washington, D. C. 2000, p. 79.
26. *Ibid.*, p. 90.
27. *Ibid.*, p. 84.
28. W. Hazlitt, <<On Reason and Imagination>>, in Id., *On the Pleasure of Hating*, penguin, London 2004, p. 88. Italics in the text.
29. A. Gewirth, *Reason and Morality*, The University of Chicago Press, Chicago 1978, p. 175.
30. H. Palmer Olsen and S. Toddington, *Law in Its Own Right*, Hart, Oxford 1999, pp. 153-154.
31. See A. Gewirth, <<Foreword>>, in D. Beyleveld, *The Dialectical Necessity of Morality*, the University of Chicago Press, Chicago 1991, pp. viii-ix.
32. *Ibid.*, p. xvi, italics in the text.
33. Cf. N. MacCormick, <<Gewirth's Fallacy>>, in *Queen's Law Journal*, Vol. 9, 1984, pp. 345 ff. A similar point is made by R. M. Hare, <<Do Agents Have to Be Moralists?>>, in *Gewirth's Ethical Rationalism. Critical Essays with a Reply by Alan Gewirth*, ed. by E. Regis Jr., the University of Chicago Press, Chicago 1984, pp. 52 ff.
34. Indeed – we may remember Sieyès' words – reason does not love mistery; it works only through expansion. Reason is eminently public: <<La raison, d'ailleurs, n'aime point le mistère; elle n'agit que par une grande expansion; ce n'est qu'en frappant partout, qu'elle frappe juste>>(E. Sieyès, *Qu'est-ce que le Tiers Etat?*, Presses universitaires de France, Paris 1982, p. 92).
35. See J. Finnis, << Natural Law and Natural Reasoning>>, pp. 139-140.
36. D. Beyleveld and R. Brownsword, *Law as Moral Judgment*, 2nd ed., Sheffield University Press, Sheffield 1994, p. 403.
37. *Ibid.*
38. *Ibid.*, p. 440; italics in the text.
39. *Ibid.*, p. 290.

40. *Ibid.*, p. 162.
41. J. Finnis, <<Law and What I Truly Should Decide>>, p. 126.
42. J. Finnis, *Natural Law and Natural Rights*, p. 16.
43. J. Finnis, <<Law and What I Truly Should Decide>>, p. 128.
44. D. Beyleveld and R. Brownsword, *Law as Moral Judgment*, 2nd ed., p. 170.
45. See for instance R. P. George, *In Defence of Natural Law*, p. 139: <<marriage, considered not as a mere legal convention, but, rather, as a two-in-flesh communión of persons that is consummated and actualized by sexual acts of the reproductive type, is an intrinsic (or, in our parlance, 'basic') human good>>.
46. *Ibid.*, p. 179.
47. See H. Palmer Olsen and S. Toddington, *Law in Its Own Right*, p. 158.
48. Beyleveld and Brownsword, *Law as Moral Judgment*, p. 161; italics mine.
49. *Ibid.*
50. J. Habermas, *Between Facts and Norms*, trans. by W. Rehg, Polity Press, London 1998, p. 14.
51. *Ibid.*
52. R. Alexy, *The Argument From Injustice. A Reply to Legal Positivism*, trans. by S. L. Paulson and B. Litschewski Paulson, Oxford University Press, Oxford 2002, p. 79.
53. *Ibid.*
54. J. N. Adams and R. Brownsword, *Understanding Law*, 2nd ed., Sweet & Maxwell, London 1999, p. 19.
55. See J. Habermas, *Facts and Norms*, Chapter 3.
56. <<Die Rechtsform als solche ist diskurstheoretisch unableitbar [The legal form as such is undeducible through a discourse theory approach]>>(K. Günther, <<Diskurstheorie des Rechts oder liberales Naturrecht in diskurstheoretischem Gewande?>>, in *Kritische Justiz*, Vol. 27, 1994, p. 478).
57. See K. Günther, *ibid.*
58. H. L. A. Hart, *Essays in Jurisprudence and Legal Philosophy*, Oxford University Press, Oxford 1983, pp. 11-12.
59. <<The moral criticism of law, he [Hart] thought, requires a clear and morally neutral way of identifying what the law is that carries no presumption of moral authority>>(Th. Nagel, <<The Central Questions>>, in *London Review of Books*, 3 February 2005, p. 13).
60. D. Beyleveld and R. Brownsword, *Law as Moral Judgment*, 2nd ed., p. 312.
61. See *ibid.*, p. 311.
62. Cf., for some inclination in this direction, R. P. George and Ch. Wolfe, <<Natural Law and Public Reason>>, in *Natural Law and Public Reason*, ed. by R. P. George and Ch. Wolfe, p. 56: <<Not all persons are equally competent to deliberate carefully when it comes to the most difficult matters. Some matters, as Aquinas suggested, are evident (or, indeed, self-evident) "only to the wise">>.
63. This seems to be Leo Strauss' position. See, for instance, his *Liberalism Ancient and Modern*, Basic Books, New York 1968, Chapter Two, or his *What Is Political Philosophy and Other Studies*, The University of Chicago Press, Chicago 1988, pp. 221-222, and cf. A. Bloom, *The Closing of American Mind*, Simon and Schuster, New York 1987, p. 279: <<So philosophers engaged in a gentle art of deception [...] Therefore philosophers allied themselves with the gentlemen, making themselves useful to them, never quite revealing themselves to them, strenghtening their gentleness and openness by reforming their education>>.

64. Cf. R. P. George, *The Clash of Orthodoxies*, p. 198.
65. See H. Arendt, *Was ist Politik?*, ed. by U. Ludz, Piper, München 1993, pp. 9 ff.
66. See *ibid.*, pp. 20 ff.
67. J. Raz, *Ethics in the Public Domain*, Oxford University Press, Oxford 1994, p. 341.
68. *Ibid.*, p. 209.
69. Put in Thomas Nagel's words, <<the process of judicial deliberation may include moral reasoning; the process of discovering what the law is does not>>(Th. Nagel, <<Raz on Liberty and Law>>, in Id., *Concealement and Exposure and Other Essays*, Oxford University Press, Oxford 2002, p. 139).
70. This is the view held by another "exclusive" positivist, John Gardner, in his <<The Legality of Law>>, in *Ratio Juris*, Vol. 17, 2004, p. 178.
71. J. Raz, *Ethics in the Public Domain*, p. 203.
72. This difficulty was pointed out by Raz himself in one of his previous works: see his *Practical Reason and Norms*, 2nd ed., Princeton University Press, Princeton, N. J. 1990, pp. 125-126.
73. Cf. J. Gardner, <<The Legality of Law>>, p. 178: <<Legal arguments [...] often need moral premisses whether or not the legal norms themselves authorise such a resort to moral premises>>.

APPENDIX B

ROBERT ALEXY'S CONSTITUTIONAL RIGHTS THEORY

I. PRELIMINARY

The main contention of this book has been that a discourse theory approach to legal reasoning, that is, focusing on and stressing, the relevance of reasoning and interpretation in the legal esperience would lead to an alternative concept of law. In particular, a discourse theoretical approach would point towards two directions that are somehow interconnected. On the other side, it would lead the way to the acknowledgment of a clear relationship between law and morality, thus opening the gate to the theory of virtues and deontology into the specific legal domain. Professional ethics in this way should be considered an integral part of the legal practice. On the other side, a principled and reasoned practice could no longer be congruent with the usual traditional instrumental notion of law in terms of command or prescription.

Now my point here is that my assumption – that of a strong link between discourse theory approach and a not-prescriptive concept of law – is confirmed by the study of the doctrine of fundamental rights by the most distinguished legal scholar who has adopted a discoursive approach: Robert Alexy. Alexy's rights theory suffers – I believe – under some strains, which are the result of a faulty conceptualization of the link between legal practice as argumentation and the very idea of what law is. That is, Alexy, though adopting a view of legal practice and of law in general as intrinsically principled and argumentative, does not draw the final conclusion from such an assumption. He sticks to a command instrumentalist concept of law, thus bringing about a set of tensions inside his own theory.

I do not intend of course to propose a theory of fundamental rights alternative to the masterly one outlined by Robert Alexy. Nor would I like to present the existing alternative conceptions of constitutional rights possibly based on some version of discourse theory. My intention in this appendix is more modest. I propose to make and discuss a list of points within Alexy's theory which may be exposed to plausible criticism, though I do not necessarily share all the critical objections presented here. These however – I believe – will finally point out the unresolved question of the concept of law within his theory.

II. THE SEMANTIC APPROACH

Doubts can be raised on the semantic notion of norm adopted *expressis verbis* by Alexy and shaped along the three deontic operators of order, prohibition and permission. <<Eine Norm ist [...] die Bedeutung eines Normsatzes>> – we read in *Theorie der Grundrechte*.[1] The first line of attack against such a view is that a purely semantic concept of a norm cannot account for rules such a as the rule of recognition, which is defined through its being embedded in a practice. And without such a rule we are not able to give the law the form of a legal order or system and to introduce and use the idea of a hierarchy of norms, which is, however, absolutely relevant in the concept of *Grundrechtsnorm*, of a "fundamental right norm" so central to Alexy's reconstruction of constitutional rights. A mere presupposed Fundamental Norm *à la* Kelsen, the famous *Grundnorm*,[2] will not do, since such norm is "presupposed", that is, in Kelsen's strategy, fictitious, a mere epistemological device. It is only by giving to the ground rule the meaning of a rule "abstracted" from a practice, in the sense, for instance, of Leonard Nelson's "Abstraktion",[3] and therefore in a sense somewhat close to the one given by Hart to his "rule of recognition", whose assessment <<can only be an external statement of fact>>,[4] that that ground rule can be conceived as a valid and effective norm – since it is the existing practice, and not mere semantical content, from which it draws its "point". So that the latter can be a matter of "trascendental" or inductive knowledge.

There is a command – says Gadamer – only where there is someone called upon to obey it.[5] That is, a command is not just a logical form or a semantic structure but is embedded in a relationship between subjects, in a practice common to them. The same holds – we might say – as far a rule is concerned. We have a rule only where we find people willing to abide by it and use it to explain and justify a conduct.

Moreover, a mere semantic notion does not explain the constitutive effects of special fundamental rules, for instance of constitutional rules, and their pragmatic character. Such a notion indeed is easily exposed to a strong metaphysical jump into normative Platonism, or normative realism, that is the assumption of deontic modalities as entities in the world (such is the outcome for instance of Kalinowsky's legal theory and somehow of Weinberger' use of Popper's "World Three" to explain the "ideal" side of norms). This has also be shown in the recent post-Hartian discussion stemming from the question of legal determinacy. A solution to such a question has been seen in proposing a semantical notion of the norm as reflecting the reality of the world, which however leads to two highly controversial theses: (a) that of meaning as corresponding to, or a picture of, states of affairs or essences in the world and further, (b) that of moral realism, that is the assumption of normative, moral things or "entities" in the world. It thus seems that a semantic theory of norms, to give them an acceptable degree of determinacy, should again embrace an essentialist approach towards language.

A semantic notion of a norm, furthermore, implies a semantic theory of rights. As a matter of fact, this implication is drawn by Alexy himself.[6] Now, this semantic theory of rights is strongly criticized by Jürgen Habermas.[7] It cannot, he says, take account of two fundamental aspects of rights: (i) first, of their pragmatic character of *claims to be right*; (ii) second, of the situation of reciprocity and mutual recognition in which rights were born and embedded. The triadic relationship around which Alexy, following Hohfeld,[8] reconstruct the position of a right, is only the representation of a situation of subordination of one party to another where no claim of correctness is raised or raisable. Hohfeld's rights (though paradigmatically "claims") do not imply any claim to be right. Which actually is the point tackled by Dworkin's "rights thesis", according to which holding or claiming a right and accordingly, denying a right, cannot be fully understood if *having a right* is not also explained in terms of *being right*. Denying a right means therefore not only damaging the individual's interests but also and above all, diminishing his moral status, by implying that he *is wrong*.

The very notion of a *Grundrechtsnorm* may be questioned, that is, one can attack the idea that fundamental rights conceptually derive from norms or prescriptions. Actually, this is one of the most controversial points of Alexy's theory with regard to the liberal notion of rights, which is openly or overtly played against the notion of a rule. The history of legal positivism can be told as a permanent attempt to tame the idea of rights and to reconduct them into the more convenient context of a norm; however, such attempts are not always convincing and their rationale is not free of strong normative and political implications.

Be that as may, is not Alexy's theory in this regard a trifle too predetermined through the doctrine held by the German Federal Constitutional Court? It is true that Alexy presents his theory as an exercise in the dogmatics of German law; however, his ambitions are clearly much stronger and in any case, his theory of law is oriented towards a *universal* configuration of fundamental legal concepts. So the question remains: does not such a theory mean an unsafe *general* reductionism of right to command? Where is, in this regard, the substantial difference between John Austin denying rights an independent legal conceptual status, and then subscribing to the conclusion that constitutional law as such is just an extra-legal enterprise, and Robert Alexy, who on the one hand prefers to speak of fundamental rights norms, and then on the other shapes fundamental rights as "commands" of optimization?

But what is a *Grundrechtsnorm*? It is – says Alexy – a norm that is correctly *grundrechtlich* founded, that is, founded through valid fundamental rights. It is explicitly affirmed that <<Grundrechtsnormen alle die Normen sind, für die eine korrekte grundrechtliche Begründung möglich ist>>.[9] However, it seems that according to Alexy *Grundrechtsnormen* are a more fundamental concept than *Grundrechte*. In fact, according to him, whenever we have a *Grundrecht*, there must be a corresponding *Grundrechtsnorm*. The opposite does not hold: there may well be *Grundrechtsnormen* without corresponding *Grundrechte*. If this is so, the question arises as to what exactly a *grundrechtliche Begründung* is and what role it plays in the production and recognition of a *Grundrechtsnorm*. Is a *grundrechtliche Begründung* a justification through fundamental rights or through fundamental rights norms? In either case, Alexy's definition of a *Grundrechtsnorm* as an entity given through a *grundrechtliche Begründung* seems to be circular.

III. PRINCIPLES VERSUS RULES

A very common line of attack is the one launched against the idea that principles and rules are two fundamentally diverse or different normative entities. This line is adopted by Hart in his *Postscript*. <<There is no reason – writes Hart – why a legal system should not recognize that a valid rule determines a result in cases to which is applicable, except where another rule, judged to be more important, is also applicable to the same case. So a rule defeated in competition with a more important rule in a given case may, like a principle, survive to determine the outcome in other cases where it is judged to be more important than another competing rule>>.[10] The point is raised against Dworkin, but it applies as well to Alexy's view – though, as we know, the latter does not distinguish between "rights" and "policies", a distinction central to Dworkin's philosophy. In particular, once we conceive principles as goals (optimization commands), which is the road taken by Alexy, the fact that rules as well as rights can be interpreted as establishing and prescribing goals (as is shown by the widely used teleological criterion for statutory interpretation), the difference between principles and rules becomes indeed thin enough.

Or, alternatively, why could we not for instance adopt Marcus Singer's view of the difference between rules and principles? <<Moral rules – he says – do not hold in all circumstances; they are not invariant; in a useful legal phrase, they are "deafeasible". A moral principle, however, states that a certain kind of action (or, in some cases, a certain kind of rule) is always wrong (or obligatory) and does not leave open the possibility of justifying an action of that kind. Moral principles hold in all circumstances and allow of no exceptions; they are invariant with respect to every moral situation. They are thus "indefeasible">>.[11] Following Marcus Singer, we might thus say that, while rules are defeasible, principles are not. In this view, principles are therefore submitted to *a greater deontological discipline* than rules.

Another point exposed to criticism is the idea that *Grundrechtsnormen* are fundamental principles. Why could they not be fundamental rules? And why should principles be conceived as hierarchically superior to rules? In Alexy's reconstruction rules offer a better protection to rights than principles. If this is so, why should we not put rules at the bottom of the system (giving stronger protection to individual freedoms) instead of principles (actually unable to guarantee freedoms in a conclusive way)?

To this question is linked the central idea of Alexy's theory, that of principles as "optimization commands". Here again – I believe – we are confronted with a reductionist (imperativistic) strategy: principles at the end of the day are made to collapse into mere command or precepts. Another objection is that principles so conceived are no longer distinguished *from policies*, and that they in any case by so doing lose their deontological character. This is in a sense recognized by Alexy himself, when he equates principles to "values", and adds that the distinction principles/rules, in the sense of *prima facie* and definitive commands, applies to values as well: <<Der Strukturunterschied zwischen Regeln und Prinzipien findet sich also auch auf der axiologischen Ebene. Den Prinzipien entsprechen die Bewertungskriterien, den Regeln die Bewertungsregeln>>.[12] However, Alexy's reply is prompt. Principles are deontological practical concepts (assuming Von Wright's terminology proposed in his *The Logic of Preference*), and optimization commands are just...commands, that is deontological entities. Now, this argument to me is not convincing.

First of all, if principles were expressing a "Sollen", were "gesollten", if thus their content were apt to be expressed through a deontic operator, deontic logic would then apply to them. In such a case, however, their application would obey an "all-or-nothing" logic, not a gradualistic argumentation leading to *Abwägung*. But there might be – I believe – a further objection. You might remember that the minimum content of natural law, its bedrock (as it were), was traditionally seen as embodied in two precepts: *malum vitandum, bonum faciendum*. This at least is Aquinas' view. Now, the question arises as to what kind of precepts these two are. Are "*malum vitandum*" and "*bonum faciendum*" possibly optimization *commands*? If you say they are, and then you add that therefore they are deontological rules, should we then forget that they are clearly expressions of a teleological morality where values and virtues are more central and relevant than rules and obligations?

Let us take another example. Let us take the principle that lies at the basis of utilitarianist moral doctrine. This – as everybody knows – is the pursuit of "the greatest happiness of the greatest number". This principle can be reformulated as the "command" that the greatest happyness of the greatest number be realized or pursued. Is the adding of the imperative form sufficient to transform a utilitarian criterion into a deontological one? Should we then say that the utilitarian principle is an expression of a deontological doctrine or that it has deontological content? Is it not rather possible that a precept as such, or better that the imperative linguistic form as such, be not yet capable of producing a deontic obligation distinct from a teleological or a consequentialist one?

On this issue – as is well known – Habermas is strongly critical of Alexy's programme. In particular, the German philosopher stresses two points. On the one side, he is very keen to point out that justice is not just a value among other values. <<Werte konkurrieren stets mit anderen Werten. Sie sagen, welche Güter bestimmte Personen und Kollektive unter bestimmten Umständen erstreben und vorziehen. Nur aus deren Perspektive können Werte vorübergehend in eine transitive Ordnung gebracht werden. Während also Werte relative Geltung beanspruchen, stellt die Gerechtigkeit einer absoluten Geltungsanspruch: moralische Gebote beanspruchen Geltung für alle und jeden>>.[13] Values are agent-relative and can be provisionally measured and traded-off from the agent's perspective and only from this. Such is not the case of justice, which is a value claiming "absolute", universal validity, that is, validity for all. Habermas' point here thus is that values are particularistic, while justice is universalistic. It is true – he adds – that legal norms are addressed to a concrete community of members. However, through their claim to correctness, which is the result of their pragmatic nature, legal norms transcend the concrete political community and somehow refer to an ideal discourse. Such an ideal discourse is not values-based, is not grounded on individual preferences, but is rather embedded in deontological requirements.

Habermas' second point is that principles, as well as rules, are not teleological devices, that is, are not optimization commands. <<Prinzipien haben ebensowenig wie Regeln eine teleologische Struktur. Sie dürfen nicht – wie es die "Güterabwägung" in der üblichen Methodenlehre nahelegt – als Optimierungsgebote verstanden werden, weil damit ihr deontologischen Geltungssinn verloren ginge>>.[14]

IV. BALANCING AND RATIONALITY

The following controversial point that I would like to point out is that fundamental rights according to Alexy are applied, exercised, or implemented through balancing, *Abwägung*. This idea deserves special scrutiny.

Balancing is again related to the discussed conceptualization of rights in terms of principles as a notion sharply distinguished from rules. The idea of rights applicable through weighing depends on the thesis that fundamental rights are ascribed through principles, and that principles are applicable only through *weighing* – an idea which is shared, as is well known, by Ronald Dworkin. Now, balancing or weighing – this is the objection – is at the end of the day a procedure consigned to judicial discretion, since it cannot be given a fully formal and rational structure. Alexy believes to solve this problem through the so-called *Kollisionsgesetz*, whose non-technical formulation reads as follows: <<Die Bedingungen, unter denen das eine Prinzip dem anderen vorgeht, bilden den Tatbestand einer Regel, die die Rechtsfolge des vorgehenden Prinzips anspricht>>.[15] Alexy's *Kollisionsgesetz*, by which from principles we can pass to definitive rules, however, is no guarantee, since the relevance of principles and the configuration of the conditions of priority of one principle over another are shaped by judiciary discretion. The *Kollisionsgesetz* gives only an appearance of rationality to a procedure which is in the end irrational and at its core decisionist.

In this respect, a further interesting objection is advanced by Habermas. The question with balancing is also that parties in a legal dispute claim each to be right and fully right and thus take the ideal stance of the one only right answer. Now, Alexy excludes – contrary to what is held by Dworkin – the ideal necessity of one such answer, though he recognizes that in easy cases it could be reached. However, there is another implication of the claim to justice raised by parties and of their presupposition of the one right answer (which is, in Dworkin's theory, the substantive core of his "rights thesis"): such an implication concerning the way a case is decided before a court. Balancing, which strikes a kind of compromise, seems to deny that parties' claim to rightness. <<Eine an Prinzipien orientierte Rechtsprechung hat darüber zu befinden, welcher Anspruch und welche Handlung in einem gegebenen Konflikt rechtens ist – und nich über die Ausbalancierung von Gütern und über die Relationierung von Werten>>.[16]

A very important criticism is the one then raised against the idea that fundamental rights can be balanced against collective goods (meant as non-distributive entities). The question here is that by so doing we are confronted with a strong re-introduction of consequentialist and utilitarian considerations in the assessment of rights. In particular, in a perspective of this kind no rights could resist a utilitarian reasoning. Rights will no longer be "trumps" (to use Dworkin's expression) against policies, and there will be no "absolute" rights whatever. Torture would thus be eventually "grundrechtlich" justified. Such a conclusion might suffice – I believe – to make Alexy's theory unpalatable to a staunch liberal.

A further critical point very much connected with the latest one is the assumption of the notion of *Wesensgehaltsgarantie* (*Grundgesetz*, article 19, section II) as equivalent to the proportionality principle. That is, the essential core of rights is to be assessed through the principle of proportionality and in the end to be considered as embedded in such principles. <<Die Wesensgehaltsgarantie des Art. 19 Abs. 2 GG. formuliert gegenüber dem Verhältnismäßigkeitsgrundsatz keine zusätzliche Schranke der Einschränkbarkeit von Grundrechte>>.[17] The consequence has already been announced: *there are no absolute rights*. <<Die Überzeugung, daß es Rechte gibt, die auch unter den extremsten Umständen nicht zuruckweichen – nur solche Rechte sind genuin absolute Rechte –, mag der einzelne, der die Freiheit hat, sich für bestimmte Grundsätze zu opfern, für sich für verbindlich halten, vom Standpunkt des Verfassungsrechts aus kann sie nicht gelten>>.[18]

Now, here the question is whether a fundamental right's fundamental task is not just to be there, that is, to protect individual autonomy and dignity, especially "under the most extreme conditions" – to use Alexy's words. Is not the function of a right to physical integrity and to dignity, of the right not to be tortured, to act as an "absolute", intangible right just for the most extreme conditions of a terrorist menace or of an impending civil war? As a matter of fact, fundamental rights apply not in normal conditions, when people recognize or ignore each other, but especially whenever there is a special occurence that endangers the peaceful co-existence of individuals. If we deny an absolute core to individual rights, what is then left of them?

Elsewhere Alexy, replying to the accusation of irrationality launched against his equivalence between *Wesensgehaltgarantie* and the proportionality principle, has connected the notion of proportionality to the intensity of their attack brought against the right. He does introduces a "disproportionality rule", which reads as follows: <<An interference with a constitutional right is disproportional if it is not justified by the fact that the omission of this interference would give rise to an interference with another principle (or with the same principle with respect to other persons or in other respects), provided that this latter interference is at least as intensive as the first one>>.[19] Here, nevertheless, Alexy does not face the fundamental problem raising from his treating rights and principles as a common unity of measure, especially given that principles are not distinct from policies. Policies and fundamental rights can thus be legitimately be introduced in a same structure of reasoning leading to a decision concerning fundamental rights: rights can be weighed and measured against policies, and the latter can overwhelm the former if the omission of the policy in question would bring about an interference with another policy which is more intensive than the interference against the principle upholding the fundamental right in question. <<Constitutional rights gain overproportionally in strength as the intensity of interferences increase. There exists someting like a centre of resistance>>.[20] However, this resistance is not "absolute" against policies. It is in the end a matter of intensity, a value indeed, which moreover allows for an intense judicial discretion. And such resistance is not absolute and really effective, because according to Alexy fundamental rights themselves are in the end conceived as policies.

If fundamental rights are seen as policies, they will however lose their point, which is the controlling and the limitation of State action. On the contrary fundamental rights shaped as optimization commands – prescriptions for positive, not omissive attitudes – would contribute to a further expansion of State powers in the social domain. One might reply to this objection by pointing out that fundamental rights are not only of the liberal kind (*Abwehrrechte*), but that there are several very relevant fundamental rights which consist of political and social rights, asking for positive action by the State. However, even after accepting such objections, a disquieting problem remains, that is, that *negative* fundamental rights too will then be conceived as claims for positive State intervention, which is by necessity tendentially expansive. Optimizing does not imply a conduct whose precinct will not expand.

And the limits of optimization – if there are some – are never stable and can always be enlarged.

Robert Alexy has recently very much elaborated on the notion of *discretion*, following a two-fold project. On the one hand he has articulated principles in two classes (i) formal and (ii) substantive and has specified the content and the shape of legislative discretion through a further distinction between (a) *structural* and (b) *epistemic* discretion. On the other hand he has introduced a "Weight Formula" based on a triadic scale, rendering it easier for constitutional adjudication to avoid a possible decisionist slippery slope.[21] However, with all these refinements, the essential critical points – that of the ascription of a common, particular, quantifiable value to all variables considered and especially that of weighing as trade-off and prudential compromise – are not really tackled.

V. A RIGHT AS POSSIBLE OUGHT

I would like to devote special attention to Alexy's three-stage theory of individual rights and his notion of a right as "mögliches Sollen". According to such a theory in conceptualizing a right we should carefully distinguish three different dimensions: (i) justification; (ii) legal position and relation; and (iii) enforcement. In this way we would be able – this is Alexy's contention – to solve the perennial controversies on the nature and range of rights. These controversies – Alexy believes – are the outcome, in fact, of a confusion of these three distinct dimensions. For instance, Windscheid's will theory would be better understood as a doctrine of the legal position dimension of rights, Ihreing's interest theory would rather offer a justification basis for them, while Kelsen's claim theory would focus on the enforcement dimension. Now, such a solution, though interesting, is not fully convincing. In particular, unconvincing is – I believe – Alexy's distinction between (i) a dimension of justification and (ii) a dimension of legal position and relation, at least as far the traditional doctrinal controversy on rights is concerned. The dispute between "will theories" and "interest theories" is not really a meaningless dispute originating from methodological confusion. In fact, it can be seen both as (a) a dispute about justification (indeed, will, autonomy, sometimes is produced as a justification for having rights) and (b) as a dispute on legal positions: interest theories usually stress more the passive element of entitlements' ascription than the active one of claim and are more willing to see as rights holders even individuals with a reduced autonomy or with no autonomy at all. Paradigmatical in this regard is the controversy about childrens' rights, which interest theories tend to affirm without additional qualifications, while will theories are embarassed to cope with.

The second highly controversial point is – I believe – the ideal of "possible or potential ought", which according to Alexy should serve to explain individual rights as powers and competences. Alexy distinguishes rights into three categories: (i) "Rechte auf etwas", (ii) "Freiheiten", and (iii) "Kompetenzen". Accordingly, a negative right against the State, an *Abwehrrecht*, the traditional type of liberal right, is according to Alexy a bundle of three kinds: right to something, liberty, power or competence. Now, according to Alexy individual rights, whatever their form, are grounded on the traditional deontic modalities, that is, commands, prohibitions, and permissions. To such reduction the right as competence or power is more resistent than the other two kinds. Then Alexy's ingenious way out is the following. A power in his view would be the possibility at a meta-level of commanding, prohibiting, or permitting. To this configuration nonetheless, one may object there there is a fourth possibility, as far as legal powers are concerned, that is, the possibility at a meta-level not only of commands, prohibitions and permissions, but of legal powers as well. Why should powers be banned from the meta-level? A (legal) power indeed may consist in ascribing a legal power, that is a power on or of power, a (legal) meta-power. That means, however, that its content would not be a traditional deontic modality. The contingent fact that the ascribed (second order) power may in its turn have as contents a command, a prohibition or a permission, is not sufficient to explain the contents of the first order power in terms of one or more deontic modalities. In any case, Alexy elsewhere admits <<the relation between a right and its subject matter is not a relation of identity>>.[22]

Alexy's explanation of individual rights in terms of traditional deontic modalities recall various legal positivistic attempts to conceptualize rights as obligations or duties and conceiving rules competence in terms of rules of conduct. Such are Alf Ross' attempts to reduce rights to "presentation techniques" of legal norms and conceiving norms of competence as "fragments of norms". Alf Ross, however, to justify his views, should finally deny that a (strong) permission, an explicit permission, is an independent deontic modality (as it was on the contrary defended by Von Wright). Ross, in the end, proposed that even (strong) permissions are to be conceived as simple negations of a command. Command here is the only pure deontic operator, the alpha and the omega of the whole of law and practical domain. Ross was therefore only consequent in defending his reductionist strategy, since according to him there held the assumption of "the unity of ought", which meant that there is one and only one supreme deontic modality, *command*. Now, the postulate of the *unity of ought* is warmly defended by Robert Alexy in terms which are identical to Ross' view. In the case of Ross it was then only a matter of course that such an authoritarian view (the centrality or the fundamentality of command), I dare call it, a real obsession, could not tolerate an independent notion of rights – which, as Vilhelm Lundstedt (another legal realist) proposed, should rather be mentioned in inverted commas.

Now, coming back to Alexy's notion of "mögliches Sollen", how should we interpret this idea? "Possible" or "potential" might be conceived in analogy to the "possibility" modality of modal logic. However, this would have as a consequence the denial of the normative character of legal powers – which for sure is not what Alexy intends to do. "Possible ought" in modal terms is equivalent to the statement "it is possible that ought", or, said differently, "it is possible that ought takes place". However, such a phrase would be trivial, since for an ought to hold or take place or be meaningful, the said ought has not to be "necessary". But if "it is not necessary that ought", then "it is possible that ought". In this sense whatever ought is a "possible ought".

If the "possibility" in question is not the modal possibility, we then have two other ways out. (i) Either "mögliches Sollen" is the deontic possible, that is, a permission, or (ii) it is a power, a competence – which is clearly not a permission. But this second way out is exactly what Alexy seems to avoid. What is left is the first way out: "mögliches Sollen" is a permission. However, if it is a permission it is not a competence or power – according to the same Alexy, who carefully distinguishes between the two positions. Moreover, Alexy in his *Theorie der Grundrechte* denies that rules of competence are equivalent to rules of conduct. Now, a permission is the modality of a rule of conduct and we have to say that if we reduce powers to permissions, we would accordingly agree that there is no rule of conduct distinct from a rule of competence and that competences are fully equivalent to permissions. An outcome, it seems, that Alexy might not be happy with.

To Alexy's (and Ross') search for the unity of ought one could reply by recalling Hart's criticism against the "fragments of norms" thesis, according to which rules *prima facie* not imposing duties, e.g., rules of competence or rule ascribing powers, would just set conditions for the holding of rules imposing duties and could thus be considered as internal to the latter rules' formal structure. Such a thesis – argues Hart – would amount to say <<that all the rules of a game are "really" directions to the umpire and the scorer>>.[23] But this would <<distort the ways in which these are spoken of, thought of, and actually used in social life>>.[24] According to the "fragments of norms" thesis, defended among others by Alf Ross, the rules of a game would not be anything but "orders" or "prescriptions" issued to the person in charge as scorer or umpire. In a similar way the constitutional rules of a country would be the only assumptions needed for the judge to inflict sanctions. In this way, however, the "puzzled man",[25] who is the subject around whom the normative experience centres, being the rules devices to orient the disorented, would see his being "puzzled" brought to extremes.

VI. JUSTIFICATION AND APPLICATION

A further possible weak point in Alexy's powerful theory is that application of law (and rights) is ruled by the same criteria required for the justification of rules (and rights). However, one could believe that the discourse of application, which should give account of the factual features of a case and of its specificity, is different from the discourse of justification assessing the validity of the final ruling. What we need in reasoning about legal facts – it has been argued – is not balancing, but coherence, or "integrity". Integrity, however, does not assume rights as optimization precepts, and coherence is sought between strong deontological criteria which exclude policies. Such seems Ronald Dworkin's strategy, later adopted by Klaus Günther and Jürgen Habermas.

Disputable is also the view that legal positivism is inclusive or rather that positivism, being necessarily inclusive (as Alexy seems to hold), it should at the end of the day be rejected (which is Alexy' contention). Indeed, we might assume that (moral) principles are included in the rule of recognition, and in this way are transformed in positivistic prescriptions. This is Hart's strategy (especially unfolded in his *Postscript* to the *Concept of Law*) in opposing Dworkin's attack and such strategy might be be also damaging as far as Alexy's idealism (the connection thesis in the dispute around the relationship between law and morality) is concerned. By their inclusion in the rule of recognition principles are legally recognizable and applicable in terms of pedigree criteria. Reference to principles accordingly, would not imply that legal argumentation should jump into moral reasoning and much less that it should be successfully justified through a substantive moral theory – both claims being raised by Alexy.

Nonetheless, should legal reasoning be doomed to be translated into moral reasoning, there is no conceptual need to connect a theory of the nature of law with a theory of legal reasoning. We can conceive the first enterprise as fully neutral and descriptive, while defending a moral and political picture of legal reasoning. This is Joseph Raz' line ("exclusive positivism") and seems to be echoed by Hart as well.

A further point concerns Alexy's discursive foundation of human rights. Only through discourse theory – one can object – we are not able to transform discursive requirements into action or conduct requirements. Alexy's three-step strategy – moving from (i) a claim to correctness to (ii) a claim to justifiability to eventually land at (iii) a claim to justice[26] – fails, since discourses are not the whole of human experience (human beings unfortunately are not fully discursive beings). Somehow connected with this objection is Eugenio Bulygin's criticism of the pragmatic assumption of a claim to correcteness embedded in legal discourse, based on contesting the meaningfulness of the idea of "normative necessity".[27]

We could add that in particular rights (as claims) cannot offer the bedrock for morality whose main task is just the control over and the limitation of, our claims and rights. "Rechthaberei", "self-righteousness", is not a moral attitude – just the opposite. The same objection could be and has been, directed against all "rights-based" theories of morality and especially against those rights theories which centre around the notion of "autonomy" and "agency".

There is a final issue to consider, which can serve as a conclusion and a coda for this appendix. When considering Alexy's views one faces – I believe – a strange incongruence between a general philosophy based on discourse and language (its Habermasian roots) and a strong insistence on a prescriptivist, behaviourist jurisprudence (centring around Alf Ross' reductionist strategies). Said in different terms, there is on the one side a development of a pragmatic, post- or anti-positivistic philosophy (whose main tenet is the idea that concepts are embedded in social practice and discourses, and that discourses are ideally free and non-hierarchical experiences) and on the other side high fidelity to a positivistic account both of social reality and of law (where the central view is that concepts are just tools external to reality and that in law the fundamental notion is command and the central experience is hierarchy and subjection). In the one corner, the Habermasian one, there is a defense of the priority and fundamentality of communicative rationality over other forms of reason; in the other corner, the Rossian one, practical rationality is only instrumentalism, *Zweckrationalität*: Alexy – it seems to me – perpetually goes to and fro between the two. Said in different terms, Alexy has not drawn all the possible conclusions from his argumentative consideration of legal practice, since he still maintains and defends a concept of law somehow based on command and instrumentalism.

NOTES

1. Suhrkamp, Frankfurt 1986, p. 43.
2. See, for instance, H. Kelsen, *Reine Rechtslehre*, 2nd edition, Franz Deuticke, Wien 1960, chapter five.
3. See L. Nelson, *Kritik der praktischen Vernunft*, Felix Meiner Verlag, Hamburg 1972 (Vol. 4 of the *Gesammelte Schriften in neun Bänden*), pp. 29 ss.
4. H. L. A. Hart, *The Concept of Law*, Clarendon, Oxford 1961, p. 107.
5. <<Einen Befehl gibt es nur dort, wo einer da ist, der ihn befolgen soll>> (H. G. Gadamer, *Wahrheit und Methode*, Mohr, Tübingen 1990, p. 339).
6. See R. Alexy, *Op. cit.*, pp. 45-46.
7. See his *Faktizität und Geltung*, Suhrkamp, Frankfurt 1992, pp. 164-165.
8. See W. N. Hohfeld, *Some Fundamental Legal Conceptions as Applied in Legal Reasoning*, in <<Yale Law Journal>>, Vol. 23, 1913, pp. 16-59, e Id., *Fundamental Legal Conceptions as Applied in Legal Reasoning*, in <<Yale Law Journal>>, Vol. 26, 1917, pp. 710-770.
9. R. Alexy, *Op. cit.*, p. 63.
10. *The Concept of Law*, 2nd ed., Clarendon, 1994, pp. 260-261.
11. M. S. Singer, *Moral Rules and Principles*, in *Essays in Moral Philosophy*, ed. by A. I. Melden, University of Washington Press, Seattle 1958, p. 169.
12. R. Alexy, *Op. cit.*, p. 131.
13. J. Habermas, *Faktizität und Geltung*, p. 190.
14. *Ibid.*, p. 255.
15. R. Alexy, *Op. cit.*, p. 84.
16. J. Habermas, *Faktizität und Geltung*, p. 317.
17. R. Alexy, *Op. cit.*, p. 272.
18. *Ibid.*, p. 272.
19. R. Alexy, "Constitutional Rights, Balancing, and Rationality", in *Ratio Juris*, Vol. 16, 2003, p. 138.
20. *Ibid.*, p. 140.
21. See R. Alexy, "Postscript", in Id., *A Theory of Constitutional Rights*, Trans. by J. Rivers, Oxford University Press, Oxford 2002, pp. 388 ff.
22. R. Alexy, "Individual Rights and Collective Goods", in *Rights*, ed. by C. S. Nino, Aldershot, Dartmouth 1992, p. 173.
23. H. L. A. Hart, *The Concept of Law*, p. 80.
24. Ibid.
25. See ibid., p. 40.
26. See for instance R. Alexy, "Discourse Theory and Fundamental Rights", in *Ratio Juris*, Vol. 9, 1996, pp. 209-235.
27. See E. Bulygin, "Alexy's Thesis of the Necessary Connection Between Law and Morality", in *Ratio Juris*, Vol. 13, 200, pp. 133-137.

AUTHOR INDEX

SUBJECT INDEX

Law and Philosophy Library

65. E. Santoro: *Autonomy, Freedom and Rights*. A Critique of Liberal Subjectivity. 2003 ISBN 1-4020-1404-X
66. S. Eng: *Analysis of Dislagreement – with particular reference to Law and Legal Theory*. 2003 ISBN 1-4020-1490-2
67. D. González Lagier: *The Paradoxes of Action*. (Human Action, Law and Philosophy). 2003 ISBN Hb-1-4020-1661-1
68. R. Zimmerling: *Influence and Power*. Variations on a Messy Theme. 2004 ISBN Hb-1-4020-2986-1
69. A. Stranieri and J. Zeleznikow (eds.): *Knowledge Discovery from Legal Databases*. 2005 ISBN 1-4020-3036-3
70. J. Hage: *Studies in Legal Logic*. 2005 ISBN 1-4020-3517-9
71. C. Wellman: *Medical Law and Moral Rights*. 2005 ISBN 1-4020-3751-1
72. T. Meisels: *Territorial Rights*. 2005 ISBN 1-4020-3822-4
73. G.W. Rainbolt: *The Concept of Rights*. 2005 ISBN 1-4020-3976-X
74. O. Ezra: *Moral Dilemmas in Real Life*. Current Issues in Applied Ethics. 2006 ISBN 1-4020-4103-9
75. N.T. Casals: *Group Rights as Human Rights*. A Liberal Approach to Multiculturalism. 2006 ISBN 1-4020-4208-6
76. C. Michelon Jr.: *Being Apart from Reasons*. The Role of Reasons in Public and Private Moral Decision-Making. 2006 ISBN 1-4020-4282-5
77. A.J. Menendez and E.O. Eriksen (eds): *Arguing Fundamental Rights*. 2006 ISBN 1-4020-4918-8
78. J. Stelmach and B. Brozek: *Methods of Legal Reasoning*. 2006 ISBN 1-4020-4936-6
79. M. La Torre: *Constitutionalism and Legal Reasoning*. 2007 ISBN 1-4020-5594-3

Law and Philosophy Library

1. E. Bulygin, J.-L. Gardies and I. Niiniluoto (eds.): *Man, Law and Modern Forms of Life*. With an Introduction by M.D. Bayles. 1985 ISBN 90-277-1869-5
2. W. Sadurski: *Giving Desert Its Due*. Social Justice and Legal Theory. 1985 ISBN 90-277-1941-1
3. N. MacCormick and O. Weinberger: *An Institutional Theory of Law*. New Approaches to Legal Positivism. 1986 ISBN 90-277-2079-7
4. A. Aarnio: *The Rational as Reasonable*. A Treatise on Legal Justification. 1987 ISBN 90-277-2276-5
5. M.D. Bayles: *Principles of Law*. A Normative Analysis. 1987 ISBN 90-277-2412-1; Pb: 90-277-2413-X
6. A. Soeteman: *Logic in Law*. Remarks on Logic and Rationality in Normative Reasoning, Especially in Law. 1989 ISBN 0-7923-0042-4
7. C.T. Sistare: *Responsibility and Criminal Liability*. 1989 ISBN 0-7923-0396-2
8. A. Peczenik: *On Law and Reason*. 1989 ISBN 0-7923-0444-6
9. W. Sadurski: *Moral Pluralism and Legal Neutrality*. 1990 ISBN 0-7923-0565-5
10. M.D. Bayles: *Procedural Justice*. Allocating to Individuals. 1990 ISBN 0-7923-0567-1
11. P. Nerhot (ed.): *Law, Interpretation and Reality*. Essays in Epistemology, Hermeneutics and Jurisprudence. 1990 ISBN 0-7923-0593-0
12. A.W. Norrie: *Law, Ideology and Punishment*. Retrieval and Critique of the Liberal Ideal of Criminal Justice. 1991 ISBN 0-7923-1013-6
13. P. Nerhot (ed.): *Legal Knowledge and Analogy*. Fragments of Legal Epistemology, Hermeneutics and Linguistics. 1991 ISBN 0-7923-1065-9
14. O. Weinberger: *Law, Institution and Legal Politics*. Fundamental Problems of Legal Theory and Social Philosophy. 1991 ISBN 0-7923-1143-4
15. J. Wróblewski: *The Judicial Application of Law*. Edited by Z. Bańkowski and N. MacCormick. 1992 ISBN 0-7923-1569-3
16. T. Wilhelmsson: *Critical Studies in Private Law*. A Treatise on Need-Rational Principles in Modern Law. 1992 ISBN 0-7923-1659-2
17. M.D. Bayles: *Hart's Legal Philosophy*. An Examination. 1992 ISBN 0-7923-1981-8
18. D.W.P. Ruiter: *Institutional Legal Facts*. Legal Powers and their Effects. 1993 ISBN 0-7923-2441-2
19. J. Schonsheck: *On Criminalization*. An Essay in the Philosophy of the Criminal Law. 1994 ISBN 0-7923-2663-6
20. R.P. Malloy and J. Evensky (eds.): *Adam Smith and the Philosophy of Law and Economics*. 1994 ISBN 0-7923-2796-9
21. Z. Bańkowski, I. White and U. Hahn (eds.): *Informatics and the Foundations of Legal Reasoning*. 1995 ISBN 0-7923-3455-8
22. E. Lagerspetz: *The Opposite Mirrors*. An Essay on the Conventionalist Theory of Institutions. 1995 ISBN 0-7923-3325-X

Law and Philosophy Library

23. M. van Hees: *Rights and Decisions*. Formal Models of Law and Liberalism. 1995 ISBN 0-7923-3754-9
24. B. Anderson: "*Discovery*" *in Legal Decision-Making*. 1996 ISBN 0-7923-3981-9
25. S. Urbina: *Reason, Democracy, Society*. A Study on the Basis of Legal Thinking. 1996 ISBN 0-7923-4262-3
26. E. Attwooll: *The Tapestry of the Law*. Scotland, Legal Culture and Legal Theory. 1997 ISBN 0-7923-4310-7
27. J.C. Hage: *Reasoning with Rules*. An Essay on Legal Reasoning and Its Underlying Logic. 1997 ISBN 0-7923-4325-5
28. R.A. Hillman: *The Richness of Contract Law*. An Analysis and Critique of Contemporary Theories of Contract Law. 1997 ISBN 0-7923-4336-0; 0-7923-5063-4 (Pb)
29. C. Wellman: *An Approach to Rights*. Studies in the Philosophy of Law and Morals. 1997 ISBN 0-7923-4467-7
30. B. van Roermund: *Law, Narrative and Reality*. An Essay in Intercepting Politics. 1997 ISBN 0-7923-4621-1
31. I. Ward: *Kantianism, Postmodernism and Critical Legal Thought*. 1997 ISBN 0-7923-4745-5
32. H. Prakken: *Logical Tools for Modelling Legal Argument*. A Study of Defeasible Reasoning in Law. 1997 ISBN 0-7923-4776-5
33. T. May: *Autonomy, Authority and Moral Responsibility*. 1998 ISBN 0-7923-4851-6
34. M. Atienza and J.R. Manero: *A Theory of Legal Sentences*. 1998 ISBN 0-7923-4856-7
35. E.A. Christodoulidis: *Law and Reflexive Politics*. 1998 ISBN 0-7923-4954-7
36. L.M.M. Royakkers: *Extending Deontic Logic for the Formalisation of Legal Rules*. 1998 ISBN 0-7923-4982-2
37. J.J. Moreso: *Legal Indeterminacy and Constitutional Interpretation*. 1998 ISBN 0-7923-5156-8
38. W. Sadurski: *Freedom of Speech and Its Limits*. 1999 ISBN 0-7923-5523-7
39. J. Wolenski (ed.): *Kazimierz Opalek Selected Papers in Legal Philosophy*. 1999 ISBN 0-7923-5732-9
40. H.P. Visser 't Hooft: *Justice to Future Generations and the Environment*. 1999 ISBN 0-7923-5756-6
41. L.J. Wintgens (ed.): *The Law in Philosophical Perspectives*. My Philosophy of Law. 1999 ISBN 0-7923-5796-5
42. A.R. Lodder: *DiaLaw*. On Legal Justification and Dialogical Models of Argumentation. 1999 ISBN 0-7923-5830-9
43. C. Redondo: *Reasons for Action and the Law*. 1999 ISBN 0-7923-5912-7

Law and Philosophy Library

44. M. Friedman, L. May, K. Parsons and J. Stiff (eds.): *Rights and Reason*. Essays in Honor of Carl Wellman. 2000 ISBN 0-7923-6198-9
45. G.C. Christie: *The Notion of an Ideal Audience in Legal Argument*. 2000 ISBN 0-7923-6283-7
46. R.S. Summers: *Essays in Legal Theory*. 2000 ISBN 0-7923-6367-1
47. M. van Hees: *Legal Reductionism and Freedom*. 2000 ISBN 0-7923-6491-0
48. R. Gargarella: *The Scepter of Reason*. Public Discussion and Political Radicalism in the Origins of Constitutionalism. 2000 ISBN 0-7923-6508-9
49. M. Iglesias Vila: *Facing Judicial Discretion*. Legal Knowledge and Right Answers Revisited. 2001 ISBN 0-7923-6778-2
50. M. Kiikeri: *Comparative Legal Reasoning and European Law*. 2001 ISBN 0-7923-6884-3
51. A.J. Menéndez: *Justifying Taxes*. Some Elements for a General Theory of Democratic Tax Law. 2001 ISBN 0-7923-7052-X
52. W.E. Conklin: *The Invisible Origins of Legal Positivism*. A Re-Reading of a Tradition. 2001 ISBN 0-7923-7101-1
53. Z. Bańkowski: *Living Lawfully*. Love in Law and Law in Love. 2001 ISBN 0-7923-7180-1
54. A.N. Shytov: *Conscience and Love in Making Judicial Decisions*. 2001 ISBN 1-4020-0168-1
55. D.W.P. Ruiter: *Legal Institutions*. 2001 ISBN 1-4020-0186-X

Volumes 56–63 were published by Kluwer Law International.

---

56. G. den Hartogh: *Mutual Expectations*. A Conventionalist Theory of Law. 2002 ISBN 90-411-1796-2
57. W.L. Robison (ed.): *The Legal Essays of Michael Bayles*. 2002 ISBN 90-411-1835-7
58. U. Bindreiter: *Why Grundnorm?* A Treatise on the Implications of Kelsen's Doctrine. 2002 ISBN 90-411-1867-5
59. S. Urbina: *Legal Method and the Rule of Law*. 2002 ISBN 90-411-1870-5
60. M. Baurmann: *The Market of Virtue*. Morality and Commitment in a Liberal Society. 2002 ISBN 90-411-1874-8
61. G. Zanetti: *Political Friendship and the Good Life*. Two Liberal Arguments against Perfectionism. 2002 ISBN 90-411-1881-0
62. W. Sadurski (ed.): *Constitutional Justice, East and West*. 2002 ISBN 90-411-1883-7
63. S. Taekema: *The Concept of Ideals in Legal Theory*. 2003 ISBN 90-411-1971-X
64. J. Raitio: *The Principle of Legal Certainty in EC Law*. 2003 ISBN 1-4020-1217-9

Law and Philosophy Library

65. E. Santoro: *Autonomy, Freedom and Rights*. A Critique of Liberal Subjectivity. 2003 ISBN 1-4020-1404-X
66. S. Eng: *Analysis of Dislagreement – with particular reference to Law and Legal Theory*. 2003 ISBN 1-4020-1490-2
67. D. González Lagier: *The Paradoxes of Action*. (Human Action, Law and Philosophy). 2003 ISBN Hb-1-4020-1661-1
68. R. Zimmerling: *Influence and Power*. Variations on a Messy Theme. 2004 ISBN Hb-1-4020-2986-1
69. A. Stranieri and J. Zeleznikow (eds.): *Knowledge Discovery from Legal Databases*. 2005 ISBN 1-4020-3036-3
70. J. Hage: *Studies in Legal Logic*. 2005 ISBN 1-4020-3517-9
71. C. Wellman: *Medical Law and Moral Rights*. 2005 ISBN 1-4020-3751-1
72. T. Meisels: *Territorial Rights*. 2005 ISBN 1-4020-3822-4
73. G.W. Rainbolt: *The Concept of Rights*. 2005 ISBN 1-4020-3976-X
74. O. Ezra: *Moral Dilemmas in Real Life*. Current Issues in Applied Ethics. 2006 ISBN 1-4020-4103-9
75. N.T. Casals: *Group Rights as Human Rights*. A Liberal Approach to Multiculturalism. 2006 ISBN 1-4020-4208-6
76. C. Michelon Jr.: *Being Apart from Reasons*. The Role of Reasons in Public and Private Moral Decision-Making. 2006 ISBN 1-4020-4282-5
77. A.J. Menendez and E.O. Eriksen (eds): *Arguing Fundamental Rights*. 2006 ISBN 1-4020-4918-8
78. J. Stelmach and B. Brozek: *Methods of Legal Reasoning*. 2006 ISBN 1-4020-4936-6
79. M. La Torre: *Constitutionalism and Legal Reasoning*. 2007 ISBN 1-4020-5594-3

FSC
www.fsc.org
MIX
Papier | Fördert gute Waldnutzung
FSC® C083411

Kolibri 360 GmbH
Ferdinand-Jühlke-Straße 7
99095 Erfurt, Deutschland
produktsicherheit@kolibri360.de